T0345233

THE ICONOGRAPHY
OF PRISTINE STATEHOOD

Painted pottery and seal impressions from Susa,
southwestern Iran

PETR CHARVÁT

Charles University in Prague
Karolinum Press
Prague 2005

Reviewers: PhDr. Jana Součková, DrSc.
Mitchell S. Rothman, Ph.D.

ISBN 80-246-0964-9

CONTENTS

Introduction – – – 7
Catalogue – – – 11
The domestic fire – – – 37
The air beneath the wings – – – 75
The water of life – – – 113
The good mother earth – – – 141
And lo! There sprang a world – – – 177
Conclusions – – – 211
Bibliography – – – 219
Index – – – 239
General index – – – 247
Appendix – – – 253

INTRODUCTION

This book constitutes the third, and, for the time being, last part of my investigations of the emergence of early statehood in ancient Mesopotamia. It thus rounds up my interpretations of the archaeological evidence (Charvát 2002) and of textual materials available for such a study (Charvát 1997).

Unlike the previous publications, this book took a much longer time to write. As early as 1995, when I closed my query of ancient Mesopotamian texts in Berlin, I realized that there does exist one important source category which I have still not adressed, and that is the iconographic evidence. The significance of this material was, in my eyes, enhanced by the fact that some parts of this evidence reached farther back in date than the earliest texts, and, in fact, constituted one of the most ancient sources of iconic nature for social processes that led to the formation of the first state bodies of the ancient Near East.

My resolution to tackle the interpretation problems of this kind of evidence led me to consider detailed studies of at least some of the seal impressions found by the French missions at the prehistoric and historic site of Susa, SW Iran. It is self-evident that little is to be added to the art-history assessment of such materials after their magisterial treatment by Pierre Amiet (1972). Nevertheless, the kind of study that I had in mind required the gathering of supplementary information not always accessible in the published works. With this purpose in mind I approached the authorities of the Département des Antiquités Orientales of the Musée du Louvre, where this material is currently deposited, and thanks to their generosity and amiability, I could study the evidence concerned during my repeated study tours to Paris in the years 1995–1997.

The questions posed by the materials did, however, take me even farther. Already at this period of time, I became aware that an appropriate interpretation of the Susa seal impressions, datable to the Early Uruk culture (early 4th millennium B. C.), taking into account their temporal and socio-

-economic contexts, must consider other, still earlier, source groups. This led me to focus on the most ellegant, justly famous but little studied painted pottery of the same site of Susa, dating into even earlier periods of time (Final Ubaid culture, late 5th millennium B. C.). In this respect also, I was greatly helped by the Département des Antiquités Orientales of the Musée du Louvre, who kindly placed at my disposal the card catalogue of their collection of the Susa painted pottery. In 1997–1998, I could also study the original publications in their well-furnished library.

Not even this, however, proved to supply entirely satisfactory results. Ultimately, I decided to pursue an even more extensive course of studies, including ethnological interpretations of some aspects of this ancient Oriental evidence. This concerned, first and foremost, some of the gestures and postures of the chief protagonists depicted by the early seal impression of Susa. Such iconic sources can be illuminated by no other kind of evidence than by combined ethnological data taken from as wide a sample of world pre-industrial cultures as possible. I am aware of the traps and dangers jeopardizing an uncritical employment of ethnological evidence. Much as Giambattista Vico, however, I am firmly convinced that if we postulate a biological unity of the *Homo sapiens* species, we must acknowledge also the oneness of the way our minds and souls worked and work.

At that time, it has been brought to my attention that there does exist in Paris a paper copy of the famous George Peter Murdock ethnological files (HRAF), which was once made for Claude Lévi-Strauss and which is to this day accessible for study at the institution the world-famous French ethnologist has founded, the Laboratoire d'Ethnologie Comparée of the Collège de France. There also, I have been accorded a warm welcome and I could round up my study in the spacious library of this institution in 1998–2002.

Some of the last touches on this work have been put in place by work in the libraries of the Laboratoire d'Archéologie Orientale of the Université de Paris – Panthéon-Sorbonne (Paris I), as well as that of the Cabinet d'Assyriologie of the Collège de France.

Acknowledgments

As will be evident, I am grateful to a host of institutions and persons without whom this book could not have been written. In obliging cooperation, both the Academy of Sciences of the Czech Republic and the

Centre National de la Recherche Scientifique of France enabled me to go to Paris by having kindly included my project in the list of officially approved Franco-Czech academic undertakings (No. 2869 of the 1996 list, and No. 4773 of the 1997 list). My thanks also go to the Ministry of Foreign Affairs of the Republic of France and to the Ministry of Education, Youth and Physical Culture of the Czech Republic, who had again the amiability to put my project on the list of those supported officially by the Franco-Czech BARRANDE cooperation programme (No. 98011 of the Ministry of Education of the Czech Republic list in 1998–1999). I render my heartfelt thanks to the Development Fund of the Universities (Fond rozvoje vysokých škol), who kindly provided funds for work connected with these investigations of mine (grant No. FRV· 1332/2000). Ultimately, I have to acknowledge my debt of gratitude to the Grant Agency of Charles University, Prague, thanks to a grant from which I could finish the work necessary for the final phases of this project (grant No. 300/2001/A-HN/PedF for the years 2001–2003).

In the course of my work there were times when I was a daily guest at the Département des Antiquités Orientales of the Musée du Louvre, Paris. It is a quite special honour and pleasure for me to render my homage for this to Mme. Annie Caubet, Conservateur-Général of the same Department, for her kind consent to allow me the study of the finds in question, as well as to Mme. Agnès Benoit who helped me with the archaeological materials which I have constantly demanded. Mesdames Patricia Kalansky and Marie-Jo Castor had the kindness to attend to the everyday routine tasks of my work at the Louvre; thanking them from all my heart, I humbly confess that I have only too often put them out of their own work by my constant demands.

To no less extent am I obliged to the Laboratoire d'Archéologie Orientale of the Université de Paris I – Panthéon-Sorbonne, where my work was much aided by the generous help given to me by my learned friend and colleague, Professeur Jean-Louis Huot. I greatly profited from cooperation and debates with other French colleagues, especially Jean-Daniel Forest, Jean-Jacques Glassner, Régis Vallet, Catherine Breniquet, as well as Bertrand Lafont and Serge Cleuziou.

I thank very much M. Jean-Marie Durand of the Collège de France for his kind permission to study in the library of the Cabinet d'Assyriologie of the above mentioned venerable institution.

I am grateful to the colleagues I met at the Laboratoire d'Ethnologie Comparée of the Collège de France, especially to Mme. Marion Abélès,

Director of the Library. At this institution, it was especially M. François Grainville who had to bear the burden of my frequent questions and wishes, all of which he bore with patience. I thank him, as well as all the other colleagues, most sincerely.

Throughout the entire duration of this project, I learned to deeply appreciate the service done to our knowledge of the material sources for the pre- and protohistory of the ancient Near East by the unquestionable mastery of M. Pierre Amiet. Though we have been meeting only occasionally – for which the fault lies entirely on me, as I invariably tried to accomplish too much during my stays at Paris – , I harbour a feeling of deep respect and sympathy to him, and I humbly acknowledge my indebtedness to his work, without which I could have not accomplish mine.

I am delighted to acknowledge my debts of gratitude to other colleagues who contributed, in one way or another, to the knowledge I was able to marshal for the benefit of this project. I owe thanks for inspiration and support to Reinhard Bernbeck, Jesús Gil Fuensanta, Mitchell Rothman, Gil Stein and Susan Pollock.

Among all the people who did help me to write this book, I am most profoundly obliged to my family. My deepfelt gratitude goes first and foremost to my wife, Kateřina Charvátová, who has gathered much more merit in the eyes of the ancient Sumerians and Susians than she is aware of. My sons, Jan and Ondřej, have been bearing the caprices of their father with patience and grace.

Prague, on 29th May 2003
Petr Charvát

CATALOGUE

The first duty of any historian worthy of that name is to marshall the basic material he or she will be working with. Pictorial sources constitute no exception to this general rule and it is therefore appropriate to open this treatise with review of the source base that I shall be using.

The most extensive and comprehensive source documentation of the painted pottery unearthed in the prehistoric layers of Susa that I came across is a card file, comprising essential information on individual items of the pottery found at the site of Susa, now in the Département des Antiquités Orientales of the Musée du Louvre in Paris. This card file gives museum numbers of all the relevant finds, as well as data on their current deposition and good-quality black-and-white photographs of the respective vessels. I decided to base all my investigations on data culled from this catalogue, as I found no other more extensive and detailed description of the entire find group.

In this investigation I am focusing on the iconography of the Susa pottery and I have therefore refrained from more detailed investigations of the vessels. I give here a representation of the motifs painted on singular dishes, bowls, pots and bottles, in a more or less standard size, omitting any reference to dimensions of the individual vessels, as well as to details of their manufacture, finish and present condition. All such data will have to be investigated in the future by an expert ceramological study.

This group of material is supplemented by documentation of figural depictions on seal impressions from Susa, traditionally classified as belonging to the Susa B phase. I have documented these finds by personal inspection in the Musée du Louvre. The results are comprised within this text.

These parts of the catalogue are followed by a list of painted-pottery items for which the photographs of the Louvre catalogue bring no complementary information. They are therefore included in this investigation at their "face value".

The serial numbers accorded to each vessel in the text that follows fall in with serial numbers marking my illustrations. In each case the vessel is identified by all the other relevant numbers noted in their files. The numbers beginning with SB are inventory numbers of the Département des Antiquités Orientales.

I could study data from the card file by kind permission of Mme. Annie Caubet, Conservateur-Général, Département des Antiquités Orientales, Musée du Louvre, for which I am profoundly grateful. I owe a debt of thanks to members of the same Département who made my study possible and who kindly took care of me during my successive stays at the Louvre museum in 1995–1999, Mesdames Marie-Jo Castor and Patricia Kalansky.

1. SB 3223 (11.623)
2. SB 4819 (12.609)
   Publication: de Morgan 1912, Pl. XVIII, No. 1.
3. SB 3194 (12.101)
   Publication: de Morgan 1912, Pl. XVIII, No. 6.
4. SB 3218 (A 7.936)
5. SB 3186 (9.794)
6. SB 3153 (11:617)
   Publication: de Morgan 1912, Pl. Va No. 1.
7. SB 3176 (A 7.011)
   Publication: de Morgan 1912, Pl. XLII, No. 2.
8. SB 3183 (12.613)
   Publication: de Morgan 1912, Pl. XVI, No. 1.
9. SB 14288 (12453, 24)
   Publication: de Morgan 1912, Pl. XIII, No. 6.
10. SB 3148 (10.026)
    Publication: de Morgan 1912, Pl. XVII, No. 5.
11. SB 14267 (12 174 = Louvre 106)
    Publication: de Morgan 1912, Pl. XVI, No. 3.
12. SB 3149 (A. 7918)
    Publication: de Morgan 1912, Pl. XVI, No. 2.
13. SB 14 383 (12695)
14. SB 3152 (12.675)
    Publication: de Morgan 1912, Pl. XVIII, No. 3.
15. SB 3144 (12.115)

16. SB 3136 (13.876)
    Publication: de Morgan 1912, Pl. XVII, No. 3.
17. SB 3161 (12.491)
18. SB 3143 (A 6.618)
    Publication: de Morgan 1912, Pl. XLII, No. 3.
19. SB 14 382 (12 487)
20. SB 3193 (12.244)
    Publication: de Morgan 1912, Pl. XVI, No. 4; Amiet 1986, 235 fig. 2
    (*in situ* sketch by de Morgan).
21. SB 3191 (12.143)
    Publication: de Morgan 1912, Pl. XLII, No. 5.
22. SB 3162 (12.693)
23. SB 14 381 (A 6568)
24. SB 3130
25. SB 19 519 (As 12 522)
26. SB 4820 (12 694)
    Publication: Le Breton 1947, 200, fig. 46: 9(?).
27. SB 3175 (11.613)
28. SB 3200 (A. 7041)
    Publication: de Morgan 1912, Pl. XV, No. 4.
29. SB 14 384 (11 619)
30. SB 3137 (12 934, A 7934)
    Publication: de Morgan 1912, Pl. XIII, No. 2.
31. SB 3134 (12 160)
    Publication: de Morgan 1912, Pl. Va, No. 5.
32. SB 3195 (13 892)
    Publication: de Morgan 1912, Pl. Va, No. 3, ibid. Pl. XLII No. 1.
33. SB 3163 (11 620)
34. SB 3140 (A 6.618)
    Publication: de Morgan 1912, Pl. XI, No. 6.
35. SB 3196 (12 218)
    Publication: de Morgan 1912, Pl. XIII, No. 4.
36. SB 3180 (Strasbourg)
37. SB 9503 (270, 16 046, 10 046?)
38. SB 14 265 (A 7045, 184)
    Publication: de Morgan 1912, Pl. XIII, No. 5.
39. SB 14 276 (12 138,25?)
    Publication: de Morgan 1912, Pl. IX, No. 8.

40. SB 3202 (12 698)
41. SB 3204 (181, 26, 13 896)
    Publication: de Morgan 1912, Pl. XVII, No. 6.
42. SB 3169 (12. 138)
    Publication: de Morgan 1912, Pl. IV, No. 6.
43. SB 3184 275 (A 7.938)
    Publication: de Morgan 1912, Pl. IV, No. 2.
44. SB 14 275 (12 138, 25?)
45. SB 14 293 (11 596)
46. SB 3199 (12 395)
    Publication: de Morgan 1912, Pl. IVa, No. 5.
47. SB 14 291 (12 591)
48. SB 3197
49. SB 14 274 (12 120)
    Publication: de Morgan 1912, Pl. IVa, No. 3.
50. SB 14 273 (12 599, 38)
    Publication: de Morgan 1912, Pl. VII, No. 5.
51. SB 3190 (12.581)
    Publication: de Morgan 1912, Pl. IX, No. 9; Amiet 1986, 235 fig. 2
    (*in situ* sketch by de Morgan).
52. SB 3145 (12.316)
    Publication: de Morgan 1912, Pl. VII, No. 5.
53. SB 3181 (13.926)
54. SB 14 272 (12 305, 58)
55. SB 3189 (12.647)
    Publication: de Morgan 1912, Pl. Va, No. 8; Harper-Aruz-Tallon 1992,
    39.
56. SB 14 269 (11 600, B1)
57. SB 3146 (12.689)
    Publication: de Morgan 1912, Pl. V, No. 3.
58. SB 3170 (12.313)
59. SB 3141 (13.906)
60. SB 3142 (12.403)
    Publication: de Morgan 1912, Pl. VII, No. 7.
61. SB 14 294 (M 237)
62. SB 3198 (A.7956)
    Publication: de Morgan 1912, Pl. IV No. 4.

63. SB 14 266 (12 330, 64)
    Publication: de Morgan 1912, Pl. VIII, No. 3.
64. SB 3206 (A 7.930)
65. SB 14 270 (12 961, 4?3, 50)
    Publication: de Morgan 1912, Pl. VIII, No. 1.
66. SB 14 290 (A 7932, 56)
    Publication: de Morgan 1912, 7, fig. 6, ibid., Pl. V No. 9.
67. SB 14 278 (12 442, 77)
    Publication: de Morgan 1912, Pl. VII, No. 3.
68. SB 14 385 (7009)
    Publication: de Morgan 1912, Pl. V, No. 8.
69. SB 3188 (12.470)
    Publication: de Morgan 1912, Pl. IX, No. 3.
70. SB 14 268 (12 494)
71. SB 3171 (A. 7957)
    Publication: de Morgan 1912, Pl. X, No. 2.
72. SB 3212 (12.121)
    Publication: de Morgan 1912, Pl. XLI, No. 1.
73. SB 14 289 (10 058bis, 94bis)
74. SB 14 292 (5?)
    Publication: de Morgan 1912, Pl. XXII, No. 9.
75. SB 14 286 (228)
76. SB 14 287 (A 6859, 229)
77. SB 14 284 (14 065, 212)
78. SB 14 285 (A 6455)
79. SB 3213 (12 618)
    Publication: Le Breton 1947, 200, fig. 46: 10.
80. SB 3187 (A 7.908)
    Publication: de Morgan 1912, Pl. IX, No. 4.
81. SB 3158 (12.410)
82. SB 3211 (12.569)
83. SB 3159 (12 348)
84. SB 3164 (12 677)
    Publication: de Morgan 1912, Pl. XIX, No. 3.
85. SB 2862 (11 385, A5)
86. SB 3123
    Publication: de Morgan 1912, Pl. XXI, No. 12.

87. SB 3125 (12 686)
    Publication: de Morgan 1912, Pl. XIX, No. 1.
88. SB 14 283 (A 6453, 260)
    Publication: de Morgan 1912, Pl. XXI, No. 7.
89. SB 14 280 (12 640, 242)
    Publication: de Morgan 1912, Pl. XXI, No. 9.
90. SB 14 386 (AS 15 460, 2)
91. SB 3155 (12.130)
    Publication: de Morgan 1912, Pl. XXII, No. 3.
92. SB 3127 (22)
    Publication: de Morgan 1912, Pl. VIa, No. 4.
93. SB 14 281 (12 339, 2279)
94. SB 3160 (13.912)
    Publication: de Morgan 1912, Pl. XLI, No. 2.
95. SB 14 282 (12 678, 254)
    Publication: de Morgan 1912, Pl. XXI, No. 11.
96. SB 3138 (A 6864)
    Publication: de Morgan 1912, Pl. XX, No. 9.
97. SB 3172 (13.922)
    Publication: de Morgan 1912, Pl. IX, No. 1.
98. SB 3166 (10 038)
99. SB 3124 (12.550), paintings of horses(?) inside
100. SB 3128
101. SB 14 277 (12 553, 97)
     Publication: de Morgan 1912, Pl. VIa, No. 4.
102. SB 3129 (10 054)
     Publication: de Morgan 1912, 7, fig. 7, ibid. Pl. XX, No. 8.
103. SB 3132
104. SB 3156 (15.316, A 7908)
     Publication: de Morgan 1912, Pl. XX, No. 10.
105. SB 3135 (12.679)
     Publication: de Morgan 1912, Pl. X, No. 1.
106. SB 14 279 (A 6879)
107. SB 19 354 (B 223 et R 773)

108. SB 2227.
Ochre to light brown colour, fine clay decomposing into tiny particles.
Imprints of the grain of wood of which the seals were cut are visible within the

impressions. Traces of fingerprints may be surviving around the more extensively preserved impression fragment. Sealing of a pot with a rim diameter c. 280 mm, tied over by a cord below the rim. Details of the cord: cord thickness 4.2 mm, strand thickness 2.4 mm, strand interval c. 15 mm, S-spin.

Publication: de Mecquenem 1943, 11 fig. 6: 11; Amiet 1972, No. 231, p. 43, Pl. 2 ad 50.

109. SB 2136.

Dark ochre to light reddish colour, fine and coherent clay. Outside surface smoothed, inside surface shows what may be impressions of a textile Impressions of a cord with the following parameters: cord thickness 3.8 mm, strand thickness 2.4 mm, strand interval 5–6 mm, Z-spin.

Publication: de Mecquenem 1943, ibid.; Amiet 1972, ibid.

110. SB 2107.

Light ochre colour. Fine coherent clay with minute pores. Outside surface carefully smoothed. On the lower part of the inside traces of textile folds ascending as far as the upper part. Likely to come from a vessel the rim diameter of which amounts to c. 130 mm. Impression of a cord tied below the rim: cord thickness 2.1 mm, strand thickness 2 mm, strand interval c. 12 mm, Z-spin.

Publication: de Mecquenem 1943, ibid.; Amiet 1972, ibid.; Amiet 1986, 37–38 and 236, fig. 4: 3; Harper-Aruz-Tallon 1992, 43–44.

111. SB 2013.

Dark and variously shaded grey-brown colour. Fine coherent clay with a tendency to form grains. Outside surface smoothed with remains of stalks(?) in the hollows. The inside surface is smooth and straight, possibly copying a wall surface. Faint traces of a cord impression in the lower part inside with only the cord thickness of 1.9 mm measurable.

Publication: Amiet 1972, No. 212, p. 40 and Pl. 2.

112. SB 2139.

Brown-grey colour. Fine, dense and coherent clay. Outside surface carefully smoothed with traces of fingerprints. On the lower part of inside surface impression of a fine textile and, in the upper part, traces of impression of a cord, possibly with a knot. Cord thickness: 2.6 mm, strand thickness: about 2.4 mm, strand intervall possibly 6 mm, S-spin.

Publication: de Mecquenem 1943, 11, fig. 6: 11; Amiet 1972, No. 231, p. 43 and Pl. 2.

113. SB 2246.

Brown-grey colour, fine, dense and coherent clay. Outside surface smoothed, with traces of fingerprints. Inside surface: lower part shows impression of folds of a pliable matter, possibly leather (not textile); upper part displays traces of a binding by three courses of a cord. Cord thickness 2.3 mm, remaining features illegible.

Publication: de Mecquenem 1943, 11, Fig. 6: 13; Amiet 1972, No. 219, p. 41 and Pl. 2; Amiet 1986, 37–38 and 236, fig. 4: 4.

114. SB 2011.

Grey-black colour, fine and dense clay flaking off in layers. Outside surface carefully smoothed with traces of fingerprints. Inside surface also smoothed, with traces of fine lines, possibly also from human fingers(?).

Publication: Amiet 1972, No. 212, p. 40 and Pl. 2.

115. SB 2061.

Ochre to brown-grey colour, fine and dense clay tending to form grains. Outside surface carefully smoothed, with traces of fingerprints. The inside surface shows traces of upper part of a jar and of its mouth closed by some kind of organic material held in place by a cord. Cord thickness 3 mm, strand thickness 2.5 mm, strand interval 11–12 mm, S-spin.

Publication: Amiet 1972, No. 212, p. 40 and Pl. 2.

116. SB 2048.

Brown to brown-grey colour, fine to medium coherent clay with a tendency to flake off in layers and to blurr outlines of the seal carving. Outside surface smoothed. Inside surface: lower part displays what appears to be a shoulder of a rim with a clear impression of a fold of textile. Upper part broken off but a cord impression survives. Cord thickness 4.6 mm, strand thickness 3.5 mm, strand interval about 10 mm, Z-spin.

Publication: de Mecquenem 1943, 11, fig. 6: 13; Amiet 1972, No. 219, p. 41 and Pl. 2.

117. SB 2010.

Grey-black colour with a brown hue. Fine and coherent clay with a tendency to flake off in layers. Outside surface smoothed, with traces of fingerprints. The lower part of inside surface displays impressions of folds of a pliable material, most probably leather enclosing a mouth of a jar the diameter of which amounts to about 180 mm. No traces of cord.

Publication: de Mecquenem 1943, 11, fig. 6: 2; Amiet 1972, No. 215, p. 41 and Pl. 2.

118. SB 2012.

Black-grey colour, fine and dense clay with a tendency to form grains. Outside surface carefully smoothed, with traces of fingerprints. Inside surface shows folds of a pliable matter, likely to come from a leather sack tied over with two courses of a cord. Cord thickness 3.2 mm, strand thickness 2.5 mm, strand interval about 8 mm, S-spin.

Publication: Amiet 1972, No. 214, p. 40 and Pl. 2.

119. SB 6941.

Light red to ochre-brown colour, fine to medium clay with admixtures, a tendency to form grains. Outside surface carefully smoothed. Inside surface broken, with impression of a peg with two courses of cord. Peg diameter 24 mm. Cord thickness 2.9 mm strand thickness about 2.3 mm, strand interval more than 5 mm (no strand survived entirely), probably S-spin.

Publication: Jéquier 1905, p. 5 fig. 11; Amiet 1972, No. 226, p. 21 and Pl. 2.

120. SB 6943.

Ochre to light red colour, fine and dense material with a tendency to crackle. Outside surface carefully smoothed, with traces of fingerprints. Inside surface smooth and showing traces of three cords meeting at angles of c. 90, 140 and 130 degrees. Cord thickness 2.3 mm, strand thickness 1.7 mm, strand interval 2–3 mm, Z-spin.

Publication: Legrain 1921, No. 209, p. 52 and Pl. VIII; Amiet 1972, No. 224, p. 42 and Pl. 2.

121. SB 6936.

Grey colour with a lighter hue inside. Fine dense clay with tiny crackles. Outside surface carefully smoothed, inside also smoothed, parts broken off.

Publication: Amiet 1972, No. 214, p. 40 and Pl. 2.

122. SB 6938.

Ochre to light grey colour, fine dense clay with pores, a tendency to form grains. Outside surface carefully smoothed. Inside on surface impressions of folds of pliable material such as leather, tied over with two courses of a cord. Cord thickness 1.6 mm, strand thickness about 1.4 mm, strand interval about 7 mm, probably Z-spin.

Publication: Jéquier 1905, p. 5 fig. 11; Amiet 1972, No. 226, p. 42 and Pl. 2.

123. SB 5300.

Light ochre colour, finde, dense and coherent clay. Outside surface carefully smoothed. The inside surface copies a rounded object tied over with two courses of a cord. Impression of a fold of an organic texture-like material covering the cord is also visible inside. Cord thickness 1.5 mm, strand thickness 1.1 mm, strand interval 4 mm, Z-spin.

Publication: de Mecquenem 1943, 11, fig. 6: 10; Amiet 1972, No. 218, p. 41 and Pl. 2.

124. SB 5301.

Ochre colour with a brownish hue. Fine and dense clay with a tendency to flake off in larger areas. Outside surface carefully smoothed. The inside surface displays traces of pliable material forming larger and soft folds and, in some spots, impressions of a thin and short textured surface. Both planes so marked form a right angle but if this was a leather sack, no traces of the closing cord have survived.

Publication: Amiet 1972, No. 215, p. 41 Pl. 2.

125. SB 6940.

Ochre colour with a brownish hue outside. Fine and dense clay with tiny cavities, large broken areas. Outside surface smoothed, with traces of fingerprints. The inside surface is made up by a smooth area with traces of crossing bands of parallel grooves, as well as with traces reminiscent of lifting the clay with a flat tool.

Publication: Jéquier 1905, p. 5 fig. 11; Amiet 1972, No. 226, p. 42 and Pl. 2.

126. SB 2267.

Ochre colour with a brownish hue visible in the broken section. Fine dense clay breaking in large areas. Outside surface carefully smoothed, with traces of fingerprints. Inside surface covered by mineral deposits; a smooth plane appears to have been tied over with a cord. Only the cord thickness of 2.5 mm could be measured.

Publication: Amiet 1972, No. 230, p. 43 and Pl. 2.

127. SB 2266.

Ochre colour with a whitish hue. Fine, dense clay with a tendency to form grains. Outside surface carefully smoothed, with traces of fingerprints. Inside surface broken; legible traces include a conical smooth surface, possibly a rim of a jar, in the upper part, and impression of a rounded object with horizontal grooves in the lower part. The contact line between both these configurations displays traces of several courses of a cord of which only the cord thickness, 2.6 mm, could be measured.

Publication: Amiet 1972, No. 230, p. 43 and Pl. 2.

128. SB 2248.

Light ochre colour with a brownish hue. Fine, dense clay with traces of short parts of vegetable stalks, with a tendency to form fine grains. Outside surface carefully smoothed, with traces of fingerprints. The inside surface probably copies rim and upper part of body of a pottery vessel. No measurements can be taken and no traces of any binding devices are visible.

Publication: de Mecquenem 1943, 11, fig. 6: 13; Amiet 1972, No. 219, p. 41 and Pl. 2.

129. SB 2229.

Grey-black colour with irregular light red streaks. Fine, dense clay with a tendency to form grains. Outside surface carefully smoothed. The inside bears traces of two conical surfaces displaying folds of pliable material covered by textile imprints, most probably of a sack or bag. This may once have been tied over by a cord of which only the cord thickness, 3.6 mm, is visible.

Publication: Amiet 1972, No. 212, p. 40 and Pl. 2; Amiet 1986, 37–38 and 236, fig. 4: 1.

130. SB 2228.

Ochre colour with a whitish hue. Fine, dense clay with crackles and breaking into irregular fields. Outside surface carefully smoothed. The upper part of inside surface bears traces of folds of pliable material without any traces of texture, the lower inside part has once adhered to a rounded smooth surface.Most probably from a pot, the mouth of which was closed by leather or a similar substance. The contact line of both surfaces bears indistinct traces of a cord. Cord thickness 3.1 mm, strand thickness 2.6 mm, strand interval 5 mm, S-spin.

Publication: Amiet 1972, No. 213, p. 40 and Pl. 2.

131. SB 2247.

Grey-black colour. Fine, dense clay with a tendency to form grains. Outside surface carefully smoothed, with traces of fingerprints. The inside copies a biconical surface bearing traces of pliable matter without recognizable texture. Was this a leather bag? Traces of tying with three courses of a cord. Cord thickness 4.2 mm, strand thickness 3.1 mm, strand interval about 7–9 mm, probably S-spin.

Publication: de Mecquenem 1943, 11, fig. 6: 13; Amiet 1972, No. 219, p. 41 and Pl. 2.

132. SB 2245.

Light red-brown colour, darker inside. Fine, dense clay with a tendency to form grains. Outside surface carefully smoothed, with traces of fingerprints. The inside has preserved traces of a biconical surface showing impressions of very coarse textile. Most probably a textile sack or bag tied over with a cord. Cord thickness 2.5 mm, strand thickness 1.7 mm, strand interval 3 mm, Z-spin.

Publication: Amiet 1972, No. 231, p. 43 and Pl. 2.

133. SB 2265 (two fragments.)

White to ochre colour. Fine, dense clay breaking into larger areas. Outside surface carefully smoothed, with traces of fingerprints. The edge and centre of the image side display dimples 3 mm deep. Inside covered with mineral deposits, the only legible trace being a cord impression. Only the thickness of this cord, 2.4 mm, can be measured.

Publication: Amiet 1972, No. 230, p. 43 and Pl. 2.

134. SB 2265 (two fragments)

Ochre to whitish colour with a brownish hue. Fine, dense clay with a tendency to form grains. Outside surface carefully smoothed, with traces of fingerprints. Inside surface broken, with only a cord impression legible. Cord thickness 1.5 mm, strand thickness 1.2 mm, strand interval 3 mm, S-spin.

Publication: Amiet 1972, No. 230, p. 43 and Pl. 2.

Some details explaining my description of the cord impressions deserve explanation here. *Cord thickness* means the overall thickness of the cord, equal to the shortest posssible distance between its two edges. *Strand thickness* denotes thickness of the individual strands out of which the cord is wound, as far as measurable. *Strand interval* means the largest measurable distance between the two most distant points on one strand, making up the cord in question. The last two items obviously refer to the quality of the cord in question. *Spin* marks the direction in which the cord was twisted which may be read off the impression when positioned vertically. I am giving the spin as visible in the impression so that the true twisting direction is always the opposite.

In resorting to these categories I am following the practice introduced by Roger Matthews in his artifact descriptions, acknowledging my debt of gratitude to him in this place (Martin-Matthews 1993, 37).

Examples of Susa pottery that have been already published with sufficient clarity of illustration, and are therefore **not included in the above series,** consist of the following items:

135. SB 3174
     Publication: Harper-Aruz-Tallon 1992, 32–33.
136. SB 3157
     Publication: Harper-Aruz-Tallon 1992, 33–34.
137. SB 3168
     Publication: de Morgan 1912, Pl. IVa: 1–2; Harper-Aruz-Tallon 1992, 34–35.
138. SB 3131
     Publication: Harper-Aruz-Tallon 1992, 36.
139. SB 3178
     Publication: Harper-Aruz-Tallon 1992, 36.
140. SB 3208
     Publication: Harper-Arruz-Tallon 1992, 37.
141. SB 3154
     Publication: de Morgan 1912, Pl. XVII: 2; Harper-Aruz-Tallon 1992, 37.
142. SB 3165
     Publication: de Morgan 1912, Pl. XLI: 4; Harper-Aruz-Tallon 1992, 38.
143. SB 3179
     Publication: Harper-Aruz-Tallon 1992, 38.
144. SB 3167
     Publication: Harper-Aruz-Tallon 1992, 39.
145. SB 14 271
146. SB 3182
     Publication: Harper-Aruz-Tallon 1992, 41.

147. de Morgan 1912, Pl. XIX: 8; Amiet 1986, 235 fig. 2 (in situ sketch by de Morgan).
148. de Morgan 1912, Pl. IV: 1.
149. de Morgan 1912, Pl. IV: 3.
150. de Morgan 1912, Pl. IVa: 4.
151. de Morgan 1912, Pl. V: 2.
152. de Morgan 1912, Pl. V: 4.
153. de Morgan 1912, Pl. V: 5.
154. de Morgan 1912, Pl. V: 7.
155. de Morgan 1912, Pl. Va: 2.
156. de Morgan 1912, Pl. Va: 4.
157. de Morgan 1912, Pl. Va: 6.
158. de Morgan 1912, Pl. Va: 7.
159. de Morgan 1912, Pl. Va: 9.
160. de Morgan 1912, Pl. VI: 1.
161. de Morgan 1912, Pl. VI: 2.
162. de Morgan 1912, Pl. VI: 4.
163. de Morgan 1912, Pl. VI: 5.
164. de Morgan 1912, Pl. VI: 6.
165. de Morgan 1912, Pl. VIa: 1.
166. de Morgan 1912, Pl. VIa: 3.
167. de Morgan 1912, Pl. VII: 1.
168. de Morgan 1912, Pl. VII: 2.
169. de Morgan 1912, Pl. VII: 4.
170. de Morgan 1912, Pl. VII: 6.
171. de Morgan 1912, Pl. VIII: 2.
172. de Morgan 1912, Pl. VIII: 4.
173. de Morgan 1912, Pl. VIII: 6.
174. de Morgan 1912, Pl. VIII: 7.
175. de Morgan 1912, Pl. IX: 2.
176. de Morgan 1912, Pl. IX: 5.
177. de Morgan 1912, Pl. IX: 6.
178. de Morgan 1912, Pl. X: 5.
179. de Morgan 1912, Pl. X: 6.
180. de Morgan 1912, Pl. X: 7.
181. de Morgan 1912, Pl. X: 8.
182. de Morgan 1912, Pl. XI: 2.
183. de Morgan 1912, Pl. XI: 3.

184. de Morgan 1912, Pl. XI: 5.
185. de Morgan 1912, Pl. XII: 2.
186. de Morgan 1912, Pl. XII: 3.
187. de Morgan 1912, Pl. XII: 4.
188. de Morgan 1912, Pl. XII: 5.
189. de Morgan 1912, Pl. XII: 6.
190. de Morgan 1912, Pl. XIII: 1.
191. de Morgan 1912, Pl. XIII: 3.
192. de Morgan 1912, Pl. XIII: 7.
193. de Morgan 1912, Pl. XIV: 1.
194. de Morgan 1912, Pl. XIV: 2.
195. de Morgan 1912, Pl. XIV: 4.
196. de Morgan 1912, Pl. XIV: 6.
197. de Morgan 1912, Pl. XIV: 8.
198. de Morgan 1912, Pl. XV: 1.
199. de Morgan 1912, Pl. XV: 2.
200. de Morgan 1912, Pl. XV: 3.
201. de Morgan 1912, Pl. XV: 5.
202. de Morgan 1912, Pl. XV: 7.
203. de Morgan 1912, Pl. XVI: 6.
204. de Morgan 1912, Pl. XVI: 7.
205. de Morgan 1912, Pl. XVII: 4
206. de Morgan 1912, Pl. XVIII: 4.
207. de Morgan 1912, Pl. XVIII: 5.
208. de Morgan 1912, Pl. XIX: 4.
209. de Morgan 1912, Pl. XIX: 6.
210. de Morgan 1912, Pl. XIX: 7.
211. de Morgan 1912, Pl. XIX: 9.
212. de Morgan 1912, Pl. XX: 1.
213. de Morgan 1912, Pl. XX: 2.
214. de Morgan 1912, Pl. XX: 3.
215. de Morgan 1912, Pl. XX: 4.
216. de Morgan 1912, Pl. XX: 6.
217. de Morgan 1912, Pl. XX: 7.
218. de Morgan 1912, Pl. XXI: 1.
219. de Morgan 1912, Pl. XXI: 3.
220. de Morgan 1912, Pl. XXI: 6.
221. de Morgan 1912, Pl. XXI: 8.

222. de Morgan 1912, Pl. XXII: 1.
223. de Morgan 1912, Pl. XXII: 2.
224. de Morgan 1912, Pl. XXII: 6.
225. de Morgan 1912, Pl. XXII: 7.
226. de Morgan 1912, Pl. XXII: 8.
227. de Morgan 1912, Pl. XLI: 3.
228. de Morgan 1912, Pl. XLI: 5.
229. de Morgan 1912, Pl. XLII: 4.
230. de Morgan 1912, Pl. XLII: 6.

Find-context data

Painted pottery

The excavation- and documentation methods employed by Jacques de Morgan and his team at Susa are sufficiently known to merit any further considerations (for their own description cf. de Morgan 1900a; de Morgan 1900b; de Morgan-Lampre-Jéquier 1900; de Mecquenem 1911, esp. pp. 65–66, as well as de Mecquenem hist.). The excavation in galleries, by means of which archaeological layers were removed in successive five-metre layers and which ultimately resulted in the exposure of strata with interments yielding the painted-pottery items, took place during the campaign of 1907–1908 (de Morgan 1912, 1) or 1907–1909 (de Mecquenem 1943, 5). Jacques de Morgan himself identifies the stratigraphical position of the painted-pottery items as Gallery B, at the depths of 24.9 to 20.7 metres below the summit of the Susa Acropole hill (de Morgan 1900c, 183; for the present state of the Susa tells cf. a satellite image in Kouchoukos 2001, 89).

As to the location of the cemetery area, de Morgan says that it lies on the tell's western edge and at its very base (20–25 metres below its summit, in his layer V, de Morgan 1912, 2), extending some 30 metres in width and 3 metres in thickness (a stratigraphic sketch in de Morgan 1912, 23, fig. 113). In 1907–1908, about 750 square metres of this cemetery area were reported to have been investigated (de Morgan 1912, 2). This figure is modified by Roland de Mecquenem, who estimates the overall cemetery area to have amounted to hardly more than 120 square metres (de Mecquenem 1943, 5). Excavations below the level of 25 metres under the hill summit reached the groundwater level, and de Morgan came to the conclusion that this was the subsoil, on which the first settlers of the Susa site chose elevations about 9 metres high above the river for their abodes and cemetery precincts (de Morgan 1912, 2).

Before 1910, Jacques de Morgan divided the entire Susa Acropole hill into five successive phases (I, II, III, IV and V), each five metres thick, in the descending order, from the hilltop downwards. In that year, Phase I and most of Phase-II materials had already been removed and the excavating team sunk trenches into Phase-III deposits. The deeper strata of the tell had by then been opened a) by a stratigraphic pit cut as deep as the groundwater level and b) by a complete exposure of the Chalcolithic cemetery (de Mecquenem 1911, 65). In this re-arrangement, the layer with burials naturally fell to Phase V (Toscanne 1911, 156).

The original excavator believed that some 2 000 bodies might have found their last resting place at the Susa cemetery; more than 4 000 vessels, out of which "two or three thousand" were painted, are supposed to have come forth from these interments (de Morgan 1912, 7; on the painted-pottery finds cf. also de Mecquenem 1912 and Pottier 1912).

These data are seen from a different angle in a later review by Roland de Mecquenem (1943, 5–6). While Jacques de Morgan does not give any indications as to the form of the cemetery area, de Mecquenem perceives it as a hillock in the form of a truncated cone (*une butte en forme de tronc de cône*), some 3 metres high and of a basal diametre amounting to about 12 metres (de Mecquenem 1943, 5). Pierre Amiet believes that the whole situation might have arisen through addition and superposition of individual burials, possibly laid to rest in brick casings, as the occasion might have demanded, until a true hillock of interments was formed (Amiet 1986, 33).

The burials were rather densely spaced (de Morgan 1912, 7; de Mecquenem 1943, 5). Jacques de Morgan apparently believed that most of the bodies were lying in an outstretched supine position and that the corpses went to the graves in the anatomical order, as is also shown by the only sketch of a grave surviving from his documentation (Amiet 1986, 235 fig. 2). This statement was substantially modified by Roland de Mecquenem (1943, 5). The latter author refers *expressis verbis* to secondary deposition of human bone, mentioning skulls laid in bowls and long bones in jars (ibid.). The skeletons were in a lamentable state of preservation. A single tomb that could be excavated in 1972 was apparently laid down in brick masonry and the bones were not deposited in an anatomical order (Amiet 1986, 32–33).

Most of the equipment items, consisting of bowls, pedestaled bowls, globular vases, goblets, jars and miniature vessels as well as arms, tools, ornaments and toilet articles (copper discs, interpreted as mirrors), were found by the heads of the deceased (de Morgan 1912, 7). Some of the metal implements display traces of woven textiles in which they were originally wrapped (Amiet 1986, 35; Hole 1992, 30).

Roland de Mecquenem refers to various other categories of small finds which came forth from his own excavations within the cemetery: pottery (de Mecquenem 1943, 6–7, fig. 2), clay statuettes (ibid., 7–8, fig. 3) and other minor finds of this kind such as whorls or tokens (ibid. 8–9, fig. 3 and 4).

Of particular interest is a fragment of a carving or a wall plaque displaying geometrical ornament in the form of a lattice of rectangular lines intersected by diagonals (ibid., 8 fig. 3: 4); taking up a theme well known from Halaf-age seals and sealings (von Wickede 1990, Nos. 60–223). This shows well the temporal proximity of Susa I to Halaf culture and demonstrates that Susa I is unlikely to have been very distant in time from the end of the Halaf culture.

The overall picture is completed by details furnished by another important contribution of the French team, that of Louis Le Breton (1947). We owe to him the recognition of some artifacts of more than passing interest. He has published a find of major significance for the dating of the entire Susa I cemetery, a hammer-axe (Le Breton 1947, 194, fig. 42: 13, and 195). The first hammer-axe known in Greater Mesopotamia has turned up in layer XIII of Tepe Gawra, datable to the terminal Ubaid culture (Charvát 2002, 51, 78). This fact gives us an important reference point for the dating of the Susa-I emetery to the very end of the Ubaid-culture period.

This Susa cemetery apparently entombed only remains of deliberately chosen individuals. Contemporary settlement strata revaled the presence of child burials under house floors (cited in Amiet 1986, 32).

Seal impressions

The seal impressions of Susa were found in strata overlying the ancient cemetery (Susa I) but unfortunately, very scanty data are furnished by any of the excavators (de Mecquenem 1943, 9–12). With all probability they appeared somewhere in the layer sequence about 10 metres thick which, according to Maurice Pézard (1911, 81–82), separated deposits of the two Susa epochs featuring painted pottery (the latter one belonging to the third millennium B.C.). Pézard characterized these strata summarily as containing *sortes de terrines d'argile grossières* (ibid. 82, the description presumably referring to bevelled-rim bowls). Gustave Jéquier referred to them as to layers of ashes and refuse (Jéquier 1905, 2), but his assertion that all prehistoric sealings came from one single findspot of the same level as that of tablet and cylinder-seal impression finds (ibid., 5) has been refuted by Pierre Amiet as apparently erroneous (Amiet 1972, 35 n. 6).

The chronology of seal-impression finds is far from clear. In 1921, Léon Legrain (1921) referred only to the finds of Uruk-age and later sealings, with only two earlier finds documented already by Gustave Jéquier (1905, cf. my numbers 119 and 120). Unfortunately, Roland de Mecquenem supplies only a summary of data in his successive field diaries and find lists of the twenties and thirties of the 20th century. As early as 1921, he must have explored the strata denoted by him later as 4 and 3 (de Mecquenem, s.d.) with *tablettes protoélamites* (4) and *écuelles grossières* (3), but he found *boutons et cachets à la bélière*, not impressions, in his layer 3 (de Mecquenem 1920–1921, depth 4–5 metres). In 1923, de Mecquenem found a *boule en terre crue avec empreintes*, but the fact that it was accompanied by *les bulles d'argile contiennent de petites masses d'argile crues: pastilles, cônes, boulettes*, as well as by the regularly appearing *écuelles grossières*, shows that this find came from an Uruk-age deposit (de Mecquenem 1922–1923, on 19 February, 25 February, 7 March and 10 March).

From the resumption of excavations at the site of Susa in 1920–1921, the only archaeological data source that I could find is represented by Roland de Mecquenem's archaeological diaries and find lists, referred to above, which list the individual find categories in a summary fashion by date. I believe that it will be useful to present these data in a tabellary form:

Date	Find context	Find type	Source
15 February1924	Acropole II	2empreintes sur terre crue	de Mecquenem 1924a
21 February 1924	Acropole II	1épingle en bronze à tête de colombe, empreintes sur terre crue	– " –

22 February 1924	Acropole II	1 cachet-cylindre épingles en ivoire empreintes sur terre crue	– " –
23 February 1924	Acropole II 2	fragment d'inscription élamite vases parthes	– " –
26 February 1924	Acropole	cylindres et cachets empreintes sur terre crue	– " –
27 February 1924	Acropole II 1	perles cachets empreintes sur terre crue	– " –
27 February 1924	Acropole II 2	tablette protoélamites	– " –
27 February 1924	Acropole II 3	vases grossiers silex	– " –
28 February 1924	Acropole II 1	tablettes – " – protoélamites	
28 February 1924	Acropole II 2	bulle de terre ornée à empreintes faucilles de terre cuite pour la main droite	– " –
28 February 1924	Acropole II 3	vases grossiers fragment de vase peint	– " –
1 March 1924	Acropole II 1	empreintes et tablettes proto- élamites	– " –

1 March 1924	Acropole II 2	i. a. taureau achéménide figurine parthe	– " –
1924	no data	Série F, No. 514: Lot d'empreintes sur terre crue	de Mecquenem 1924b
3 February 1925	Acropole Niveau II	bouchons terre cônes	de Mecquenem 1925
11 February 1925	Acropole Niveau II	fragments de bouchons de jarre à empreintes	– " –
16 February 1925	Acropole Niveau III	empreinte sur bouchon de jarre tranche I	– " –
17 February 1925	Acropole	fragments de vases peints faucilles fusaïoles clous bouchons de jarres empreintes sur terre crue	– " –
1926	no data	No. 515: lot d'empreintes	de Mecquenem 1926, p. 12
1927	no data	No. 373: empreinte de cachet sur terre crue	de Mecquenem 1927, p. 11
1927	no data	No. 414: empreinte de cachet sur terre crue	de Mecquenem 1927, p. 12

1928	possibly layers 4 and 3 (de Mecquenem, s.d.)	empreintes sur bouchon de jarres	de Mecquenem 1928a, p. 10
1928	no data	Nos. 495–497: empreintes de cachets – terre crue	de Mecquenem 1928b, p. 4
1928	no data	No. 503: empreinte de cachet terre crue	– " –
1929	no data	No. 200: bouchons de vase terre crue	de Mecquenem 1929, p. 3
1929–1932	no data	No. 151: bouchons de vases	de Mecquenem 1932a,
1932	no data	No. 858: fragments d'empreintes de cachets sur terre crue	de Mecquenem 1932b, p. 32
1933	no data	No. 822: 55 fragments, empreintes sur terre crue, époques diverses	de Mecquenem 1933

1934	no data	No. 556: 2 Boîtes d'empreintes et dessins, terre crue, XXX à XXII avant J. C.	de Mecquenem 1934, p. 13
1934–1935	no data	No. 517: 1 Lots de 83 empreintes terre crue XXXII et XXIII avant J. C.	de Mecquenem 1934–1935, p. 10
26 February 1936	Acropole 2 II	cylindre-cachet	de Mecquenem 1936
– " –	Acropole 2 III	empreintes bouchons de vases	– " –
27 February 1936	Acropole III	bouchons de vases, fragments empreintes, écuelles grossières	– " –
29 February 1936	Acropole 2 II	une empreinte	– " –
6 March 1936	Acropole III	fragments empreintes	– " –
16 March 1936	Acropole 2 II	empreintes	– " –
– " –	Acropole 2 III	écuelles grossières	– " –

– " –	Acropole 2 IV	fours	– " –
– " –	Acropole IV	empreinte	– " –
– " –	Acropole 2 II	empreintes sur terre crue	– " –
28 February 1937	Acropole 2 III	empreintes, écuelles grossières	de Mecquenem 1936–1937
1 March 1937	Acropole 2 II	empreintes	– " –
– " –	Acropole 2 III	empreintes, écuelles grossières	– " –
3 March 1937	Acropole III	empreintes	– " –
4 March 1937	Acropole III	fragments tablettes et empreintes	– " –
1 April 1938	Acropole 2 II	empreintes	de Mecquenem 1938
– " –	Acropole 2 II	empreintes	– " –
1939	no data	No. 175: 106 fragments, empreintes sur terre crue, XLe au XXIIIe avant J. C.	de Mecquenem 1939

De Mecquenem thus found clusters of seal impressions at various spots in his Trench One (*premier Sondage de l'Acropole*, de Mecquenem 1920–1921, de Mecquenem s.d.). His own characterization of their findspot as *la partie supérieure de la couche Suse I* (de Mecquenem 1943, 9) is, in the light of the data just adduced in the tabellary form, likely to refer to the layer denoted on his stratigraphical sketch (de Mecquenem, s.d.) as No. 2. This was comprised between the Suse I stratum, characterized there as featuring pottery kilns and painted as well as red-slipped pottery, and layer No. 3 with *écuelles grossières, vases à bec et anses, outils os, faucilles terre cuite, vases et écuelles pierre, boutons et cachets à bélière, silos, silex, obsidienne, masses en gypse, bouterolles de pierre,* likely to belong to the Late Uruk age. The excavator unfortunately offered no data on this layer No. 2, but its irregular interfaces with the above- and underlying strata and varying thickness may imply that it consisted of building- and settlement débris resting on top of the painted-pottery strata, possibly left by a residential area occupying a mild slope rising from the river bank. Its character might thus have not been very different from that of the lonely impression found in a settlement sequence by Alain Le Brun at the end of the sixties of the twentieth century (cf. infra).

De Mecquenem noted that a quantity of seal impressions appeared by the side of two big oval-shaped and wheel-turned terra-cotta jars (de Mecquenem 1943, 10, fig. 5: 2). He also pointed to the fact that a seal which left its impression at this findspot (ibid., 11, fig. 6: 4) appeared also in impressions found at Trench I at the Acropole where a large number of them rested on a plaque of fired clay close by a kiln (ibid., 11).

The author of the new excavations at the Acropole of Susa, Alain Le Brun, has noticed the presence of seals of a similar style in his layer 25, dating to the final Susa I age (Final Ubaid) or to the Early Uruk (Amiet 1986, 37 n. 6; Harper-Aruz-Tallon 1992, 44 and 45 fig. 25, with ref.).

THE DOMESTIC FIRE

Within the history of ancient Mesopotamian civilization, the Eneolithic period (c. 5500–3500 B.C.) played a role of incomparable importance. All the major discoveries constituting the foundation of Mesopotamian civilization saw the light of day in this major age of human history. For this reason, it is right and proper that we start our investigation concerning the birth of one of the earliest state and literate civilization of human history at this moment.

The above statement does by no means exclude that there were other and earlier periods of rapid change and social transformation, linked especially to sedentarization, within human history. This is especially valid for the Near Eastern region where the first cycle of sedentarization, followed by the emergence of brilliant human civilization which brought forth eternal fruit in the form of the first domestic plants and animals of the Old World, is now commonly assumed to have taken place in the pre-pottery Neolithic age, by and large, in the ninth to seventh pre-Christian millennia. Unfortunately, creators of this first cycle of human civilization did not use an intelligible set of symbols which would survive into periods of time when it would have been transformed into legible script. This could then give evidence on the spiritual world of these first sedentary agriculturalists and livestock-keepers to the generations to come.

Their successors of the Eneolithic age were more fortunate in this aspect, or perhaps we may say that they were simply nearer to the present historical time than our predecessors of the more distant past. At any rate, the Eneolithic symbol systems have survived and, having evolved into script and other interrelated means of expression, they may be subjected to a procedure attempting their interpretation, especially with recourse to the emergence of the earliest non-kinship social systems and the state in this part of the ancient world. This is the very aim and purpose of the present study.

Archaeological evidence on Eneolithic societies indicates, first and foremost, two features the relation of which presents now one of the major problems of historical research: economic intensification and sedentarization of human communities. The question which came first – intensification or sedentarization – will probably tend to divide historians into two groups according to their research orientation. Materialistically oriented colleagues would naturally say that economic intensification preceded sedentarization and, indeed, made it possible. Non-materialistically oriented scholars would say that, of course, things may not be so simple and that a reverse process – sedentarization, for whatever reasons, which brought about economic intensification as a consequence of the necessity to nourish the now much more numerous population – is equally conceivable. However that may be, let us try to see how sedentarization and economic intensification may have resulted in transformations of the modes in which human mind perceived the contemporary transformations.

Eneolithic transformations: economy

First and foremost, let us pass in review the essential changes in economic life. In agriculture, there is evidence of common use of irrigation channels and conduits evidenced first in the preceding, Neolithic age (Charvát 2002, 59). The first form of plough, commonly called the ard, was introduced in this age (Charvát 2002, 61). The first occurence of garden produce bears out a kind of economic intensification hardly conceivable without sedentarization (Charvát 2002, 60). The sphere of livestock-keeping joins the testimonies speaking up in favour of intensification, displaying higher frequencies of occurrence of pigs and cattle (Charvát 2002, 60–61). This indicates both a higher degree of sedentarization (pigs) and the need for new energy sources and traction power (cattle). Moreover, evidence for expert stockbreeding practices is available (Breniquet 1996, 66). All this fell short of lowering the significance of exploitation of uncultivated landscapes and especially hunting, which is still well-evidenced, though its nature does show changes, as we shall presently see. Instead of playing a purely subsistence-gaining role, hunting now becomes a prestige acitivity, likely to have been exercised by groups, possibly even for training purposes (also Breniquet 1996, 62; Charvát 2002, 62–63, 78–80).

All the spheres of professional transformation of natural resources, or arts and crafts, do show traces of change and intensification (Charvát 2002, 65–71, 77–78). Let us just briefly mention, by way of examples, the introduction of the slow potter's wheel, first work with stones of hardnesses measurable in degrees 4–7 of Mohs's scale, progress in metallurgy with the appearance of new metals, or the discovery of the first truly artifical materials (frit). The same goes for the areas of transport and communication. The overcoming of distances measurable in hundreds of kilometres constituted obviously no problem and first evidence for specialized means of transport – ships and, by inference, also waggons (on these cf. now Bollweg 1999) – is to be dated into this age. Indeed, the diffusion spheres of both major cultures of the day, the Halaf- and the Ubaid ones, give an eloquent testimony of the efficiency of the means of transport available to their bearers (Charvát 2002, 71–72).

Let us also make a brief reference to incipient social stratification, borne out by first finds of true sealings, that is, impressions of seals in pliable materials and accompanying supplies of material goods, or closing records deemed to have been of common interest (Charvát 2002, 86–88). The earlier, Neolithic "seal impressions" are also impressions of hard matrices into soft materials but the social contexts of this act are by no means clear. How far the first Eneolithic seals were supposed to "visualize control of, or suzerainty over, material goods on behalf of those persons claiming the former as property", as is commonly assumed, must be clarified. I shall present my own investigation of this problem in the following chapter "The water of life".

In short, Eneolithic life was not only very busy but teeming with changes, novelties and transformations. How did the Eneolithics take to the fact that their world was becoming an uneasy field of quicksands moving around them and, indeed, below their feet? How did they perceive and reflect all that was going on?

In the following investigation I am leaning heavily on evidence supplied by written sources belonging to the much later development phases of the cuneiform civilization; for comparative purposes, I then avail myself of data furnished by cultural and social anthropology, as will be seen presently. This, of course, is a procedure that would require a rigorous methodological underpinning and clear proof that the ideas surviving in the cuneiform texts actually date from such a remote period of time. It is self-evident that such a procedure cannot be applied, as no uninterrupted series of narrative sources capable of substantiation of refutation of the hypotheses presented is currently at our disposal. I shall therefore follow the example of those Assyriologists who compose the full versions of literary sources from texts frequently written hundreds or even thousands of years apart. As a matter of fact, it has already been observed that the Mesopotamian civilization displays one marked feature that distinguishes it from later human creations of this kind but makes it closer to the major civilizations of the ancient world alive today – India and China, for that matter – and that is the unusual degree of longevity and tenacity of its spiritual foundations. I shall just rely on the assumption that this feature might be projected into an even more distant past than that of the cuneiform texts, which, at any rate, is much closer to the period in consideration than the present day. In fact, we shall presently see how the iconographic evidence lends itself well not only to the "reading off" of intelligible structures from within itself but also to "mapping" by means of interlocking with departure points in the earliest cuneiform script.

Eneolithic transformations: spiritual attitudes

For the ancient Mesopotamians, all things of the outer world were charged with supernatural power. Just to begin with agriculture, grain was supposed not only to incarnate the life force itself but even to represent an embodiment of a divinity (Vanstiphout 1989; Alster 1991). In ancient China, the very cultivation of landscape and creation of an irrigation network was perceived as a humanizing and civilizatory task (Puett 1998, 447). The same supernatural strain lies in the conceptualization of some kinds of garden produce, especially for the date palm, "Heir of the Underworld" (Horowitz 1998, 276; details on date-palm cultivation cf. Zettler 1992, 136 n. 41). At least some animals were perceived as living "ghosts" of gods: donkey of Enlil, wolf of Anu, gazelles as daughters of Anu (Horowitz 1998, 6). This, by the way, explains why bovine horns constituted emblems of divine status in Mesopotamia: much as human hair represents a visible excrescence of an "inner nature" of any individual human personality, the divine nature that a bovid carries within itself springs forth in such protuberances of his body as the horns. Horns associate with religious matters not only in Mesopotamia but also in Elam (Vallat 1990). The stars of heaven are sometimes likened to cattle (Horowitz 1998, 255). Let us remark here that in other cultures, the uncultivated nature is also full of souls of deceased humans (Central America: Austin 1988, 374–375).

For a long time has it been known that hunting activities symbolized a major aspect of activity of early Mesopotamian rulers – that of mastering and "humanizing" the wild, untamed and hence inhuman and potentially dangerous aspects of the natural world (cf., in general, Watanabe 1998).

A good example is provided by an Uruk-age cylinder seal depicting what seems to be a symbolic hunting expedition in the mountains designated as KUR, in which four emblem-bearers assist a fifth man who shoots and arrow from his bow; all the participants are naked (Rova 1994, 95, No. 777). Even manipulations with the uncultivated landscape had to take into consideration aspects of mythology and related spiritual constructs supporting the Mesopotamian way of life: in Old Babylonian Sippar, a judiciary oath was taken by the symbol of Shamash, the sun god of justice, in a room revetted by reed stalks (or in a reed hut), and even the kings of Assyria marked out a "sacred area" where they deliberated upon the affairs of state, by a reed fence (Reiter 1989; Reiter 1991).

This sacrality of the natural world may be extended into the sphere of the arts and crafts as well. The well-known epic glorifying the pursuits of the god Ninurta, Lugale, depicts him as a champion who overwhelms certain aspects of untamed nature and becomes master of a series of stones and kinds of wood – that is, natural resources for such occupations as the art of the lapidary or metallurgist. "Decreeing their fate", Ninurta defines, in fact, the economic-cum-cultural role that these resources, and hence also the products thereof and those persons who worked with them, were to play in Mesopotamian society. In this manner, the extraction of raw materials which may serve for various economic and social purposes is also perceived as an activity with a strong supernatural aspect (cf. Streck 2001, esp. pp. 514–517; Horowitz 1998,6).

The dangers inherent in the transport and communication sphere, requiring its agents to overcome long distances and to pass through lands which may be inhabited by strange and potentially dangerous humans and other creatures constitute the thematic range of such Sumerian epics as the "Enmerkar and the Lord of Aratta" cycle, as well as "Lugalbanda in the tenebrous mountains". Let us adduce a most eloquent modern parallel:

" 'Over the mountains of the moon,
O'er the valley of the shadow,
Ride, boldly ride' the shade replied,
'There, there lies Eldorado' ".

Or for those who prefer a more modern poet:

"Not fare well,
but fare forward, voyagers."

Now it may be argued that perceiving the visible world as an arena of divine powers, the ancient Mesopotamians saw in its mastering and harnessing for the good of the human race a pursuit that required not only an ordinary talent, but a nearly superhuman endowment of any primeval entrepreneur who dared to fare beyond the visible horizon, beyond the frontiers of the everyday routine. Those who found their home under the starry sky of Mesopotamia might have felt inclined to hold in high esteem, and to ascribe a special supernatural mission to, any of their fellow personages who pioneered efforts which, though previously unheard of, ultimately brought good to their entire home communities. This special honour and privilege, that the primeval entrepreneurs might have at first enjoyed only in the form of prestige, could in time have been transformed by some of them them into a more permanent base on which such personages, together with their home communities, gradually built up structures of social and civic life that were to give birth to one of the pristine state- and literate civilizations of mankind.

Does there exist evidence that may substantiate such a hypothesis?

The painted pottery of Susa, which constitutes a hub of my investigations in this book, has been preceded by one single phenomenon which might possibly have had a comparable social role. This is the exquisite ornate tableware of the Halaf culture to which our attention must be turned at first. Let us therefore see how far an analysis of data offered by the decorated pottery of the Halaf culture.

Let us first ask a question how far any of the considerations with which we have been preoccupied so far may eventually find reflection in Halaf pottery. Can any informations as to the behaviour and value scales of the highly ranked groups of Halaf-culture be "read off" the exquisitely decorated dishes, bowls, pots and jars?

Message of the painted pots

First and foremost, there is the question of the three colours appearing on the Arpachiyah painted pots and bowls of Max Mallowan' s stratum TT 6. Upon consideration of the overwhelming presence of the trichrome decoration in TT 6 I have suggested that it represents a more widely conceived spiritual construct, standing perhaps for a coherent system of perception and explanation of the nature of both the human and the non-human world, in other words, for one of the first known more universal religions (most recently Charvat 2002, 92–93). This assumption of mine met with some scholarly opposition. I now wish to point to the fact that the highest of the three heavenly regions of Mesopotamian mythology, that belonging to the primeval god An, was supposed to be built of a *luludanitu* stone that displays the above cited three colours – white, red and black, also supposed to belong to An (Horowitz 1998, 9–10). Veneration of the supreme god An and the original version of the Mesopotamian cosmology might have thus have started as early as the final phase of the Halaf culture. This gives us also a clue as to the linkage of the painted pottery to ideational constructs of a higher order.

The ornate tableware thus refers to pristine religion and (one of) its gods. Do we have any indications that it also pertained, in one way or another, to the emerging highly ranked groups, the focus of whose social activities is now seen in rank conferment and their ritual roles? (on this cf., for instance, Mosko 1992). In his re-excavations of Tell Arpachiyah, Ismail Hijara found an incomplete burial, consisting of a human skull deposited in a painted pot (Charvat 2002, 42, 90; cf. also Breniquet 1996, 99 and 133–137 for a list of such cases from among Halaf burials). This is the first clearcut evidence linking non-average human beings with exquisitely painted pots. This is also the first known instance of a custom well-evidenced at Susa, as we have already heard.

To what extent can painted pottery give evidence on other spiritual and social aspects of Halaf culture – in other words, does it convey any intelligible message, does it have a semantic function?

Shamsuddin Tannira

In fact, it may. To begin with, the Halaf-culture Syrian site of Shamsuddin Tannira is distinguished among others of its kind by a high percentage of hunted game among the animal bones found here (Uerpmann 1982, esp. the tables on pp.9–10,12, and pp. 43). I take the liberty of reiterating my earlier assumptions here. The hunting of gazelle and onager, the most frequent species attested to at Shamsuddin Tannira, is a fairly complex affair requiring plenty of experience, as well as careful organization of, and a fairly high degree of cooperation among, the group of hunters. Such animals are, in fact, best hunted in great quantities by being driven into corrals, traps or to difficult places in which they can be more easily disposed of (Charvát 2002, 27, 33). This makes it likely that, in accordance with the conclusions of Pierre Ducos, this may be a case in which hunting activities are to be comprehended as an act of prestige (Breniquet 1996, 62). I dare to suggest that another factor may be at play: hunting is the "best peacetime training for war", be it for the training in lightning action of a hunter who confronts really dangerous prey such as the wild boar, or for development of managing and commanding capacities in those who direct the whole business, or ultimately for training in the coordination of activities of the necessary "task force", numbering many participants.

It may, then, not be a mere coincidence that among the 7,437 sherds of painted pots from this site, donminated by lineally disposed bands of abstract ornament (Gustavson-Gaube 1981, esp. the table on p. 31), the bucranium motif represents one of the few ornaments that fall out of the monotony of purely non-figurative designs. It appeared in 13 examples, making up 0.175% of the whole group. Though this seems a minimum number, over one half of the Shamsuddin Tannira patterns fall into the linear-arrangement category while the rest is made up by groups numbering single percenta or even their fractions. The interesting thing about the bucranium is not only the fact that it does figure prominently in later Halaf-culture contexts, such as Arpachiyah. In view of the particular character of activities carried out at Shamsuddin Tannira, we may surmise that the bull-head icon may convey the idea of strength and controlled, and hence civilized, violence against the inhuman world here.

Let us also notice that one of the Halaf-culture ornaments with a great future, the chequerboard (cf. infra), also appears at Shamsuddin Tannira in 10 examples (0.134% of the whole).

The stippled circles, "one of the more characteristic 'types' in the Shams ed-Din Area A ceramic chronology" (Gustavson-Gaube 1981, 39) are present in the pre-TT 6 layers of Arpachiyah in 9 examples (20.00%). In the TT 6 stratum, only four examples have been documented, but these occupy a highly prestigious position: they all figure on the large exquisite dishes with the rosette centres, in three cases along the outer edge of the whole composition. Whether they do carry any message or can be interpreted semantically is not clear at present; how rich insights into native mythology even simple geometrical patterns can offer is well exemplified by the decoration of locks and keys of the Dogon of Western Africa (Dieterlen 1970).

It is probably of relevance that rosette patterns are not attested to at Shamsuddin Tannira.

Arpachiyah

The earlier (pre-TT 6) strata of Arpachiyah show a preponderance of panel decoration (all data from Mallowan-Rose 1935). Of the 45 items depicted by the authors of the excavation report and expressedly designed by them as coming from pre-TT 6 strata, the most numerous motif groups are those displaying linear arrangement of ornament on body (13 items, i.e.28.90%). Disposition of ornament in panels follows with the same number of examples (13 = 28.90%). The rest is made up various much less numerous groups, among which the more prominent ones include stippled circles (9 examples = 20.00%) lozenges or rhomboids (7 items = 15.55%), bucrania (3 items = 6.67%), with the chequerboards, abundant in TT 6, making up no more than 2 items (4.44%). It must be noted, though, that these data are probably flawed, as the composition of patterns attested to on "Pottery of the Tall Halaf period" plates without further specification is quite different (cf. infra) and chequerboard motifs play a much more important role there. Most of the patterns present in these early strata probably cannot be interpreted as intelligible messages, as the ornament seems to be of purely decorative character, sometimes perhaps copying plaited containers of organic materials or technical finish of metal vessels (shape of the "cream bowls").

The only type of ornament that can possibly carry a message comprehensible today is the chequerboard. Robert Englund has shown that in early cuneiform numerical systems, this pattern served for the construction of artificially high numbers (cited in Charvat 2002, 155). In addition to this, the chequerboard pattern is borne by the proto-cuneiform sign KID, making up the second component of the earliest documentable form of the divine name Enlil, in fact, EN:KID (ibid.). The chequerboard can thus either mean something like "everything, everybody, the sum total of beings", or, alternatively, the capacity to produce such high numbers of entities. In other words, it may refer to fertility, in the sense of the Biblical command to "be fruitful and multiply"; indeed, its character, making it very easy to propagate itself in any direction desired, lends itself readily to such an interpretation. An Egyptian statuette of a lady of rank, wrapped in a veil, the hem of which bears a chequerboard pattern, found in one of the tombs of layer II in the middle part of the cemetery U at Abydos – Umm el-Ga'ab, dating to the First dynasty, does not contradict such an assumption (Leclant-Clerc 1998, 370, fig. 26). In a highly significant fashion, a simplified form of chequerboard, combined elsewhere with "hourglass" motifs, associates with an erotic scene in an, admittedly much later, archaic Ur seal impression (Legrain 1936, Nos. 239, 368).

On the other hand, TT 6 pottery, with its trichrome decoration alluding perhaps to the god An, displays a quite different character. Among the 32 examples denoted by the excavation-report authors, the chequerboard patterns, numbering 12 items (37.50%), assume the leading position. Rosettes, attested to in 10 cases (31.25%) occupy the second place while various forms of Maltese crosses, rather likely to represent a particular form of what I call a "rosette" here, constitute the third most numerous category with 9 examples (28.13%). Let us notice that at Arpachiyah, the Maltese cross must have served as a kind of emblem worn on the body or clothing, as is shown by one of the female statuettes found there (Mallowan-Rose 1935, fig. 45: 10).

Just for the sake of clarity: while a beautiful "rosette" can be seen in the frontispice of Mallowan-Rose 1935, they give a lovely example of a "Maltese cross" on their plate XVII (b). The rest is again represented by much less numerous patterns. Here the motif combinations are also interesting and eloquent: rosette combines most frequently with chequerboard (in 6 cases = 18.75%). Maltese-cross patterns associate most frequently with lattice ornaments (3 items = 9.38%) and then with chequerboards (2 times = 6.25%). If the Maltese cross really represents one of the forms of a rosette, this makes the rosette-chequerboard connection even stronger, as lattice can be viewed as an "empty chequerboard".

I have noted above that the chequerboard patterns can refer to fertility, or to the capacity of multiplication. As to the rosette and the Maltese cross, the conclusions that these might refer, in one way or another, to the notion of the four quarters of the world, so well known from later Mesopotamian literature (Horowitz 1998, 298–299), lies at hand, at least with such examples as Mallowan-Rose 1935, pl. XIX: 3 and fig. 61: 2. In Uruk- and Jemdet Nasr-period seals, the rosette incarnates the divine aspect of the plant world, present also in early Egypt (Rova 1994, 95, Nos. 172 and 175).

We can thus try to summarize at least the message of the rosette-cum-chequerboard pattern as "let the properly structured (= civilized) world multiply and keep growing", or, shorter, "let civilization prevail". A person eating from a vessel so decorated could then be presumed to participate in a ritual, setting him or her into a proper relation to the ordered structures of a civilized world which were supposed to last in time.

Needless to say that the sanctification of such a ritual by carrying out the bowl designs in the three colours of An greatly enhanced its magical potential.

It is somewhat unfortunate that by far the biggest group of Arpachiyah pottery (78 items) has been published only with the summary designation"Painted pottery of the Tall Halaf period" without reference to its stratigraphical position. Among these, chequerboard patterns prevail visibly (20 items = 25.64%). The next most numerous category is that of panel layout of decoration (9 instances = 11.54%). The rest is made up by groups numbering one to three examples, with one single rosette item (1.28%). Interestingly, figural depictions of animals also occur: horned quadrupeds (one instance), felines (one instance), birds (3 instances = 3.85%) and a single snake. All these motifs will be of relevance to the assessment of the later painted pottery from Susa.

The high frequency of the chequerboard motif makes it an interesting target of investigation, especially with recourse to the fact that it tends to combine with other motifs (Mallowan-Rose 1935, fig. 78). The individual component fields can also assume a triangular shape. As to the patterns with which it associates, such ones as dotted circles, "hourglass", lozenges with central points, rosettes, quadrilobes (= four-petalled rosettes), combs, circles with rays, dotted areas, St. Andrew's crosses and the chequerboard motif itself may be registered. If the above proposed interpretation of the chequerboard pattern referring to the proliferation capacity is valid, then all these motifs can be interpreted as symbols of benign entities the multiplication of which was a desirable fact for the bearers of Halaf culture.

Again, one would wish that the authors of the excavation report would not have treated the bucranium (bull's head) motif in a separate fashion, as a self-standing artistic entity (Mallowan-Rose 1935, pp. 154ff. figs. 73, 74 and 75). Most of the examples were thus torn out of their original contexts and their interrelations with other patterns of Arpachiyah pottery rendered very difficult to disentangle. As to the combinations, the bucranium associates with chequerboard and lattice patterns and with dotted fields; in most cases it apparently occupied a position of an element making up linear alignments ornating bowls or pots. We have presently seen that the materials from Shamsuddin Tannira may get us a bit closer to the understanding of this distinctive motif.

The site of Arpachiyah has thus shown that there are certain possibilities of semantic intepretation of pattern on Halaf-culture painted pottery. While the earlier strata are characterized by pottery bearing decorative patterns, with possibly one single motif referring to fertility, or to multiplication capacity (chequerboard), things changed considerably in the time of the TT 6 house.

At that time, the painted bowls probably not only displayed the three colours that were to become the ensign of the sky god An, but bore patterns signifying the desire that the Halaf-culture ordered universe continues in time. Their use as ceremonial tableware probably indicates that the participants of these banquets wished to partake of a substance carrying this "civilizing" message. Such an activity would be very difficult to dissociate from spiritual activities of the highly ranked groups whom ethnographic analogy credits with just this kind of enterprise (cf. infra).

Khirbet Derak

Another hint is supplied from the small but highly interesting site of Khirbet Derak, excavated by a French mission directed by Jean-Daniel Forest in 1983 and published by Catherine Breniquet (1996, 40–47 and 107–109). This site, which has yielded four different kinds of painted pottery (Halaf, Ubaid, an unknown Halaf-related group and a possibly Iranin Dalma-related group) was supplied by an economic network delivering goods in containers (pots and possibly chests) closed with Ubaid-style seals. Stylistic parallels in pottery decoration show that the site might have been active in time of Tepe Gawra XIII, XIIA and XII and thus contemporary with our Susa material. The publisher included in her treatment 53 Halaf-culture sherds, 25 Ubaid-culture ones, 17 Halaf-related and finally 4 Dalma-related examples. The Halaf-culture fragments bear, as the most frequent forms of decoration, lattice patterns (11 examples = 20.75%), followed by straight lines (9 items = 16.98%) and by chequerboard motifs (7 cases = 13.21%). Maltese crosses and quadrilobes together make up 3 cases (5.66%) and there is just one rosette and, tellingly, one single stippled circle. Some of the ornaments are nonetheless carried out with considerable sophistication and it is likely that they could compare with the major works of the master potters who supplied the Arpachiyah centre (for instance, Breniquet 1996, Pl. 11: 6).

In this particular instance it strikes the eye that a site obviously occupying a major position in a redistribution network, and hence presumably linked with pursuits of highly ranked groups, displays exquisite Halaf-culture pottery of a character well comparable to TT-6 Arpachiyah with its "civilizing" mission.

Archaeology: Conclusion

So far, I have tried to show that there are signs of interconnection between highly ranked groups of the Halaf period and painted pottery in several interrelated areas. Such pottery is present on sites with special positions in redistribution networks (Khirbet Derak), and thus links up with the economic roles of the highly ranked groups of Halaf culture. At the site of Shamsuddin Tannira, painted pottery has been used by a group indulging in non-subsistence hunting, perhaps as a sign of its nature-taming, and hence "civilizing", mission. Finally, the site of Arpachiyah shows a development from a generalized use of painted pottery, perhaps with an eye on securing fertility, to its highly specialized and ritualized use at the time of the TT 6 phase. At that time, the exquisite painted tableware, displaying the colours which were to become the ensign of the sky god An of the Sumerians, is likely to have been used in a "civilizing" ritual involving ceremonial partaking of food endowed with peculiar properties thanks to the patterns painted on the vessels and intended to induce in the participants the harmony of their inner self with the properly ordered structure of the universe (for a different approach to the same problem cf. Forest 1993).

How instructive are ethnographic parallels for the reconstruction of behaviour of the highly ranked groups of these early ages, especially with reference to ritual and to ceremonial commensality? Can they help us to shed at least a little more light on events which happened so long ago – in the darkness of the prehistoric era?

Ethnology: Emergence of the highly ranked groups

One of the best areas of the pre-modern world for studies of the emergence of highly ranked groups is ancient China. The students of her civilization, availing themselves of a rich array of sources, have contributed major treatises on Chinese traditions of rulership and emergence of the state. For the ancient Chinese, civilization came forth most definitely as a construct of a sage or sages sent to this world by the gods who wished civilization to come forth.

One of these traditions refers to three sages of Chinese mythology: the first defined the rules of life of human society, the second put earth and the watery kingdom in an ordered state and gave them their names, and the third taught people how to live by agriculture. These sages disposed of a power over such elements of the world as fire or water. Gradually, these mythical "founding fathers" have merged into a single mythical personage who, putting his inner self "in tune" with nature, created laws for human society. In this manner, a myriad things emerged out of the shapeless and silent darkness and began looking for proper relationships among one another. This brought forth both harmony and disharmony. The sages promulgated the relevant laws in accordance with nature and thus not necessarily with recourse to ethical rules; violence was conceivable, and, indeed, possible in this early state of things (Puett 1998).

However this early construct may or may not correspond to reality, the chief argument to retain is that early Chinese thinkers perceived their civilization a) as a work of singular personages who formulated laws of civilized life in accordance with the laws of nature, and b) as a construct of mythology, not of brute force or economic coercion.

Once in position, these primeval highly ranked groups lived a busy and dynamic life. Chinese kings of the early ages (Western Chou, 1045–771 B.C.) instituted their own courtly ritual above a whole series of local and regional rituals. They venerated especially illustrious persons with banquets in their honour and bestowed on them gifts, i.a. of bronze vessels, whereby they let them partake of the royal supernatural powers.

After the eviction of the Western Chou dynasty from their ancestral land in 771 B.C., a process of deep-reaching transformation took place. The fact that local notables usurped the ancient royal prerogatives is clearly evident both from the menus of the banquets they instituted and especially from inscriptions on bronze vessels. The original process of conferment of "royal glamour" on recipients of kingly gifts was now reversed: instead of receiving supernatural sanction from the king, the local rank individuals now claimed their privilege to acquire such blessings in their own right and by their own initiative. In cooperation with the ancient Chou-dynasty ceremonial officials, the new lords acquired a sanction of their power in two ways. First and foremost, a number of them initiated public feasts in which the original divine sanction of the Chou royal power was re-enacted by means of song, dance and public performances. Subsequently they set up bronze vessels, bearing inscriptions giving full reports of these proceedings to the ancestors of the groupings, in their clan shrines. The ultimate sign of establishment of full-blown statehood on behalf of these new highly ranked groups were the "altars of soil and millet"; a destruction of such an altar or removal of its "propitious metals" deprived the relevant ruler of legitimacy (Overmyer et al. 1995, cf. also Emerson 1996, esp. pp. 539–541).

At this moment, let us notice one single detail. All narratives concerning the emergence of early Chinese civilization lay great stress on music, considered to be a perfect model of harmony into which both the new human being and the new world was supposed to fit (Emerson 1996, 542–543; Overmyer et al. 1995, 149). How far does the fact that perhaps the very first sophisticated musical instrument of the ancient Near East, which left behind a set of bone tubes with a mouthpiece of grey limestone found at Arpachiyah (Charvat 2002, 43), belongs to exactly this period of time, point in the same direction? At any rate, the phenomenon itself is conspicuous.

Here again the process of re-distribution of power and re-stucturation of the political scene is constructed as a purely mythological and symbolical discourse, involving a najor role of both commensality and public ceremonies.

A similar perception of the role of the earliest historically documentable highly ranked groups prevailed in ancient India (Yelizarenkova 1993, 10–16). The need to renew orderly life at the start of each year, when life was believed to relapse into the original chaotic state, resulted in a series of restoration rituals including sacrifices but also, for instance, chariot races. Ritual was conceived there as the ultimate source of earthly happiness, validity of laws, balance of power and material welfare.

It is perhaps relevant to add at this point that a similar definition of the crucial task of highly ranked groups of the early ages brought no substantial innovations. In the hunter-gatherer groups of Amazonia, the chiefs managed the survival of their groups by applying magical knowledge which had a direct bearing on the fertility of both nature and people (Granero 1986). Modern research points to the conclusion that in many aspects, the pretended "revolutions" of later historical periods represent hardly more than development of attributes of early, and frequently even hunter-gatherer societies. In the case of some of these it can be demonstrated, for instance, that they display a visible social stratification and even hold slaves (Gronenborn 2001, esp. pp. 10–21).

It should be added here that in what follows I do not take into consideration the economic aspects of emergence and activities of the early highly ranked groups, as this is a subject too vast to be included here. One of the possible conceptualizations of this problem has been most pertinently submitted by Reinhard Bernbeck (1994) and most exhaustive treatments have now been furnished by Gil Stein (1998; 2001).

51

The highly ranked groups of early ages thus presumably acquired their positions, "speaking through" elaborate rituals, which could nonetheless also work as battering rams, dislodging the old cliques from power and enabling the takeover of public offices by fresh candidates. In what manner did the commoners, who probably watched this drama, which could at times turn either into tragedy or into a grotesque, with amusement or with horror, conceive their own relations vis-a-vis the power holders? How were the essentials of social life, especially of subsistence, managed and handled?

Soil, and especially arable earth, were perceived by most pre-industrial cultures as the creation of primeval elements such as heaven and earth, of divinities or at least of divinized heroes. Earth belonged properly to the gods and people were there just to take it in custody and to manage it. In most cases, soil is reported to have been inherited from the ancestors who had received it from the gods (Kank 2000 [1992], esp. pp. 64–69).

How this was done in practice may most instructively be seen from the results of Sir Edmund Leach's magisterial study on the states of highland Myanmar (Leach 1968). In the mythology of the Kachin, inhabiting the woodland hills on the border between China and Myanmar, above the well-watered river valleys, dwellings of the sedentary agricultural population of Shan, the highest among all the supernatural beings are the spirits of the sky. The youngest among these is Madai, who married his daughter to a human male and thus became the ancestor of the Kachin chiefs. These chiefs are in-laws to Madai and only they are entitled to sacrifice to him and to turn, by his mediation, to Shadip, the highest of the land spirits and incarnation of the primeval creator, a binary and bisexual divinity. Shadip is the lord of fertility and well-being (Leach 1968, 175).

This high social status pertains not only to the chief in question, but to all his family and progeny. Collectively, this kinship group are then known as "hunch-eaters" because they have the right to demand a portion of game from every hunting expedition undertaken in Kachin territory. (An interesting sidelight on the Sumerian sign UR2, "portion", "share".) All the "hunch-eaters" have two altars in their houses: on one they sacrifice to the spirits of the chiefly lineage, on the other to Madai, lord of heaven (Leach 1968, 155–156, 175–176).

The "chief's political authority is based ... on his ability to preserve the prosperity of his domain by making sacrifices to the sky spirit, Madai, and to the earth spirit Shadip" (Leach 1968, 129). This is so because the welfare of all the inhabitants of the region in question depends on proper performance of these rituals.

This essentially kinship-based social construction is so strong that any Kachin, while identifying himself, will give evidence on his or her lineage – unlike the Shan who will, in such circumstances, give evidence on their birthplace (Leach 1968, 107). A meaningful distinction to which we shall return later.

Ethnology: Landholding through ritual

In kinship-based societies, property and social recognition is thus achieved by means of respecting the spiritual structure that puts things in proper places. We now have the chiefs with the shamans, the commoners, and the land, all held together by the proper performance of rituals. Nevertheless, it would be somewhat difficult to maintain the collective rights to land solely on the base of human words and deeds, as life was fragile by then as it is now and an entire human group could have been wiped off by a single catastrophic event. For this reason, people began to label the property of their territories by material markers, though of a most peculiar kind. The following paragraph does not, strictly speaking, have a direct bearing on the highly ranked groups of Halaf-culture Mesopotamia. It is nevertheless so interesting for any students of early human territorialization that I deem the data to be worth a brief overview.

A number of human groups living in the Lelet Plateau of central New Ireland in Papua, New Guinea, view as the clan's most cherished possessions huge shells which they jealously guard. Such shells, embodying the origin and story of the relevant clan, are supposed to lie without motion and in many instances biographies and genealogies of clan members who hold them are inscribed on them. Such "bones of the clan" are charged with magical power which may work both benignantly and malignantly. They pass from father to son as inheritance; when they are lost, the clan "has nowhere to sit" and "is worth nothing" (Eves 1998, 142–147, 243–244).

A site-bound variant of these huge shells is represented by magical boulders supposed to bring fertility to taro gardens. These are normally to be found in the household courtyards, where they have been deposited upon holding of a ritual. They must not be removed lest the hunger strikes the household. If any unauthorized person touches such stones, he or she will die a terrible death (Eves 1998, 217–219).

In addition to these material markers, all local clans venerate the larada, "tutelary guardians, rooting particular clans in certain bounded locales". If the larada sit motionlessly, their clans remain sedentary in their abodes. When, however, the larada stand up, leave their site and go away, their clans must follow. In fact, the tales of journeys of the larada constitute a means through which, when skilfully managed, land can be claimed (and possibly also obtained).

Here we clearly see how mythopoeic thought operates in order not only to secure positions of rank, but also to substantiate landholding of commoners. Representing in all its aspects spiritual constructs, mythology can nonetheless acquire well visible and discernible material correlates even in shifting-agriculture societies. Archaeologists must be aware of similar cases in order to at least attempt as exhaustive assessment of their evidence as possible.

Ethnology: Ritual and the human body

Once settled in their proper place, both the rank individuals and the commoners begin to think about the world which surrounds them and about its form. In a number of instances, the world is conceptualized as having the form of, or having been created out of, a human body, or alternatively, a body of a being sacrificed for that purpose, perhaps a victim of a mythical conflict or war. This idea is known from Vedic India (Yelizarenkova 1993, 42–43), but in some instances it takes on a rather unexpected turn. Some New Guinea tribes believe, for instance, that cultivated edible plants first grew out of a body of a wife murdered by her husband and buried by him in a forest (Godelier 1992, 8).

Let us, however, focus on another idea concerning the human body, which is of great interest to us here. This has been documented among the Lelet Plateau groups whom we have already visited (Eves 1998, 34–35). They are convinced that the strength of an industrious human body ultimately results in the material output of its exercise, be it harvest of the gardens or meat of livestock. In this vision, the fruit of human labour is conceived as segments of a human personality which have sprung forth from it and which represent it, both in exchange and in circulation of goods. The Lelet-Plateau groups view affluence as a visible and perceptible manifestation of previously hidden human qualities, so that "social life consists of making the internal capacities of persons visible" (Eves 1998, 35). This is very relevant to studies of prehistoric cultures of the Near East: we must be aware that the food eaten from the exquisite painted tableware might have represented, in addition to the powerful magic of the world-ordering ritual, a "detached segment" of somebody's personality and that something is likely to have been given in compensation for this benefice.

However, we would probably go too far to ascribe to the bearers of Halaf culture an individualism similar to that of our own. The nearly perfect aniconicity of Halaf-culture pottery shows that we are still operating in categories of the mythical, universal body constructs and not in deliberately used notions of personages. The cardinal moment of many pre-industrial cultures, in which a human individual constitutes an intersection of social linkages of diverse sorts and in which therefore the discovery of the body results in the recognition of a unique human individuality, had not yet occurred in Halaf-culture thought (Emerson 1996, 533–539).

Short of being perceived as individuals, bearers of the Halaf culture could have made their bodies carriers of most diverse cosmic forces. A supernatural, invisible substance of divine origin which brough to actual action the potential of the ruler's power, has been documented both in China (*de*) and in Oceania (*mana*; Kryukov 1995). Another similar case, pertaining to the abovementioned mana of the Polynesian Tonga island, has been evoked recently. The local chiefs, holding mana from their deified ancestors, were able not only to fertilize the soil of commoners' fields, but also to activate the process of fecundity in women of their own group (Douaire-Marsaudon 2001, 23 n. 28).

Ethnology: Conclusion

This section may now be concluded with the observation of the pervasiveness and universality of ritual in early pre-state societies (on this cf. also Hicks 1999). Incipient ranked groups assume their places by means of a ritual, exercise their functions through ritual and are replaced by others with deployment of the relavnt rituals. Commoners hold their land and exercise their skill and talents in a space defined by ritual coordinates. The ritual actions pertain mostly to human minds and only gradually do they acquire also the relevant material appurtenances.

A considerable role is played in ritual by the human body. On one hand, the fruit of human labour is viewed as the manifestation of the personage's hidden qualities, and consequently, as his or her "externized segments". On the other hand, the human body assumes the function of a carrier of supernatural forces, especially the body of an individual of high rank. This force can choose the body of a particular human individual in order to affect the well-being of his or her whole group.

Ethnology: Fire and cooked food

We now know something about the role of ritual, of its material appurtenances and of the human body in ritual of the pre-state societies. The next issue that I now wish to address is the question of commensality, of exceptional interest and significance for the development of early social complexity in the ancient Near East (Charvat 2002, register, esp. pp. 80–85).

Much as water symbolizes numerous aspects of fertility and proliferation in many ancient societies, fire, an essential element for preparation of cooked food, has been interpreted symbolically as an agent of a series of (also mythological) transformations by them.

In ancient Greece, fire was held to be helpful both in down-to-earth pyrotechnological procedures. In affairs supernatural, it could serve as a means of communication with the sphere of superhuman beings, but it also conferred immortality on children of earthlings held by goddesses above it. "Greek fire" destroyed to elevate: his own cremation set Hercules free of all his earthly bondage and allowed him to be elevated among divinities (Kirk 1970, 196).

Claude Levi-Strauss has also pointed to this transforming role of fire in a number of ethnologic societies: changing raw into cooked food, fire can be perceived as an element linking heaven and earth, nature and culture, or life and death. Fire can even be acquired from animals such as a jaguar of vulture (Kirk 1970, 66–67).

The "communicator" role of fire finds a good illustration in traditional myths of Central America in which supernatural sanctification of the kingly mission is conceived of as "divine fire", supposed to fill the bosom of earthly rulers. Laws promulgated by the ruler consitute sparks ignited from this divine fire, much as conferring of a higher social status on some individual is literally called "filling with fire" (Austin 1988, 399–400).

On the other hand, fire is considered to be such a firm and integral part of human life that curses against enemy realms may contain the clause "let fire vanish from his land". This is attested in an Aramaic inscription of the 8th century B.C. from Iranian Azarbaijan (Lemaire 1998, 23).

Fire is thus an all-purpose communicator and convertor. Let us now target another major issue: human food, "embodying social relationships" (Eves

1998, 38). Partaking of food constitutes an embodiment that is, "a process of internalizing that which is external, making it consubstantial with the body", a procedure "by which the outside is made inside and the uncanny made canny" (Eves 1998, 41). This appropriation of external entities and their integration into human personality does not concern food only: it also includes sensual aperception, knowledge and learning including bodily movements in space (Eves 1998, 40–43). Such an appropriation, necessary for the knowledge of entities previously unknown and thus potentially dangerous, which must be studied and "given a name" in order to integrate them into coherent and "civilized" human universe, occurs as early as the Sumerian literature, an eloquent example being provided by the myth of "Enki and Ninhursag" (Kirk 1970, 91–98, esp. pp. 95, 97).

A beautiful example of what has just been said is provided by Edmund Ronald Leach (1968, 280). In 1836, ruler of Burma accepted the oath of loyalty of both Shan and Kachin groups resident along the Sino-Burmese border. In the course of the ceremonial confirmation of this oath, a buffalo was first killed and eaten. Then the chiefs surrendered their arms to the spirits of the chiefly lineage and these spirits were honoured by sacrifices. Subsequently, all the participants took a handful of rye in their hands and then, kneeling down and clasping their hands above their heads, they listened to the text of the oath. The text was then burned, the ashes mixed into water and the resulting potion given in cups to the chiefs. The chiefs promised again to remain faithful to the oath and drank their cups, whereupon they all sat down and ate from one huge bowl a common meal. Here the internalizing process is made quite plain by digestion of a text which was supposed to become part of the personality of each dignitary present.

The embodiment process of food digestion can sometimes lead quite far. In the Trobriand Islands, Bronislaw Malinowski has noticed that a shaman pronouncing a magical formula unites himself with the ancestor spirits in the act of partaking of food which he has received from the community "in payment for our magical services"(Malinowski 1935, 254).

The food which is eaten becomes an integral part of the eater's personality (Jacobson-Widding 1990, 50). The exchange of food therefore requires complete trust among the donor and recipient, as a human being may be subjected to another human being by means of food, a clear example being offered by love magic in which partaking food containing (concealed) parts of the body of the sorcerer entails falling in love with him (or her) on behalf of the bewitched person (Eves 1998, 60–61). In a transformed manner, this idea of identity of a person with the food he or she is partaking of appears in the 11th–12th century A. D. in early fathers of the medieval Catholic Church of Europe. Petrus Damiani does not hesitate to liken a glutton's mouth to a vagina: "per os ergo cibum tamquam semen delectabiliter edendo concipiunt" (Tramontana 1999, 197). The "second founder" of the Cistercian order, Bernard of Clairvaux, says that whoever eats his food with gusto and enjoys it, "effudit super cibum animam suam" (Tramontana 1999, 197).

This section may then be concluded by an observation that within the ritual procedures of early societies, fire plays frequently the role of both sacred and profane communicator and convertor. Used for cooking food, it assists the process of human embodiment, or integration of edible entites which were originally external to humans (raw, presumably non-human and therefore potentially dangerous) and which, having undergone the process of cooking and comestion, become an indivisible part of a human personality. To a certain extent, "you are what you eat" in pre-state societies.

Ethnology: Commensality

The offering of food is commonly considered a deed of merit and a donor of food enjoys prestige and fame as a great, affluent and beneficent man (Malinowski 1929, 441). Yet, true commensality is not a characteristic of simpler pre-state societies where people commonly ate in private, even during great feasts and banquets (Malinowski 1929, 442).

In other cases, commensality represents a "constitutive principle of both incorporation and authority", offering the participants the acquisition, or reiteration, of their social personalities. For inhabitants of early modern India, the fact that someone was fed and clothed meant that he was accepted into the relevant kinship group as member. Eating at one common table or one common meal meant the same thing (Chatterjee-Guha 1999, 168–169).

Food can also act as an ethnic marker. When a baby is born in a village of the Minangkabau people of western Sumatra, the parents feed him or her rice porridge, bananas and a bit of coconut with red pepper at the age of about six months. All these foods are considered as typical Minangkabau dishes and the baby thus becomes a true Minangkabau only after the comestion of them (Sanday 1997, 32, fig. 9).

One of the most renowned cases of commensality, uniting all the principles that have been cited until now – social, ethnic and spiritual – is, of course, represented by the ceremonial drinking of a beverage prepared from the roots of *kava* in the Polynesian island of Tonga (from the abundant literature, cf., at least, Gifford 1929, esp. pp. 93 and 157–168; James 1991; and Douaire-Marsaudon 2001). *Kava* (Piper methysticum) is a shrub about 1.2 to 3 metres high and the substance used for preparation of the drink was obtained from its roots. These were originally chewed but now they are crushed in a mortar. The mashed substance was then poured over with water and passed through a sieve or strainer. Various side dishes were usually served together with the *kava* drink, including, for instance, pork meat.

The ceremonial drinking of *kava*, instituted either by the king or by any of the chiefs, included once a libation to the gods; after conversion to Christianity, it has been marking major political events such as diplomatic visits, assumption of office or transfer of official competences. The ceremony may, however, have been held in other circumstances as well: when the land is in danger (during illness of the king, for instance,) before or during a war, prior to a long-distance voyage, before a major work project or if one of the king's wives expected a baby; last but not least, by the graveside of a recently deceased chief. Universal peace must be observed during the *kava*-drinking ceremony.

The *kava*-drinking chiefs are seated in two large semicircles facing each other, forming thus a big oval space. The highest dignitary, usually the king, flanked by two attendants, assumes a place at the centre of the main semicircle. Other chiefs with their masters of ceremony sit at his sides in the descending hierarchical order. The commoners' places are either outside the oval or within it.

The ceremony is opened with toasts held by all the important participants including, of course, the king. Next, the *kava* is poured into a dish while one of the officiating courtiers proclaims this to be a *kava* of the king. Consumption of the drink and food follows.

It is interesting to observe that the cups for drinking *kava* are made either of banana leaves tied over with a string or of coconut shells. The utensils can thus be quite plain and unprepossessing and the Halaf-culture painted pottery might well have been preceded by receptacles of organic matters such as basketry, as seems to be implied by the decoration of some examples.

All the students of this colourful Polynesian ceremony have concentrated particularly on the ritual meaning of *kava* drinking. The roots of the *kava* shrub are perceived as bones of ancestors, containing a kind of seed including a "life-transmission element". The crucial moment of the ceremony comes when the (new) king drinks from his cup. At this moment he becomes mystically reunited with his ancestors who had held the title before him, as far as the goddess Hikule`o, "sister to his father". From this moment on he is also the bearer of the substance called *mana*, enabling him to trigger off both the fertility of the soil of his realm and the fecundity of women of his group (Douaire-Marsaudon 2001, 23 n. 28). The king's union with the supreme goddess of the Tonga pantheon confers upon him the privilege to collect yearly first-fruit offerings. As to the chiefs, they invoke their own ancestors and, in turn, become their avatars after having drunk from the *kava* cups. The ritual is supposed to transmit an idealized form of virility and is strictly confined to males capable of exercising the kingly and chiefly functions.

Archaeology and ethnology: Conclusions

All in all, what has come forth from this lengthy exposition with so many digressions? The highly ranked groups of the Halaf culture, in whom a connection with the exquisite painted pottery may be surmised, introduced the first discernible traits of Mesopotamian religion, venerating, at the very least, the sky god An. They apparently exercised functions putting them in connection with redistribution practices. They might also have indulged in non-subsistence hunting, perhaps in a ritual role of humanizing the wild nature. They are rather likely to have instituted a complex set of ceremonies including music and solemn commensality involving (symbolic?) partaking of food from the beautifully painted tableware.

From its own side, ethnology says that the highly ranked groups of early ages were born with ritual, they lived by ritual and died by ritual, much as the commoners of their groups. Originally, the rituals dwelt solely in human minds; only slowly did they acquire also material appurtenances, of which one of the most important was the human body. In early societies, the human body frequently carried a twofold mission: first and foremost, by applying its strength and know-how it transformed nature, making thus its inner qualities manifest. Second, it acted as a transmitter and amplifier of superhuman forces which found their way into the visible world through it.

The human body must be nourished and here the food cooked on fire comes to the fore. The fire, a sacred and profane convertor and communicator, helped to provide the eating table where the food comested fulfilled again a double purpose. First, it served as a means to integrate entities which were originally external, and possibly uncanny, into the human person and to make them consubstantial with the body. Second, partaking of food created new groupings – social, ethnic, or spiritual, whatever the particular case might have been.

Does all this help us somewhere with our Halaf-culture problems? It seems that Halaf culture is "prehistoric" in the sense that its bearers have still not made the "discovery of the body", at least as far as its nearly perfect aniconicity can show. We now know that both the highly ranked groups and the commoners of the Halaf-culture are likely to have "set a great store" by ritual. Nevertheless, out of all interpretation possibilities, we must acknowledge our confinement to the sphere of painted pottery. In this aspect, at least three observations may be made:

a) the occurrence of pottery bowls, pots and jars presupposes the existence of both solid and liquid food, most probably cooked with the aid of fire. Thus the chief form of transformation of natural resorces – and also of economic surplus – is likely to have been constituted by various foodstuffs, brought to the high-rank households to be consumed there;

b) the common partaking of food must have generated solidarities, though of what kind we cannot say. The hypothesis that results of the primeval entrepreneurs' efforts, perceived as materialized manifestations of their exceptional personal qualities and endowments, were "embodied" by their followers desiring to "eat the chief's *mana*" in the food provided by him, is possible but cannot be proven;

c) as to the possible spiritual or mystical dimensions of Halaf-culture commensality, we are entirely in the dark. Still, there goes the Polynesian kava-drinking chief, united with the supreme deity and thus acquiring mana, thanks to which he can not only trigger off the fertility of the soil but also the fecundity of women. Moreover, he is collecting the yearly first-fruit offerings. All this is so dangerously close to what will be usual in the Uruk-culture world, as we shall presently see, that the urge to resist the hypothesis-building temptation must be very strong.

Archaeology and ethnology: Combs and what they stand for

A particular motif deserves attention here, and that is the image of a comb. It does not figure with any particular prominence on Halaf-culture pottery; at Arpachiyah, one single instance of a comb component in a chequerboard matrix has been documented (Mallowan-Rose 1935, fig. 78: 28). Nevertheless, a bowl from the eponymous site of Tell Halaf in Syria displays two opposite-lying combs as the principal filling motif (illustrated in Charvát 2002, 62 fig. 4.13). As, however, combs will constitute one of the chief decorative elements on the painted pottery of Susa, it may be of interest to take a closer look at them now, in a moment when they first enter our field of vision.

The issues concerning human hair and its symbolic interpretations are manifold and complex and some colleagues have voiced their conviction that in view of this fact, a case-by-case approach seems the best advisable (e. g. Williamson 1979, with a bibliography on the theme on p. 395 n. 3; cf. also a summary of earlier research in Leach 1999 [1958]). If I dare to go beyond this recommendation here, I am guided solely by my desire to push forward the frontiers of our knowledge, by way of something that may prove to be a futile undertaking, though I have decided to include it here, simply for the sake of experiment. The lure of Sir Francis Drake's maxim of "plus ultra" is too strong.

In order to include in my investigations the widest circle of human cultures possible, I have decided to take my samples from communities at maximum distances from one another, to ensure that they could not have come into mutual contacts and that they can thus furnish mutually disjunct examples of hair symbolism. The location of Susa induced me to seek motifs of Iranian lore, which quickly proved to be rather limited in extent. I complemented these by materials from the ethnography of Africa and Oceania and by a rather loose array of similar data from the cultures of Europe, India and America. Let us now pass the results in a brief overview.

Ethnology of combs: Iran

Historically, the amount of Iranian iconic evidence for the interpretation of combs and comb imagery is extremely limited, chiefly because of the prevailing Shi'ite attitude towards images. Yet, some regions of Iran have retained a certain amount of carved tombstones yielding comprehensible evidence (Massé 1938). In addition to inscriptions, such tombstones may show instruments of the deceased's trade or profession, or, alternatively, a string of beads, indicating the piety of the interred person. Moreover, male burials are designated by images of razors and, especially in the Isfahan region, also by means of combs. In the latter case, the comb, signalling piety, is supposed to refer to the deceased's custom to comb his beard before praying

(Massé 1938, 104). This interpretation is presumably based on the fact that there exists a female comb symbolism as well and that cosmetic devices, including combs, sometimes do appear also on female tombs (Masse 1938, 497). Funerary monuments of strong men may carry images of lions, or of horsemen piercing lions with spears, or, alternatively, of rams (Massé 1938, 105–106).

Some interesting data are furnished by Iranian folklore. After the first forty days of life, a bath is prepared for a newly born baby. At this moment the child must have his or her own comb on which a prayer may be inscribed. The comb is immersed in water forty times and the baby's hair is combed (Donaldson 1938, 32). Another custom of relevance to my investigation here was to shave the child's head every Wednesday to ensure his or her survival; for a more insightful interpretation of this practice we would have to know more about the popular calendar of Iran, here it may suffice to note the close connection between hair and human life (Massé 1938, 824).

The rather widespread custom of burying nail- and hair clippings, as well as extracted teeth, for fear of bewitchment effectuated by means of these personal excrescences worked by a sorcerer into a statuette, which is then stabbed or melted to work ill effects on the bewitched person, is attested to in Iran as well (Massé 1938, 304).

Scanty as the Iranian evidence may be, it does bear out a connection between hair and life, life force and positive personal qualities of human beings. Manipulation of hair can influence these personal characteristics, for better (combing of the newborn baby) or for worse (bewitchment).

Ethnology of combs: Africa

Much as the anthropology of state origins is indebted to ancient Chinese sources, general physical and cultural anthropology owes much to archaeological and historical sources of ancient Egypt. Symbolical operations with human hair characterized the Egyptian civilization all along the three millennia of its existence (Tassie 1996). One of the chief rituals playing a key role in the life of every Egyptian, the hair-cutting ceremony marking the attainment of the adult status, included the sacrifice of the "Hair lock of childhood" to the god Horus. In another instance, during the so-called name-giving ceremony, a lock of hair was given by the person who received a new name to his or her tutelary divinity. In general, ancient Egyptians offered their hair clippings quite frequently, and that from the late prehistoric period

(Naqada II and III, 4th pre-Christian millennium: Tassie 1996, 61). Some of the highest-rank Egyptians even went to their graves with their hair offerings interred separately in diminutive coffins (Tutankhamun: Tassie 1996, 64). Human hair was also included in offerings and magical devices of other kinds: it was worked into pottery fertility figurines, as well as into the mysterious clay balls containing human hair and stamped with seal rings found at el-Amarna (Tassie 1996, 60).

In general, hair meant two things to the ancient Egyptians: it was identical with a part of human personality, and, moreover, it symbolized their life force. In Egypt, human hair identified both an individual human being and a whole interrelated group (Tassie 1996, 60, 65–66).

This interpretation is in full accordance with hair symbolism which is still alive in some parts of Africa, for instance, in the Congo region (Jacobson-Widding 1990). Together with human shadows, photographs of human beings, their personal names, bodily excretions, digested food, as well as sweat-drenched clothing, the human nail- and hair clippings are considered as "incarnation of the emic notion of individual personhood", referred to here as nvumbi, vital essence (Jacobson-Widding 1990, 50–51).

The extent to which human hair represents an integral part of a human personality, excrescence of his or her innermost and therefore invisible nature, comes to full recognition in African transition rituals pertaining to temporal stations in which humans change their status in life.

Shearing of hair occurrs in the initiation rites of many African tribes; for instance, the Afikpo people of the eastern Ibo tribes take the hair shorn from the heads of initiated boys to the village cemetery where it is left (Ottenberg 1975, 194A). An even more elaborate ceremony of this kind has been documented by the Lobi people: for the collective initiation rite of dyoro, the candidates must wear nothing but a cord around their waists and have their heads shorn. Receiving a new name upon accomplishment of the rite, they depart for the bush where they undergo a training lasting about two weeks. After this they return to the house of their patriclan but they behave in a reversed manner – talk nonsense, eat with their left hands, clutch the hoe by the blade, etc. In this phase they have their heads shaved alternately on one or the other half. Only after all this does the final ceremony take place (Ovesen 1990, 153–155).

Other instances in which manipulation of the hair plays a similar role include a change of an individual's social status. Persons reduced to slavery by the Dogon people, for instance, take a ceremonial bath, are shorn and shaved and receive a new name. The reverse process takes place when they are manumitted, or when captives are set free: the ceremonial bath is followed by a shearing of the person's head, donning a new robe and receiving a new name, usually that of the royal lineage (Holder 1998, 94–99).

A whole series of ritual proceedings surrounds death and burial in Africa. Hair and nails of any deceased person are clipped and buried at an intersection of two roads or, burned in the bush (Pradelles de Latour 1996, 139). Among the Marachi people of western Kenya, the heads of the widow and of all close relatives of a deceased man are shorn prior to a ceremonial bath; here we can clearly see how human hair identifies not only an individual but his or her whole group. After the widow has initiated her new life with a relative of her deceased husband obliged to take care of her, she dons a new robe, her head is shorn and she calls on her family, presumably to give evidence of her new status (Whyte 1990, 97–100). To the same circle if ideas belongs the assumption that a definite break between a husband and a wife who has left him has occurred only when she refuses to come shave his head after his death, current among the Ibo people (Thomas 1914, 17).

An unusually clear example of hair manipulation linked to a change of status concerns the inthronization ceremonies, by which the Ibo of the Awka neighbourhood (Onitsha) confer office on their Obi (ruler). The head-shaving ceremony takes place at the shrine of the Udo spirit, situated in a thick undergrowth by a termite hill where the first Obi is believed to have been buried and where the ruling Obi comes to consult his ancestors (Nzimiro 1972, 166–167). In the course of the rites carried out by the Eze Udo, chief priest of Udo, of the Obio lineage, one of the elder members of this lineage shaves the future king's head. Following this, part of the shaved hair and the king's old loincloth are deposited in the termite hill, which means that they have been transferred to the world of the spirits. The remaining part of the king's shaved hair is deposited in a sacred grove (*okwu*) of Udo (Henderson 1972, 305). In this manner, the king's life is directed by the Udo spirit from this moment on. The ruler then receives a new loincloth while these words are said to him: "Eze, now you have deposed the attire of suffering and poverty", whereupon he answers: "Now I have deposed the attire of poverty and suffering" (Meek 1970, 186).

Even the process of shaving the ruling Obi's head is a sacred proceeding. A sacrifice of food take place in its course and no one is allowed to enter the room where the shaving is taking place, though recently the king's wives have been allowed to carry out this procedure. The king himself brings his shaven hair into the bush and deposits it on a wooden board resting on four poles where no one is allowed to touch it (Thomas 1913, 53).

In terms of the African material, my findings can now be summarized in much the same manner. In Africa, too, human hair is, first and foremost, an excrescence of the innermost, invisible nature of human personality, comprising all its manifold aspects including the life force of the individual in question. Any change of the individual's status, be it of age (including death) or of social standing, entails cutting his or her hair, to reflect the person's new character. In Africa, human hair can refer not only to individuals but to whole groups to which they are closely related.

Ethnology of combs: Oceania

In the area of the Pacific Ocean, the relationship towards human hair has been marked by a rather peculiar dichotomy. On one hand, hair, and especially that growing on the body, represented an entity viewed as undesirable and hardly ellegant, being removed whereever possible (Malinowski 1929, 300). On the Tonga island, men shaved their legs and women got rid of both their pubic hair and the axillary hairs (Gifford 1929, 231). On the other hand, inhabitants of the Pacific islands tolerated hirsute appearance in creatures appearing in myths and fairy tales, from whom grotesque and perverted behaviour could be expected (Malinowski 1929, 300), and, in actual fact, in their own chiefs, whose persons enjoyed so much prestige that it was virtually impossible to touch their heads (Firth 1970, 41). In the Tonga island, the Tui Tonga, supreme chief of the realm, had to suffer his hair and beard to be burned by glowing charcoal pieces (Gifford 1929, 74, 286). Only the closest family members, such as the high chief's wives, were allowed to cut his hair and in some places they insisted on this privilege even if they had transferred nost of the other duties of the house mistresses to other members of the great household (Mead 1975 [1928], 108).

Non-elite men and women did, of course, display their hair proudly and took care to keep it in good state (Gifford 1929, 286). Most of the commoners used combs which might have been simple products made of coconut teeth bound with twine (Gifford 1929, 117); the chiefs might have availed themselves of accomplished implements made of hard wood or tortoiseshell and bearing decorative patterns (Gifford 1929, 117). As elsewhere, combs were considered a powerful instrument of magic and figured prominently in acts of sorcery aimed at enhancing female beauty (Malinowski 1929, 300). In the Tonga island, local fashion commanded soaking the hair in coral lime to make the hairdo stand upright (Gifford 1929, 232). This custom was so widespread that both the chiefly and the commoners' language possessed expressions for this procedure (Gifford 1929, 121).

A fairly clear idea of the symbolism of human hair integrated into a life cycle of a nomadic group may be obtained from data on the Umeda of Papua, New Guinea (Gell 1992, Chapter 5, 36–53). These people who live by shifting agriculture, hunting and food-collection, hold a yearly ceremony called *ida* which constitutes a unifying principle of all their society. The colour symbolism of the *ida* dance is based on reality: the Umeda are born with a light complexion, sometimes even with red hair which turns dark as they grow more mature in age. For the Umeda, black colour stands for adult age, independence bordering on asocial manners, war, ancestor spirits and the forest, as well as for the luxuriantly growing hair of adult men. The participants change their body-paint colours from black to red as the dance proceeds, symbolizing thus the backward progression from adulthood to youth and from the wild and untamed human temperament to behaviour meeting an acceptable social norm.

Each age group of the Umeda wears a particular and distinctive hairdo. Adolescent youths are cropped short; young men keep their hair long and tie it into a sort of chignon on the top of the head while adult men wear long and unkempt hair (Gell 1992, 42–46). Here it is interesting to note that in the Tonga island, old men and women also wear their hair cropped short (Gifford 1929, 231); we could thus speculate on how far they are socially considered in the same degree as children.

Here it is again the innermost nature of the human personality that is symbolized by human hair, human character as defined by the age, sex and presumed nature of the individual in question.

The identity of the essential symbolic interpretation of human hair is confirmed by the witchcraft and sorcery practices involving it. In the Lelet Plateau groups of Papua, New Guinea, hair clippings, among other parts of the body of the initiator, are burned and mixed with food eaten by the person to be bewitched as a love charm (Eves 1998, 60–61). The same thing goes, of course, for an evil spell: burning someone's hair will result in his or her death (Eves 1998, 63).

The form of hair distinguishes human and non-human beings. In the Lelet Plateau, the laga demons can assume human form but in this case their hair reaches down to their knees and they have claws instead of fingernails (Eves 1998, 156–163).

Thus the Oceanian evidence again confirms that even there, human hair represents the excrescence of the innermost human self, of the immaterial personal nature in its manifold aspects. This "inner human self" may be affected and influenced by magical procedures including the use of combs.

Ethnology of combs: Europe, India, America

Let us finish this investigation, becoming somewhat repetitive, by passing in review at least a sample of data from other continents.

There is no need of stressing the importance of historical sources of ancient Greece for general studies of human civilization, and it is no wonder that Greek evidence falls in with what we have been observing here. An excavation of a temple of Demeter and Persephone outside the city walls of Cyrene in Libya, of the Archaic period (6th–5th centuries B.C.) has brought forth a number of "small finds" including cultic gifts, personal ornaments and locks of hair or receptacles for them. Much as in ancient Egypt, the local boys and girls left locks of their hair in the temple after completion of rites marking the passage to adulthood (Warden 1992, 54, a silver imitation of a lock of hair in p. 58 fig. 17). This is another testimony in favour of the "change of state" argument whereby the change in human character is marked by cutting of the hair, containing the "human being of the past", no longer in existence.

The European medieval culture does not offer many examples that would be of relevance to my argument. Hirsuteness as a personal character of some European ruling families, such as the counts of Barcelona, does nonetheless appear in written sources and enjoys a high esteem (Aurell 1998). It is, however, not clear how far the hairiness of Guifred le Velu, which ultimately earned him the count's stool, may be brought in connection with the rather peculiar bodily characteristics of the Merovingian kings, who are reported to have had hair growing in two zones along the vertebral column (Aurell 1998, 15). In this instance it may legitimately be asked whether this was not a genetic trait transmitted within a particular lineage group, in our case a dynasty of counts or kings. The fact is that in times of the Han dynasty of China (207 B. C. – 220 A. D.), exuberant growth of bodily hair, including beard and eyebrows, was considered a mark of a great personage, but this opinion was limited to the Han-dynasty age only (Bielenstein 1997, 39). Other specialists have pointed to the conclusion that combs, featuring rather frequently in the attire, as well as burial goods, of medieval European élites 'may allude to wearing elaborate forms of coiffure, which is also a trait peculiar to prominent individuals in a number of pre-industrial societies (Clarke-Heald 2002, esp. p. 86).

A fairly eloquent testimony, bearing out the basic observation made here, is offered by East Slavic, and specifically Russian, ethnography (cf., in general, Tolstoy-Usacheva 1995, 105–107). In Russian combs, practical properties cannot be differentiated from their sacral aspects (Kondrat'yeva 1999). The nature of combs tends to be determined by the purpose to which their proprietors put them: Russian medieval episcopal combs frequently bear carved images of such liturgical items as mitres, crosses, staffs of office or candlesticks (Kondrat'yeva 1999, 83). Wedding combs, on the other hand, show such scenes as ceremonial drinking of tea, a holiday voyage, but also a winged heart on an altar, a couple of pigeons, a wreath of garlands in the shape of a flat-lying figure-of-eight, or even an anchor.

During the wedding ceremony, the bridegroom gave his bride a comb, and that in a box, in a special holder, on a tray or even on a mirror (Kondrat'yeva 1999, 84). In weddings, combs played a rather prominent role on the occasion of combing the bride's hair. The focus of the young lady's life force was seen in the hair and her combing was accordingly likened to the triggering off of both her own well-being and general fertility. Combing the bride was supposed to bring forth good harvest and passing of the comb teeth through her hair was likened to streams of rain penetrating the soil; ultimately, the bride's plaited hair was equalled to a loaf of bread. Soaking of the hair in mead or wine prior to combing, done as a metaphor of irrigation of the "good field", or the bride, brought the fertility symbolism to the top. On the other hand, a comb, together with soap and a mirror, made up the washing kit for a wedding bath (Kondrat'yeva 1999, 84).

In the Volga-river region, house mistresses wore combs on the chest and at the waist for magical protection (Kondrat'yeva 1999, 85).

It must not be forgotten that combs played a role also during funerals; for the burial, the deceased received from his or her family a comb laid again on the chest or at the waist, "for the journey" (Kondrat'yeva 1999, 85). The African burial of the corpses's hair is approximated by the custom to bury combs and vessels used for the last washing of the deceased's body. These were thrown out or broken but the combs might have been buried in their own right, in a cup (Kondrat'yeva 1999, 86).

An interesting parallel to the use of true combs in Russia is represented by the comb-like instruments used for weaving cloth and their symbolism.

A custom widespread in Russian popular culture forbade the exchange of various household items on major feast days or on particular occasions, "lest the good luck and fertility forsake the household". This concerned especially work tools and particularly weaving implements such as a spindle, a distaff, a weaving sword, warp threads and combs; if these articles left the household, it could be befallen by misfortune (Plotnikova 1999). This shows very well the longevity of ideas, linking the procedure of weaving with the structuring of human life, and especially of its initial and final moments, which we also know from ancient Mesopotamia (cf. infra, Breniquet-Mintsi 2000).

Thanks to Gananath Obeyesekere, we can adduce here some rather instructive parallels from the world of the Indian subcontinent (Obeyesekere 1981). The Sri Lankan prophetesses, constituting the subject of Obeyesekere's research, all marked their religious vocations in one or another way by adjustments of their hair (Obeyesekere 1981, 26–32).

The first of them, Karunavati Maniyo, was given by her protector and guardian deity, Huniyan, seven locks of hair after a pious pilgrimage, during which she dedicated herself to the service of this deity, as a sign of his *sakti balaya*, power of his creative force. Her hair, considered to be identical with the deity and called *ista devata* accordingly, also bore the name of *dhatu*, meaning sacred relics, but also essence or life force.

The second prophetess, Nandavati Maniyo, cut her hair quite short after having received the religious vocation.

The third prophetess, Manei Nona, grew her hair "when the deity entered her", and let it grow freely.

In the light of what has repeatedly been observed here, I do believe that the hypothesis of the growth of hair as a "divine gift" by which the deity gives compensation for the termination of sexual life, may provide one of the possible answers (Obeyesekere 1981, 34–35). I assume that it is equally possible to see in the hairdo transformations evidence for the change of the "inner nature" of the prophetesses in question. Having become followers of the deity, they transformed their "innermost self" and thus have to get rid of their hair, still containing their nature of the past which was no longer in existence.

The American evidence start with the hunter-gatherer tribes of Amazonia, showing more or less what can now be legitimately expected. The body of the *bari*, shaman of the Bororo tribe, belongs to the spirits with whom he has concluded a treaty and to whom his soul will depart after his earthly death.

This relates also to the clippings of the *bari's* fingernails and hair, as well as to his broken arrows and crockery sherds (Levi-Strauss 1966, 165).

The rich Mesoamerican data have been most conveniently summarized by A. L. Austin (1988). The ancient Nahuas located the seat of the immaterial substance of human life, including consciousness and reasoning, into the upper part of the head including its top, the face and the hair (Austin 1988, 172, 198–199). Human head also contained the life force of the individual and if a captive's lock of hair was cut off, this meant that the winner had got hold of the loser's life force (Austin 1988, 207). An enslaved person had his or her hair cut on top of the head (Austin 1988, 402). Hair was, in general, a "recipient of power" here (Austin 1988, 221). Human hair, especially that from the top of the head, had a close relation to what was called *tonalli*, soul or life force of a human being. The first hair cut from a boy's head protected the household; human hair was thrown into maguey plants to protect the person(s) from wounds of the head. In sick people, the hair was let to grow freely and then it was cut and hidden or buried. On the other hand, burning of someone's hair entailed the person's death (Austin 1988, 220).

When a death occurred in an ancient Nahua family, a lock of hair was cut off the deceased's head. The body was subsequently cremated and the ashes deposited in a container of pottery, wood or stone. In its turn, this was then put into a wooden likeness of the deceased person, kept in the household. In addition to the ashes, the receptacles were made to contain both the first lock of hair cut off the deceased's head when he or she was a child, and another lock of hair cut off the dead head. The sepulchral monument thus enshrined remembrances of the individual's whole life and this practice kept the deceased person's *tonalli* with the family. When any of the descendants of the family received the ancestor's name, his or her *tonalli* became activated and the ancestor "came back" (Austin 1988, 322–323).

A very interesting list of those parts of the body, which the Nahuas considered to be especially powerful magic, is represented by the flattering epitheta by which members of highly ranked groups were addressed. Men and women of consequence were thus called "hair of the people", "fingernail of the people", "particle of the people", "part of the people", "blood of the people", "colour of the people", "beard of the people", or "eyebrows of the people", "backbone of the people" (Austin 1988, 392).

Ethnology of combs: conclusions

In a remakable unity, human hair stands for the "innermost human self", the invisible and probably immaterial essential structural characteristics of every human being, including its manifold aspects (life force), all the world over. Summarizing the individual categories of hair semantics laid bare by earlier research, Sir Edmund Ronald Leach (1999 [1958], 235) observed that human hair stands for

- the royalty of kings,
- the divinity of gods,
- the fertility of crops,
- the power of sorcerers, and
  the mana of heroic warriors.

As the outer manifestation and excrescence of this "innermost self", it reflects changes in the personal status and must be shorn if this status has changed. Human hair symbolizes not only its individual bearer but the whole group of his closest kith and kin. The "innermost human self" can be influenced by hair manipulation including the use of combs, and that for better or for worse (various magical practices including bewitchment).

It may thus legitimately be supposed that the comb images on Halaf painted pottery refer to the "innermost human self" of such like personages as those of whom we spoke above, and whose superior endowments, or rather the material fruits thereof, were shared out to be "embodied" by their followers as food served on such painted tableware. The chequerboard-comb combination may be expressing wishes to amplify the capacities of the "innermost human self" of the initiator of the ceremonial banquet. The bowl with two combs may allude to a pair of such personages, and thus possibly to a ritual employing two members of a highly ranked group; securing of fertility? an embryonic "sacred marriage rite"?

Archaeology, ethnology and the Halaf culture:
general conclusions

The time has now come to summarize the conclusions of this chapter.

1) The highly ranked groups of the Halaf culture are likely to have perpetuated not only their positions, but also the internal structuring and coherence of their community, by ritual proceedings, probably including music.

2) The key component of the Halaf-culture ritual life was constituted by ceremonial partaking of food cooked on fire, involving the use of exquisite painted tableware. The hypothesis that such food represented the fruits of labour of the highly ranked groups of Halaf culture, in fact, the primeval entrepreneurs, and thus the external manifestation of their superior inner qualities, which their followers wishes to "embody" and to make consubstantial with their own bodies, is possible but cannot be proved.

3) Of the rituals involving painted pottery, only a few elements may perhaps be illuminated by iconic analysis. The colours of the final phase of the Halaf culture allude to the cult of the later Sumerian sky god, An. As to the particular decorative components pointing to the directions of the ritual, we may discern

    a) the use of bucranium, which may be connected with the nature-taming and humanizing activities of the highly ranked groups of the Halaf culture;

    b) the chequerboard pattern, addressing possibly the sphere of (the discharge of?) fertility and proliferation faculties;

    c) the rosette-cum-chequerboard motif, which may link up with the properly ordered structure of the Halaf-culture "civilized world".

    d) at the site of Khirbet Derak, the same motif has appeared in a milieu chracterized by coexistence of several painted-pottery traditions, as well as by the presence of impressions of Ubaid-style seals. This implies a more coherent form of furnishing the material appurtenances of such rituals;

4) at least in two instances, Halaf-culture pottery displays comb patterns. As the comb enables the manipulation of human hair, excrescence of the "innermost human self" all the world over, the relevant ritual was likely to enhance the endowments and capacities of the "innermost human self" of a concrete and particular human personage, most probably the high-rank initiator of the ritual proceeding. This makes the link between highly ranked groups of the Halaf culture and their painted pottery visible and discernible. The other instance, involving the motif of two combs, may allude to sexual symbolism, perhaps in connection with securing fertility.

In this manner began the great story of creation and establishment of the first discerinble state in human history, in a deeply prehistoric age and in a region distant from those we deem to be of consequence today. The first agent, one without whom no states will ever be built in the future, is already on the stage now. Specialists in things spiritual, those who walk with gods, eat and sleep with the gods and, if necessary, devise gods have left us an eloquent testimony of their labours in the symbols ornating Halaf-culture pottery and in the colour triad referring probably to An,. the highest Sumerian god. Thus enter our field of vision those champions of the human cause the later followers of whom will, in distant India and in faraway but foreseeable future, call themselves brahmanas, the mediators between humankind and the divine world.

THE AIR BENEATH THE WINGS

The painted pottery of Susa (on which cf. more recently Carter-Stolper 1984; Harper-Aruz-Tallon 1992; Berman 1994; Matney 1995, 31–32; Pittman 1997; Potts 1999) has constituted a target of numerous investigations and research ventures. In most cases, the authors have tried a modern, stylistic approach to its ornamentation, dwelling particularly on the comparative and aesthetic aspects of this exquisite tableware.

In this contribution, I perceive the images painted on the Susa pottery from the viewpoint of ancient semantics. I am trying to build my assumptions on the observation that at least the pottery from Susa displays a visibly standardized set of ornament components and compositions, combining on the individual bowls, jars and pots to form a kind of "language", the message of which I attempt to decipher.

The individual motifs which I shall take up to demonstrate my proposals are 1) the cross, 2) triangular compositions, 3) the chequerboard, 4) animal themes including quadrupeds, birds and reptiles, 5) arms and armaments of which spears and arrows in quivers may be distinguished, 6) combs, 7) rectangular fields filled in with wavy lines which I have chosen to refer to as "gipar", 8) motifs likely to denote water, 9) configurations like unto ears of corn which may represent cereals, 10) the "butterfly" or rather "hourglass" ornaments, 11) singular or multiple crescent-shaped arcs and 12) "sun" motifs. I shall now proceed to comment upon these components of the painted-pottery decoration one by one.

The Cross

It goes without saying that the cross, appearing so many times on Susa painted pottery, deserves a considerable amount of attention. In very frequent cases it appears prominently at the very centre of many ornamental compositions, especially on the ornate bowls in which many a head of a major

75

prehistoric personage may be assumed to have been lain after the individual in question had left this world. Let us therefore see how far we may identify any possible semantic connotations that the cross motif may carry.

Association table 1 (p. 96) demonstrates that cross motifs figure most prominently on bowls. From among their associations, those with comb-, animal, chequerboard- and gipar patterns are the most frequent. This is likely to point to activities of "city" founders who may have wished to commmemorate their acts of establishing properly the foci of "civilized" life, surrounded by uncultivated landscapes with wild animals and, ultimately, with substances of mythical or divine origin (chequerboard; cf. Wiggermann 1996). Foundations of cities with participation of more household units may be symbolized by the gipar-cross units.

Thanks to the efforts of the Berlin team directed by Hans-Jörg Nissen, a complete repertory of the earliest signs of the cuneiform script, dating back to the third quarter of the 4th pre-Christian millennium, has become available to scholars in the field (ZATU). It may be useful to inquire how far any motifs on Susa painted pottery may perhaps fall in with the data of this list.

It does not come as a particular surprise that the cross sign figures prominently in the ZATU, and that under several headings. In addition to the BAD3 sign (ZATU No. 44 p. 179, cf. also Steinkeller 1995, 698 sub No. 44), it is especially the EZEN sign (ZATU No. 150 p. 201), which yields the greatest amount of information, together with the ŠENNUR sign (ZATU No. 522 p. 286). Data subsumed under the abovementioned captions indicate clearly that this sign is to be understood as "a city, a settlement focus", undoubtedly established in accordance with the customs and manners of the "civilized" world in the form of a centre joining the four cardinal points (on the "four cardinal points" cf. Wiggermann 1996, 208–209; Horowitz 1998, 298–299). One of the clearest indication that we possess is the sign LAL2 + EZEN (ZATU No. 326 p. 238), which shows a large drawing of an EZEN sign, situated in what appears to be an area defined by a confluence of two watercourses, on the reverse of a tablet. Here we really cannot get rid of the impression that a "map" of a site relevant to the data on the tablet's obverse has been intended. And, in fact, the often central position of the cross on Susa pottery, and the fact that it is surrounded by symbols which may refer to the civilization's "outer zone", such as animals or birds, may well constitute an argument in favour of the identification of the cross sign as a "city, settlement focus".

This "civilizing" character of the cross signs in the proto-cuneiform writing is enhanced by the fact that as early as this age, the lexeme probably also carried the connotation of feast ("isinnu", CAD I/J s.v. isinnum, 195–197). This is borne out by an Uruk/Jemdet Nasr seal image in which the EZEN sign denotes a scene involving music playing and merrymaking (Rova 1994, 311, Tav. 5 No. 81). This phonetic value for the EZEN sign is present as early as the Ebla texts (24th century B.C.: Glassner 2000, 190). The foundation of a "civilized city" in the quincunx form obviously required the ceremonial surrender of the new foundation into the hands of the gods by means of a special "dedication" festival, which is precisely indicated by the "isinnum" lexeme (CAD I/J pp. 195–196).

The importance of the fivefold disposition of components of this sign is indicated by the variant ezen-nun, for i-nun, a geographical name (Ešnunna?), where "i" is a sign of five horizontal strokes (ZATU No. 259 p. 223).

The cross symbols do appear also in Proto-Elamite script. Their presence is attested to at Susa, Tall-i Malyan and Tepe Yahya (Damerow, Englund and Lamberg-Karlovsky 1989, 61 n. 165). In Susa texts, such images take place of headings in lists qualifying measures of grain and also numbers of decimally counted animals and humans (ibid., 43 n. 131). One of the Susa texts places the cross sign after an individual entry qualified by the triangular "tasselled banner" emblem, bearing a quadrilobe inside (ibid., p. 44 n. 131).

The Proto-Elamite cross sign may thus denote here one of the "cities", foci of "civilized" life, constituting a component of a network of cooperating communities, referred to, on the superior level, by the triangular "tasselled banner" signs.

The fourfold structure of the world, including the central part, belongs to ideas of the widest conceivable circulation throught humankind; it is present on the other side of the globe, in the Palaeoamerican civilization, as well (Austin 1988, 58–59).

The Triangle

Ornaments and ornament schemes employing the triangular principle are not particularly frequent in prehistoric Near Eastern art and it is therefore of exceptional interest that the masters who painted the Susa pottery employed them with some frequency.

Triangular motifs appear most frequently on bowls and combine more often with chequerboard-, cross-, comb- and "gipar" patterns (Table 1). Associating thus with the ideas of singular personages (combs), households or families (gipar), settlement foci (cross) and fertility/proliferation (chequerboard), it may refer to a sort of a comprehensive notion covering the idea of "one of the universal aspects of our, i.e. civilized, world".

Some insights pointing in this direction may be gleaned from triangular images appearing on Uruk- and later-age seals from Susa (Legrain 1921; Damerow, Englund and Lamberg-Karlovsky 1989, 12 n. 30). The seal of Legrain's fig. 53 on Pl. III associates the triangular symbol with fish and it is possible that deliveries of fish or fish products might have been marked in this particular way. This is at least implied by other, similar instances: Legrain's figs. 266 and 268 on Pl. XVII show what may be contributors of supplies to the central polity, denoted by triangular symbols containing an object of a herring-bone appearance, and alluding possibly to another member community of the corporate polity united under the triangular "tasselled banner" symbol. The contributors, either animal-looking demons themselves or people in animal disguise, associate with KUR-like signs on fig. 266 and may thus stand for one of the montane tracts included in the "triangular-banner" confederation. The martial aspects of this political body are brought to the fore in Legrain's fig. 330 on Pl. XXIII, in which the "banner" with the herringbone symbol denotes a double scene in which a mighty bull packs two lions by his forehooves while another impressive lion does the same to a couple of bulls.

In the cylinder-seal images, the body symbolized by the "triangular banner" thus includes both montane tracts and fish-producing areas and seems to insist on their aggressive and belligerent nature.

Triangular compositions re-appear in Proto-Elamite texts, serving both at central (Susa) and at peripheral sites (Tall-i Malyan, Tepe Yahya: Damerow, Englund and Lamberg-Karlovsky 1989, 12 n. 30). It seems that a triangle-shaped "tasselled banner", enclosing a quadrilobe, is present in texts from Susa., Tall-i Malyan and Tepe Yahya (Damerow, Englund and Lamberg-Karlovsky 1989, 61–62, n. 165). As against this, a triangle containing a trilobe shows up at Tepe Yahya only, together with other related variants of this emblem (ibid., 67–68, signs s.v. MDP 31: Cp. 1836ff., 1849-asterisk, 1877 and 1877-asterisk). Such signs do not form a component of either personal names or individual titles (Damerow, Englund and Lambert-Karlovsky 1989, 16). This may mean, as Robert Englund remarks, that they stood for an institution or institutional set (R. Dittmann's "tribal confederation", ibid.,

p. 16 n. 43), signifying perhaps one of the highest-order entities of contemporary "civilized" world.

A triangular sign has also been used at Susa for an entity falling within a sexagesimal system for counting of discrete objects, of which the field of application was obviously more restricted there than in contemporary Sumer (Damerow, Englund and Lamberg-Karlovsky 1989, 22 n. 67). It may have referred to KUR, a "juvenile worker/slave" (ibid., 24 n. 76).

The triangular sign appearing in protocuneiform writing (ZATU No. 679 p. 320) seems to refer to a metal object and may thus stand for a furniture item (a tripod?).

Chequerboard

The chequerboard patterns, occurring fairly frequently among the ornaments present on the Susa pottery, have already been commented upon. Connected closely with Enlil, one of the supreme gods of the Sumerian pantheon, in Late Uruk texts (Charvát 2002, 154–155, cf. also Matthews 1993, 38 s.v. Cities 2, and Krebernik 2000, esp. pp. 452 and 459–460), they may, by their very nature, convey the idea of "endless propagation", and thus also of "fertility, proliferation capacity". A simplified chequerboard pattern, combined with the "hourglass" motif and associated with an erotic scene, alludes undoubtedly to fertility symbolism in an archaic Ur seal impression (Legrain 1936, Nos. 239, 368).

In some instances, the proliferation idea can be viewed as a desire linked to the images borne by the respective vessel. The chequered rhomboid corresponding to the herd of cattle(?) in my No. 5 may mean something like "may your herds be always plentiful". The bowl of illustration No. 18 places a chequerboard field into the very centre of the composition and encloses it in concentric zones consisting probably of an inner "cereal ring" (ear-of-corn image?), a water channel and an outer "cereal ring". Chequerboard patterns may nonetheless appear even at the centres of triangular configurations (my No. 25), as well as within cross-shaped motifs likely to represent "cities" (my No. 48). Chequerboard triangles or rhomboids with "palm branches" growing out of their corners, like those of my Nos. 19, 27 and 28, may invoke the abundance of harvested crops. On the jar of my No. 47, the chequerboard, "tagging" what seems to be an image of mountain ranges, joins a panel depicting a series of "hourglass" signs issuing one big and two small watercourses. Are Enlil and Ninhursag referred to here? Overflowing water resources and the ensuing fertility of adjoining fields may have been implored by compositions linking a prominent zigzag line with chequerboard fillings of the triangular fields defined by the "watercourse". We know six very similar examples of this, borne by jars and goblets (Nos. 62, 63, 64, 149, 153, 170). In one instance, this is combined with a military-triumph scene, where quivers with arrows alternate with chequerboard fillings in the triangular fields (No. 149). Did inter-community disputes for water-use rights result in armed conflicts?

The general character of the chequerboard motif may be outlined in comparison with patterns borne by emblems contained within the curvature of horns of quadrupeds appearing on a number of Susa vases, and thus presumably in identical contexts. It shares this position (Nos. 138, 143, 148) with ears of corn (Nos. 43, 135), gipar oblongs (Nos. 39, 40, 44) and cross patterns (No. 53).

A special reference should be made to pot No. 93. The filling motif, consisting of a chequerboard square enclosed from two sides by latticed rectangles, alludes so strongly to a chequered reed mat (Sumerian KID, Krebernik 2000, 452), that a citation of the divine name Enlil must be suspected here. A similar combination appears on the goblet No. 106, but there the composition may reproduce a pattern copied from a vessel made of organic matters, such as intersecting bark strips or similar materials.

Appearing frequently on bowls and less so on jars, chequerboard patterns associate with cross-, water-, animal and cereal motifs (Table 1). This, I believe, does not contradict the "be fruitful and multiply" explanation, as related both to "cities" and to cultivated and uncultivated landscapes.

Let us notice that Piotr Michalowski (1998, esp. pp. 241–242) proposes to see in Enlil a divinity belonging to a stream of traditions of Semitic-speaking population groups who saw in him the Supreme Deity, "god of gods" (Illil, hypothetical il-ili). He also suggests that Enlil might have replaced the earlier vegetation- and fertility god Enki, dominating the earth with his spouse Ninki (ibid. pp. 239–240), or Ninhursag (ibid., 244). This would accord well with the ubiquity of chequerboard patterns on the Susa pottery, as well as with the belligerent assertivity of some of the pattern linkages (chequerboard with arms). In fact, Michalowski's idea of a "bundle of religions", a band of intersecting and intertwining spiritual traditions existing side by side and influencing and inspiring one another mutually, provides a perfectly fitting explicative model for the semantics of the Susa painted pottery, on which such currents of local/regional traditions are well discernible.

Michalowski's suggestion has been criticized recently by Manfred Krebernik (2000, 453, 459), who prefers not to take any too rigid stance. At any rate, the connection of the earliest form of Enlil's name with a reed mat bearing a chequerboard pattern seems to be accepted without doubt (Krebernik 2000, 452, as well as 459–460).

This may be a place to recall that in the Pacific-ocean islands, reed mats belonged to the property of the respective gods and enjoyed a high measure of prestige. Every local lineage was centered upon a deity served by a specific priest who cared after the sacred property of the respective divinity (*fakafaonga*). If the god or goddess chose to appear to the mortals, a mat was invariably spread for them to sit upon, and the mat thus acquired a status of the deity's shrine, having been practically equated with it. This, however, related to the tutelary deities of chiefs or lineages, not to those of particular places (Gifford 1929, 317, 319).

The Pacific-ocean inhabitants distinguished nonetheless carefully between the external garb which a supernatural being (the *fakaata* spirit) can, at the moment of its own choice and for a period of time which it deems appropriate, assume, such as that of a bird, an animal or a human, from a permanent seat of a such a spirit (*fakatino*) (Firth 1970, 119).

Animals (quadrupeds, birds, reptiles)

The paintings on the Susa pottery vessels abound in all sorts of depictions of wildlife, including horned quadrupeds, dogs, birds, snakes and reptiles of various kinds. In view of the fact that most of the relevant icons depict carefully chosen samples of the denizens uf untamed nature, it seems likely that a symbolical aspect is present in the selection of the individual species depicted. Let us pass this evidence in a review.

Several categories of animals may be combined within one single icon. On the bowl of my No. 1, the dog, likely to represent tame animals and thus the "civilized" world, chases a stag on whose back a bird is sitting. The dog may appear as a sole decorative element on a single vessel (my No. 97). We do nonetheless possess scenes in which a herd of domestic animals guarded by a dog may be meant (cattle or pigs?, my No. 5). Mostly, however, the Susa paintings feature quadrupeds with the high arching horns of the mouflon type, possibly wild goats or ibex (Hole 1992, 36).

Most of the Susa birds are depicted either flying with spread wings, sometimes also as standing (or swimming) in rather dense rows, the latter case pertaining especially to birds wading in shallow waters of the heron type. Both flying and standing birds may sometimes be shown together, as on my Nos. 56

and 180. The bowl of No.136 displays three birds and a scorpion, disposed on four sides and thus presumably referring to the quadruple structure of the "civilized" world.

As to "all that creepeth upon the earth", a depiction of a large lizard or turtle at the centre of a composition, in which two combs figure prominently, may imply a reference to fertility expected from the union of two human personages (my No. 16). On the bowl numbered 136 here, a scorpion seems to represent one of the "four quarters of the world", the remaining three being symbolized by birds. The snake icons are sometimes done with a frightening accuracy, enabling their biological identification (my Nos. 61 and 137); they depict poisonous saw-scaled vipers of the *Echis carinatus* or *Echis coloratus* species, living especially in the loose sandy soils of northern African and Near Eastern landscapes (Hole 1992, 34).

The snake goblet No. 137 displays, as a second image, a likeness of a joiner's or carpenter's borer. This offers a fascinating parallel to the protocuneiform sign UŠUMGAL (ZATU No. 607 p. 308), also showing a boring instrument, this time probably a stonecutter's one, with the phonetic complement GAL (cf. also Glassner 2000, 209).

Animal motifs appear most prominently on jars and bowls and combine, first and foremost, with the cross emblem. Their next most frequent associations link them, in the descending order, with water motifs, "hourglass" images, combs, chequerboards, cereals, and gipar icons (Table 1).

A conspicuous difference between the Susa-pottery images and proto-cuneiform animal signs may be observed. While wild-animal images predominate at Susa, tame and domestic animals take a close second in the Uruk IV texts. Here we have the dog (ŠUBUR, ZATU No. 539 p. 290), pig (ŠÁH, ZATU No. 508 p. 281), cattle (GU4, ZATU No. 234 p. 218) or donkey (ANŠE, ZATU No. 32 p. 176). In Late Uruk, wild animals repeatedly appear in toponyms: images of a lion and a horned animal stand for the TIDNUM (GÌR + PIRIG; ZATU No. 552 p. 294), an onager(?) emblem for KIŠ (ZATU No. 297 p. 232) and an icon composed of a head of a gazelle(?) and the AB structure for the city NERGAL-x (ZATU No. 392 p. 253). Signs for other wild animals include those for a ibex (?, ŠEG9, ZATU No. 519 p. 285), gazelle or stag (DÀRA, ZATU No. 70 p. 184) and lion (PIRIG or ALIM, ZATU No. 428 p. 263).

The same seems to go for birds, most of which are represented by signs referring to domestic sorts: GUN3 (a duck? ZATU No. 254 p. 220), MUŠEN (also a duck?, ZATU No. 376 p. 249), and UZ (a goose? ZATU No. 611 p. 309). A wild bird may be depicted by the NAM or SIM sign (ZATU No.

383 p. 251). The hydronym IDIGNA is represented by a spread-eagled bird image (ZATU No. 261 p. 223).

As to snakes and other reptiles, a healthy respect commanded inclusion of a cobra-snake sign into Late Uruk repertory (BU, ZATU No. 56 p. 181). That its likeness was used mostly as an emblem is shown by a series of signs of possibly toponymic function (ZATU Nos. 57, 58 and 59 on p. 182, as well as KITI, ZATU No. 299 on p. 232).

It must be pointed out that wild animals inhabited a mythological world full of wonders even in the later ages of the cuneiform civilizations. Written texts indicate well how their abodes were ambiguous, as they could protect but also endanger the human species (cf. Wiggermann 1996, and, more extensively, Wiggermann 1992). Neither is it commendable to forget that even Sumerian kings of the mythical antiquity bore names denoting wild animals (Glassner 1993, 75–76).

Frans Wiggermann has pointed out that an ibex belongs to the god Enki/Ea (quoted in Michalowski 1998, 244), and that a stag is an animal of the goddess Ninhursag (Wiggermann 1996, 215–216). Lady Ninhursag is also known to have preferred open landscapes (Heimpel 2000, 381). On the other hand, there exists a rather interesting link between birds, especially those of the sea coast, and the Lagashite goddess Nanshe (Maxwell-Hyslop 1992, esp. pp. 80–82). The fact that the ancient Mesopotamians imagined their dead in the underworld "clothed with a garb of feathers" (Horowitz 1998, 349) could indicate that bird depictions on Susa pottery may be brought into connection with the realms of the dead, and thus fall within the sphere of ancestor worship, as in many preindustrial cultures of the world (Slavic folklore cf. Vinogradova 1999, Pacific ocean: Firth 1970, 119, also Mander 1999, 98).

Wild animals were thus clearly part of the mythical world, that between full civilization and the primeval chaos, figuring upon a scene where both gods and devils were at work.

At least some of the original respect to those animals, which we now perceive as particularly repulsive, has survived into later periods, albeit in most peculiar forms. The snake has won reputation as an attribute of the Old-Testament witch (I Rg XXVIII, 3–25), asked by Saul to bring the soul of the prophet Samuel back from the nether world. For this "mulier habens pythonem", the snake represented undoubtedly one of the tools of her sinister trade (Ruhe 1993, 74).

A remarkable development has taken place between the final Ubaid (Susa) and final Uruk age. The animal images of Susa referred. first and foremost, to the wild and untamed world, constituting a target of "civilizing" expeditions of the high-rank personages of Susa. Contrastingly, the Late Uruk managers were interested primarily in economically relevant domestic animals, pushing the images of the wild ones into the safely controlled margins of geographical vocabulary and retaining only the essential names referring to the most frequent or most formidable denizens of the natural world.

Arms

The presence of various types of arms, likely to announce the military triumph over the community's enemy force, may be legitimately expected in a number of monuments of both prehistoric and historic art and the Susa pottery constitutes no exception to this. Several bowls bear the eloquent image of a personage armed with two spears (my No. 136), who may be replaced by an icon of the two spears (my Nos. 24, 32), but sometimes of one spear only (my No. 205). This kind of motif has been duly noted by Jacques de Morgan (1912, fig. 2, p. 6), who, however, saw in the spear *la lance du dieu Marduk*. Another type of weapon that may herald the idea of the military triumph is the bow and arrow, shown either in the hands of presumably military personages or, alternatively, in the abbreviated form of a quiver full of arrows (my Nos. 30, 141, 145, 149).

As to the individual cases, the bowl illustrated as my No. 15 here shows more or less clearly a personage with a marked hairdo or head covering, holding a bow. The emblems depicted on the bowl displays such a measure of uniqueness and individuality that they may well represent military ensigns under which this particular chief led his followers to war and won battles. In some instances, weapon images associate with latticed oblongs implying perhaps the offering of (victorious?) arms on mats, perhaps to gods (my Nos. 39, 94). A possible offering(?) of arrows (or maces?) in front of what appears to be a shrine constructed of light materials with an image of an incarnation of the female procreative force inside remains mysterious to me (my No. 107).

Images of weaponry appear most frequently on bowls and associate frequently with the cross-, chequerboard- and comb icons. This implies celebrations of triumphs of individual personages, victories over "cities" and perhaps wishes that the military power of the donor of food eaten from the painted tableware grow beyond measure (or an allusion that military power belongs to the realms of Enlil?) (Table 1).

Such outfitting of the Susa chiefs and their military retinues finds some parallels in the protocuneiform script. Image of the bow serves there as a carrier of the lexeme ERIM or ERÍN (ZATU No. 143 p. 199), denoting, probably as early as this, representatives of the broad masses of the population called upon by their governments to render corvée or military service. In general, the bow image served as a sign of sovereignty throughout the ancient Near East including Egypt (Keel 1990, esp. pp.278–279) and India (Jamison 1999, 258-270). The spear image has nonetheless vanished and its place has been, to a certain extent, occupied by the icon of the mace. This follows out of the graphical carrier of the lexeme MÈ = *tāhāzu*, "fight" or "struggle", depicting a bow and a mace (ZATU No. 359 p. 245).

Let us take notice of a rather colourful ethnographic parallel illustrating the use of twin spears as an attribute of power. During the inthronization of one of the last queens of the Pacific Tonga island,on 9 December 1918, one of the Queen's warriors, a dark-faced man, carried two spears with coloured streamers in the inthronization procession. In the course of the coronation banquet, this herald picked out especially tasty morsels, harpooned them with his spear and offered them to the Queen (Gifford 1929, 94–95).

Combs

Images of the comb, the semantics of which have been investigated at length in the foregoing chapter, play a major role in the decoration *répertoire* of the Susa painted pottery. I believe that it is not necessary to dwell on their significance at length, as I have developed my idea concerning the significance of the comb depictions above. In the text which precedes this chapter, I have submitted my opinion that the symbol of the comb, representing a tool for manipulation of human hair, is very likely to stand for the "innermost human self" of any human personage to which the imagery of the painted tableware is adressed or which it in any manner involves. It thus alludes to the great and elusive entity of historical research of these remote ages of mankind – the human individual, the singular personality.

Two things stand out clearly in questions concerning the presence of comb motifs on the Susa painted pottery. Table 1 shows that comb images were very popular in prehisotric Susa, appearing often on bowls and associating most frequently with cross- and animal patterns. This is likely to bring out the connection between prominent personages and establishment of cities (foci of "civilized life", cross patterns), as well as between such personages and "civilizing" incursions into uncultivated landscape, most probably, to hunting trips (animal images).

No comb-related images appear in either protocuneiform or proto-Elamite script. The only sign that may be of some relevance to comb images is ZATU 661 and 662 (p. 318), referring presumably to a comb-shaped instrument used in the textile industry, for instance, for carding.

One of the signs of Proto-Elamite script, attested to at Tepe Yahya and denoting the smallest unit of the decimal ŠE system there (1/24 of the basic unit), does display a form of a comb. In this it clearly differs from Susa orthography in which this sign assumes a different form (Damerow, Englund and Lamberg Karlovsky 1989, 30, 43 and 75 s.v. ATU 2: 39b var). No connection is apparent to me.

It is interesting to observe the traces of the original significance of the comb (hair = "innermost human self"; comb = a tool to manipulate it) in the cuneiform texts (Edzard 1976–1980). In them, the comb appears as a tool of personal cleanliness, as well as of specialized textile work (wool-carding), but also of magical procedures. Nevertheless, the cuneiform sign ZUM, equivalent of the Akkadian verb *mašādu* = to comb hair, and depicting, in its original form, a comb with female pudenda, is also used to transcribe the word *šassūru* = womb, or a mother goddess (CAD Š II, s.v. šassūru A, pp.145–146). Here we have a clear proof that human hair, symbolized by a comb sign, was originally also considered the excrescence of the "innermost human self" in Mesopotamia, though it survived only as an ensign of femininity.

Rectangles filled in with wavy lines (gipar)

This word is borrowed from the Sumerian denomination of a peculiar feature which I have commented upon already (Charvát 2002, 101–102). It refers to an image assuming the form of a rectangle filled in by wavy lines, which I assume to depict a mat woven of reeds in the same manner as can be seen on some surviving examples of early Mesopotamian matting (Jemdet Nasr: Charvát 2002, 160 Fig. 6.1). If my intepretation of the original "gipar" sememe as a reed mat, standing for a nuptial bed of a master and a mistress of a household as a source of fertility and abundance for all those who live in the same household (Charvát 2002, 101; cf. also CAD G s.v. "giparu", 83–84) holds good, then this sign may symbolize a household- or "family" unit (whatever may hide under this rather nebulous expression) and thus reveal another rather important social category represented on Susa painted pottery.

A juncture with prominent families founding "cities", such as, for instance, my Nos. 10, 11, 29 or 146 here would be logical. Two human personages are likely to be involved in the case of my No. 12, linking a gipar image at the centre of the bowl with two prominent combs (but also with two *saluki* dogs). Another couple seems to be alluded to by the beautiful pattern on my No. 46, a jar linking the "nuptial chamber" image with an "hourglass" sign. An information set of unusual clarity seems to be offered by my Nos. 33, 34 and 38. All these cases display the same kind of compositions consisting of three elements each, likely to constitute a related, if not identical, coordinate system. These three circles feature pairs of combs, likely to refer to human couples (No. 33) and what seems to be a simplified version of the wavy-line gipar sign (No. 34). (In this connection, let us take account of such triangular compositions joining true gipar signs such as my Nos. 182, 183 and 230). In the last case (No. 38), the ears of corn contained within each of the three circles convey the idea of fertility and proliferation- as well as procreation capacity. All these images thus strongly suggest an interpretation of human couples, releasing fertility by embracing on the reed-woven mats.

It may be noted that we sometimes see the gipar signs associating freely among themselves and thus possibly signifying alliances of (highly ranked?) families. These are the cases of my Nos. 156, 157 and 191, linking probably four (No. 157), five (No. 191, a clear mistake, originally proposed as a fourfold combination), and even six (No, 156) such emblems. In my No. 189, two gipar signs enclose a lattice-filled rectangle which may, in fact, be a depiction of another kind of mat and thus allude to a marriage union between the two families.Can remote ancestors of the "alliance" coats-of-arms of European medieval aristocracy be seen in such ensign combinations?

The association with wildlife is less transparent. Perhaps we may assume an allusion to fertility, manifested in the abundance of the forms of life of uncultivated landscape. This may be the case of the horned quadrupeds with gipar signs in the curvature of their horns (my Nos. 39, 40 and 44). A wider interpretation of signs so positioned also follows out of the cross signs ("civilized world"), occupying the same place within the curvature of a quadruped's horns in my No. 54. In the cases of the *saluki* dogs, such as my No. 12, referred to above, these may be an attribute of the high-rank position of the individuals denoted by the comb images. A similar idea may lie behind the gipar image "guarded" by two saluki dogs and combined again with the "hourglass" sign in my No. 142.

Association table 1 shows that the gipar motif appears frequently on bowls, less so on jars, associating most frequently with the cross- and the animal motifs.

A semantically related concept is carried by the protocuneiform lexeme of EZINU (ZATU No. 158 p. 202). The ear of corn growing out of the reed-woven mat implies the idea of fertility and proliferation force.

Water

A number of wavy-line patterns visible on Susa pottery are likely to link up with water and watercourses, as is clearly the case with Uruk-age cylinder seals (Rova 1994, 94). The connection is sometimes difficult to confirm, but at least in some instances this interpretation seems probably. I have pointed out above that I perceive in the oblongs filled with wavy lines a category apart, which I have termed "gipar". Three other cases I include under the "water" heading: a) spouted pots with wavy-line decoration where the ornament seems to allude directly to the vessel's contents; b) patterns with genetic relationship to signs of the protocuneiform script; and c) images in which landscape segments with watercourses are likely to be depicted.

We may have a pristine image of the civilized world with a cross-shaped centre and the five major rivers flowing out of it – or towards it – in my No. 17. Classical Mesopotamian images have four rivers (Wiggermann 1996, 209, 228 Fig. 2). The following No. 18, in which two concentric "grain rings", separated by a wavy-line intervening zone, encircle a chequerboard centre, is also rather likely to refer to water bringing life to crops. The jar of my No. 47 bears a framed image of what may well be a montane landscape, out of which both rivers and creeks flow into the lowlands. Similar pattern in which depictions of watercourses may be suspected appear in Nos. 51, 53 (again with mountains? and mythical ibexes), 54, 65, 78, 91 (both pots), 163, 173, 174 and 175 (four jars). We have already referred to a series of six jars and goblets with depictions of a zigzag line with filling motifs in the triangular fields, which I believe to be showing a winding watercourse (Nos. 62, 63, 64, 149, 153 and 170). A related pattern may be borne by a jar No. 180. A case also likely to pertain to water is the pot of No. 74 with a zone of wavy lines on which birds with long necks seem to swim. Spouted vessels with wavy-line patterns include my No. 96.

The jar of my No. 66 bears an image of a winding watercourse with islets of watermeadow-area undergrowth which is very likely to relate to the protocuneiform sign RAD (ZATU No. 432 p. 264). This lexeme occurrs in the title PA.NAM2.RAD title, in which the RAD is likely to refer to land situated close to the river banks (the watermeadow area), while NAM2 may refer to regularly tilled and well-watered fields above the watermeadow limit (Charvát 1997, 42).

Association table 1 shows that images linked with water appear most often on jars and less so on pots. They associate most frequently with animal-, chequerboard- and "hourglass" motifs.

In the light of Piotr Michalowski's observations (1998, esp. pp. 239–240 and 244) and of what I shall have to say about the "hourglass" motif (cf. infra), I feel tempted to link our water imagery with the god Enki who could well have been known to the users of the Susa painted pottery. Some of our images seem to refer to fertility, and would thus fall into Enki's sphere, much as the depiction of the ibex, a creature of Enki. The association with chequerboard does nonetheless show that the two gods got along quite well in social landscapes surrounding prehistoric Susa.

Rituals of unidentified character were performed by female officiants called *kezertu*, the "curly ones", in the free and by watercourses at Old Babylonian Kish (Yoffee 1998). Unfortunately, no information on their character or purpose is available.

Let us add here, just for the sake of elucidation of the relationshop of inhabitants of Iran to water, that water and salt, the "marriage settlement" of Fatima, spouse of Ali, are sacred and can be denied to no one. In Iranian folklore, all watercourses and bodies of waters enjoy supernatural protection (Massé 1938, 225–237).

Cereals

A series of depictions on the Susa painted pottery refer to images linked with cereals, in particular with ears of corn. Two types of such motifs can be discerned: a "herringbone" configuration with a central stalk out of which branches issue on both sides in an oblique fashion, such, for instance, as on my No. 26 (a bowl) or No. 50 (a jar). The other type shows a thicker cluster, which may consist of two such "herringbone" patterns laid side by side but without the central stalks, just as on my No. 52 (a jar).

In some instances such images are supplemented by filling motifs which may contribute towards their better understanding. The small black triangles accompanying the huge ear of corn in the jar of my No. 59 may stand for heaps of threshed corn and the rectangular area containing the depiction of the ear of corn may thus symbolize the threshing ground. Even more explicit in this sense are the images on a jar of my No. 150: the dark triangles, showing in this case a net-like structure, are flanked by U-shaped implements which may be suspected to have served for winnowing the threshed grain. Ears of corn growing out of what seems to be a winding watercourse, accompanied by chequerboard fields invoking perhaps the fertility of a ground newly acquired for agriculture, possibly show the concern with fields brought freshly under the plough along the river banks (my No. 64). The curious depiction on a painted sherd, showing a skirted figure "giving birth" to an ear of corn, may allude to a personification of female procreative force (my No. 107); similar symbols invoking the fertility of human marital embrace have already been commented upon within the gipar section (my Nos. 33, 34 and 38). A wish for abundant harvests may be visualized by paintings on my Nos. 161 and 187, where two ears of corn are flanking a triangular "heap" filled in by a chequerboard pattern. Procreative forces active within uncultivated landscapes may be symbolized by ear-of-corn images contained within the curvature of the horns of quadrupeds (my No. 135), at the same place where gipar- and cross-shaped signs have appeared (cf. under the respective headings).

In some instances a causal connection may even be suspected behind the symbols painted on the prehistoric pottery. My No. 224. a spouted biconical pot, shows an image of a large ear of corn on the upper part of body. Here I feel tempted to postulate a fertilizing ceremony, in which a symbolic sprinkling by water was supposed to bring about the growth of corn.

The cereal symbols figure prominently on jars and less so on bowls. They associate markedly with the animal icons, with chequerboard-, "hourglass" – and cross motifs (Table 1). All this probably links them to fertility symbolism.

In cylinder seals of the Uruk/Jemdet Nasr age, the ear of corn is an attribute of the priestly king who gives it either to her divine female partner, or to animals as fodder (Rova 1994, 96).

Similar motifs may usher in a predecessor of the commonly occurring proto-cuneiform sign of ŠE, also showing an ear of corn (ZATU No. 511 p. 283). The essential nutritional function of this plant is clearly indicated by a series of signs featuring the ŠE close to the mouths of humans (ZATU No. 274 p. 226) or even to those of beer jugs (ZATU No. 288 p. 230), as well as to the snouts of animals (DÀRA = ZATU No. 72 p. 185, or GÌR = ZATU No. 220 p. 215) and to the beaks of birds (UZ = ZATU No. 611 p. 309). A symbolical function of the ŠE sign, implying possibly fertility- and proliferation force, seems to be featured in the EZINU sign, showing an ear of corn growing out of a reed mat, possibly in consequence of a (fertility-triggering?) ceremony (ZATU No. 158 p. 202).

The second, "denser" image of the Susa pottery may lie behind the protocuneiform sign LUM, GÚM or GUZ (ZATU No. 335 p. 240).

A rare instance, in which a Susa emblem constitutes a direct ancestor of a protocuneiform sign, is represented by the ZAR = LAGAB + ŠE(+ ŠE) sign (ZATU No. 616 p. 311). The sign ZATU No. 657 (p. 317), showing the ZAR within a storage structure of light materials, offers proof that a building is not meant by the rectangular frame enclosing the ear-of-corn image. The complete pedigree of this sign does nonetheless reach even farther into antiquity: one of the signs carved on the Ubaid-style seals which left their impressions at the site of Khirbet Derak is likely to represent its even more remote ancestor (Breniquet 1996, 108–109, Pl. 62 No. 1).

In view of the agricultural character of these prehistoric civilizations it comes as no wonder that a similar sign is also attested to in Proto-Elamite script. The first, stalked variant of this sign strongly resembles the Sumerian ŠE sign, but the authors hesitate to assign a "grain" value to it (Damerow, Englund and Lamberg-Karlovsky 1989, 32, 69). Its second, "denser" form, does denote a cereal product (Damerow, Englund and Lamberg-Karlovsky 1989, 17, 68, 74).

"Hourglass"

I am using this term to denote a configuration consisting of two triangles, the bases of which run parallel to each other and which issue from a common point where their tips come into contact with each other. In fact, this ornament could also be termed "butterfly", but I think the "hourglass" denomination fits its shape better.

The "hourglass" intervenes fairly frequently in jar decoration where it is inserted between particular ornament fields or frames as a filling motif (Nos. 43, 44, 46, 48, 49, 59, 60, 65, 66, 67, 68, 72, 142, 148, 150, 160, 162, 163, 168, 169, 171, 173, 175). Pairs of doubled triangles on a common base take over this role in the jar of my No. 47, with chequerboard panels intervening in between them. In other cases we see vertical belts of triangles fulfilling the same function (my Nos. 53, 78). There exists an instance in which the chief decoration panels, occupied by vertical zones of superimposed triangles, are separated by "hourglass" fillings (No. 162). The painter of a bowl of my

No. 165 decorated it with an image of a beast of prey, possibly a feline, accompanied by "hourglass" ornaments.

Association table 1 shows that the "hourglass" ornament occurs chiefly on jars and by far less commonly on bowls. It is more frequently found in association with animals, water- and cereal motifs.

The cumulative evidence thus links this motif with what appear to be images of mountains, but also with water- and cereal icons and especially with depictions of animals, chiefly wild ones.

All this does point in the direction of a symbol of a fertility goddess, possibly Ninki or Ninhursag, "Lady of the Foothills" and mistress of wild animals (Wiggermann 1996, 216; Michalowski 1998, 239–240 and 244; Heimpel 2000, 379). She might have been a partner of Enki, represented on the Susa pottery by the water-related icons. The stag, present on my No. 1, is an animal of Ninhursag (Wiggermann 1996, 215), and, as late as the 6th century B. C., king Nabonid renewed the "stag-ornated doors of cedarwood" in the Dingirmah (= Ninhursag) temple of Babylon (Heimpel 2000, 379–380). The goddess Ninhursag displays an affinity to open landscapes (Heimpel 2000, 381).

Her cult seems to have reached a respectable antiquity, as an "hourglass"-shaped pendant turned up in the TT6 "Burnt House" of Arpachiyah (Mallowan-Rose 1935, Fig. 51:5). At that time it was certainly not an exclusively male-related amulet, as is shown by another find of this kind from the same context, depicting an erect penis (ibid., fig. 51: 6, and also: von Wickede 1990, Pl. 168).

On the other hand, "hourglass" icons, associated with a simplified chequerboard pattern, turn up together with an erotic scene in an archaic Ur seal impression (Legrain 1936, Nos. 239, 368). This may suggest an alternative to the interpretation proposed above, but it certainly confirms the linking of this symbol with the fertiltiy sphere.

Arc

In this particular instance it is greatly regrettable that we do not dispose of any more detailed information sources, as this emblem may well have developed into one of the signs of the protocuneiform script. A configuration which I have termed "arc", of the shape of a circle segment, appears on some Susa pottery, in a singular or repeated form. The object is so smooth that it does not offer any hints as to its possible meaning and any attempts at an interpretation must needs rest on guesswork.

The linkage of this sign with cereal motifs may suggest, in a most straightforward and thus possibly simplistic way, that it copies the form of a sickle, even perhaps that of a pottery sickle (my Nos. 58, 60).

The arc figures prominently on jars and associates more frequently with "hourglass"-, cereal- and animal motifs but it may also appear quite alone (Table 1). The combination of arc- and sun images is reiterated by a Late Uruk/Jemdet Nasr cylinder seal with a file of "heraldically" arranged animals (Rova 1994, 557 Tav. 31). The arc motif probably stands for an idea linked with the world of fertility and proliferation force.

This symbol displays an apparent connection with the proto-cuneiform sign RU (ZATU No. 435 p. 265). The sign is featured in some toponyms such as Aratta (LAM + KUR + KUR + RU, ZATU No. 35 p. 176) and Šuruppak (KUR + RU, ZATU No. 544 p. 291), where it may have played the role of a phonetic complement. Of particular interest in this context, however, is the existence of the NI + RU lexeme in the Jemdet Nasr period. In fact, the NI sign, frequently confused with the GAR/NINDA one, may depict a tall beaker or jar of the type so frequently occurring at Susa, not only among the painted-pottery items, but also later, in the hands of attendants of the supreme Susa chiefs on the seal impressions found in strata overlying those with the painted-pottery finds (cf. infra).

In the Jemdet Nasr texts, the NI + RU obviously represents a "common fund of goods", shared among a group of member communities. Each of these communities singled out some of her production facilities for the preparation of NI + RU goods at her own expense, and exchanged some of the fruit of such labours with the other members of the group, probably identical with the "city league". This circulation of goods was closely supervised by NI + RU officials (SANGA) and approved of by impressing the relevant texts registering movements of such commodities with the "city-league seal". The origin of this institution, likely to have had a symbolic significance in view of the modest quantities of the goods exchanged, in the Late Uruk age cannot be excluded (Matthews 1993, 29–30; Charvát 1997, 15–18).

As this is one of the very first common institutions linking together various member communities, and therefore of exceptional interest for the origin and emergence of the first states in the region, it merits a closer attention. In fact, the NI + RU sign group may actually derive from an image of a beaker denoted as "the RU beaker" – which, in fact, is the case of our tall jars and beakers with this sign painted on. The interpretation must take into account the semantics of the RU lexeme, meaning, in fact, something like "donated, dedicated, consecrated". Here we may think of such phenomena as the "im-ru-a" – literally "consecrated clay", "clans" of the Fara texts (Charvát 2002, 205), or the "a ru-a (Akk. *širku*)", persons consecrated to the Mesopotamian temples. The verb RU = Akk. *šaráku* means, first and foremost, "to dedicate something to a deity", as well as "to offer prayers or sacrifices" (CAD Š II s.v. *šaráku*, 40–48, esp. pp. 41–42). It is interesting to observe that the signs GAR (so easily confused with NI or Ì, which may well be an image of a tall beaker) or GÁ are also translated into Akkadian as *šaráku*.

Concerning the commensality at Susa, it should not be forgotten that we are moving somewhere in the period when grape wine (*Vitis vinifera*) was first cultivated and doubtlessly also consumed. At Susa itself, wine deposits have been identified in vessels of the Late Uruk age and the site has yielded one grape pip, published very recently (McGovern et al. 1997, 14–16).

It may thus be legitimately asked whether the ancestor of the RU sign on our beakers and jars from Susa does not refer to their contents as "consecrated, holy", and whether it thus does not indicate a sacral aspect of the ceremonial commensality in which this fine tableware served. Such dedication of the contents of the drinking vessels might have pointed to a rather important change in the nature of substances entering the bodies of the banquet guests. While they might have wished to "eat and drink the chief's mana" before, they could now assume that a divine element was entering their insides, whereby they also become charged with a dose of supernatural force.

The eventual confirmation of this hypothesis would contribute most important historical material for the nature and development of ceremonial-commensality practices in the epoch prior to the emergence of the pristine states of the Orient.

"Sun"

I have chosen the "sun" denomination as pure convenience, as this ornament does actually consist of a bigger circle in the middle surrounded by smaller circles along its perimeter. This is a motif known from Halaf-culture pottery, reminding us again that for the painters of the Susa pottery, the Halaf-age artistic tradition was by far not extinct.

Being a rare phenomenon, the "sun" occurs on one bowl and one jar. It combines once with an arc (my No. 57) and once within a triangular composition (No. 193).

The combination with the arc image is interesting insofar as this could refer to the "consecrated" (RU) drink. This connection could imply that the "sun" represents an ensign of a deity but no firm proof can be adduced. Let us, however, notice that the same combination occurs on a Late Uruk/Jemdet Nasr cylinder seal with a file of "heraldically" arranged animals (Rova 1994, No. 557 Tav. 31). On the other hand, a "landscape motif" on a Late Uruk/Jemdet Nasr cylinder seal shows sunlit mountain ranges and makes it likely that the "sun" icon meant actually a depiction of the foremost heavenly body (Rova 1994, No. 705 Tav. 41).

A sherd found at Tepe Gawra in layer XIII (Terminal Ubaid date) bears a sculptured depiction of what appears to be a sun, a moon crescent and two knobs, standing perhaps for female breasts (Tobler 1950, pl. CXXXII: 234). Sucha a combination of features could point to a "bi-sexual" character of the deity concerned. A connection with liquids, and thus presumably with a (female?) fertility cult may be surmised in the case of a goblet from layer XIA of the same site (Tobler 1950, pl. CXLIV: 377, p. 156), pressed to form a spout and bearing sun-shaped stamped ornament.

The "sun" signs appear in Proto-Elamite script as components of a sexagesimal system used to count volumes of grain, denoting 1/6 and 1/12 of the basic unit (Damerow, Englund and Lamberg-Karlovsky 1989, 24–25). One of the Tepe Yahya texts is supposed to indicate that a grain measure, denoted by the "sun" sign, may equal a daily ration for a working maid (ibid., 27 n. 89), about 0.7 litre (ibid., 60 n. 164). This may imply that the sign could actually refer to a "sun" as a time unit and stand for the idea of one day = one revolution of the sun. This hypothesis will have to be confirmed.

In fact, given both of the observations referred to above, it may be interesting to speculate whether a rather straightforward interpretation, seeing in the "sun" an emblem and symbol of the god An, could not be proposed. The reverence of An is likely for the Halaf-culture age, as I have pointed out above, and this identification might well be the one that does the minimum harm to the known facts. Both Enlil and Enki, as well as Ninki/Ninhursag, would bear their colleague An good company. At any rate, it is an interesting possibility.

Table 1 Association table of motifs from Susa pottery excavated by the French missions (1897–1939)

	Pot	Jar	Bowl	"Sun"	Arc	"Hgl"	Cer	Wat	Gip	Comb	Arm	Anim	Cheq	Tri	Cross
Cross	0	3	61	0	0	1	5	4	10	28	6	20	18	4	0
Triangle	0	0	14	1	0	0	1	0	3	4	0	0	5	0	
Chequerb'd	2	13	25	0	0	4	7	10	1	4	5	10	0		
Animals	13	39	25	0	2	16	9	17	9	12	2	0			
Arms	2	2	8	0	1	1	1	2	1	4	0				
Combs	0	0	32	0	0	1	0	0	2	0					
Gipar	1	4	16	0	0	2	1	0	0						
Water	16	24	3	0	0	6	1	0							
Cereals	2	14	8	0	2	6	0								
"Hourglass"	0	23	2	0	3	0									
Arc	0	6	0	1	0										
"Sun"	0	1	1	0											
Bowl	0	0	84												
Jar	0	64													
Pot	26														

The Susiana sites

In any evaluations of the Susa pottery it must be clearly stated that stylistically speaking, this exquisite class of tableware had sprung forth from predecessors on the Susiana plain, classified chronologically as belonging to the Ubaid age and preceding the foundation of Susa as a (supra-)regional centre (Berman 1994, 25 and 29 with ref.). Some of these tells, among which Djaffarabad, Djowi and Bendebal have yielded materials sufficiently abundant and preserved to an extent which allows comparison with the Susa-cemetery pottery.

First and foremost we have to take into consideration a fact, supplied recently by the neutron-activation pottery analyses carried out by Judith Berman, which I believe to be of considerable historical significance. While the contemporary red wares show a micro-chemical composition bearing out the most varied origin of the individual items, black-on-buff wares exhibit a different pattern. In Period 12, just prior to the establishment of Susa, such painted wares were made of clays which display a remarkable homogeneity all over the region in question (Berman 1994, 27). This clearly means that the production of tableware of a certain style was, at that particular moment, tied with one single source of material which is also likely to suggest one single production tradition founded on one single spiritual construction. This tells a great deal about the oneness of the legitimation source of the highly ranked groups of Susiana.

However, the image offered by the following, Susa A period, is again quite different. At least some of the painted tableware from the Susa cemetery could be demonstrated to have been made from visibly different sources of clay (Berman 1994, 28). Judith Berman brings this fact into connection with the transport of deceased members of the "country élite" to Susa, for burial in the prestigious cemetery. This conclusion carries a great deal of a convincing value.

In view of the fact that in the Susiana painted pots we probably have ancestors of the Susa tableware, is is self-evident that their iconography should be taken into consideration as well.

For the first of the sites, **Djaffarabad**, we have at our disposal both the original publication by Louis Le Breton (1947) and that of the new excavations by Geneviève Dollfus (1971). We shall treat them in a separate fashion, as they represent two distinct groups of source material.

The general characteristics of the first Jaffarabad material group do show a degree of difference from the Susa material. First and foremost, some of the motifs characteristical for the Halaf-culture leftovers in the Northern Ubaid ceramic tradition, as outlined by Catherine Breniquet (1996, 120 – latticed lozenges, for instance, even a bucranium (Le Breton 1947, fig. 13: 16), and cf. also the "sun"(Le Breton 1947, fig. 15 Nos. 9 and 10). Patterns likely to reproduce files of human figures, sometimes holding each other's hands, may invoke the magical power of dance, donor of well-being and fertility in ancient Mesopotamia (Charvát 2002, 157, fig. 5.18 with ref.; for earlier Iranian examples cf. Garfinkel 2000). They come in quite naturally on pottery used in a settlement site, and not destined for funerary use.

On the other hand, some images approximate those of Susa, and even complement them in a marvellous fashion. The vertical zigzag line on a beaker, for instance (Le Breton 1947, fig. 9: 8), does certainly recall some of the water motifs present on Susa pottery. At Susa, we could only wish for a wonderful depiction of what bears a strong likeness to a double building with two entrances, likely to have been built of perishable matters and embedded in a large chequerboard oblong (Le Breton 1947, fig. 14: 6); one could not imagine a better illustration of the fertility- and proliferation forces emanating out of a gipar structure than this. The vessels bearing large zigzag lines with the intervening triangular fields filled in either by chequerboard patterns or by depictions of arms find a perfect counterpart in a pattern which was most repeatedly reproduced at Susa (six times, cf. supra; Le Breton 1947, fig. 14 Nos. 7 and 10). Both images also show the objects protruding from the quivers to be, in one case, arrows (ibid. fig. 14: 10) and, in the other case, what may be a curving metal blade set on a long pole. Such arms as the latter, being destined both for fighting at close quarters and enabling even a successful repulsion of a cavalry charge (like the halberds of medieval Europe), bear out a surprisingly high level of sophistication of contemporary military gear. What these conquests were aimed at, is boldly indicated by the triangular emblem hovering over the quiver of fig. 14: 10: the whole wide world, symbolized by the same sign which was to become the "tasselled banner"! A bowl with oblique dotted lines, displaying, in its middle part, an enormous chequered snake (Le Breton 1947, fig. 14: 13) is closely replicated by an item from Susa (my No. 97), the only difference being that a file of dogs occupies the central horizontal zone on the Susa example. The Jaffarabad snake is clearly denoted as a benign creature by the chequered pattern it bears; let us not forget that the ibex-god (Enki/Ea) is a master of snakes (Michalowski 1998, 244).

Association table 2 shows the differences between Jaffarabad and Susa clearly. The stresses are quite different: at Jaffarabad, animals are the most frequent motif, combining on bowls and pots with chequerboard and "hourglass". The most conspicuous absences are those of cross- and comb motifs (Table 2).

The site of **Djowi** has, in addition to examples of painted pottery, yielded a sizable group of decorated spindle whorls which might be of interest here. Images which they bear may, in fact, relate to the spiritual world of ancient women and housemistresses, in whose hand they turned innumerable times, providing clothing for their families (Le Breton 1947, fig. 18; on the links between women and weaving cf., among many others, Gaydukevitch 1952 for the Greek and Roman world; for our area recently Breniquet-Mintsi 2000, esp. pp. 350–353). Of the motifs that interest us here, ears of corn (ibid., 3rd row from up, first from the right, 4th row from up, 3rd from right), combs (ibid., 4th row from up, first and second from left), and stars (ibid., 4th row from up, second from right) are displayed by them. Such images are thus unequivocally identified as benign.

Table 2 Association table of motifs from the pottery excavated by the former French mission at Jaffarabad (Le Breton 1947)

	Pot	Jar	Bowl	Sun	Arc	"Ho"	Cer	Wat	Gip	Com	Arm	Ani	Cheq	Tri	Cro
Cross	0	0	1	0	0	0	0	0	0	0	0	0	1	0	0
Triangle	1	0	0	0	0	0	0	1	0	0	1	0	0	0	
Chequerb'd	5	0	0	0	0	0	0	1	1	0	2	2	0		
Animals	4	0	3	0	0	1	0	0	0	0	0	0			
Arms	2	0	0	0	0	0	0	2	0	0	0				
Combs	0	0	1	0	0	0	0	0	0	0					
Gipar	0	0	0	0	0	0	0	0	0						
Water	2	0	2	0	0	0	0	0							
Cereals	0	0	0	0	0	0	0								
"Hourglass"	2	0	2	0	0	0									
Arc	0	0	0	0	0										
"Sun"	2	0	0	0											
Bowl	0	0	8												
Jar	0	0													
Pot	10														

The general characteristics of the Djowi pottery are again consistent with the prevalent usage, yet individualistic. The presence of the "traditional" Halaf-culture rudiments (latticed lozenges, chequerboard patterns consisting of "hourglass" motifs) is here well discernible also. Of the emblems found at Susa, we notice the cross, virtually absent at Djaffarabad (Le Breton 1947, fig. 21: 5, ibid., fig. 23: 11, ibid., fig. 24: 16, ibid., fig. 28: 5), and a variety of water-related patterns (Le Breton 1947, fig. 28: 10). The local comb patterns do bear a rather peculiar stamp, being unlike those of either Susa or Djaffarabad (Le Breton 1947, fig. 28: 23). A particular form is also assumed by the "sun" motif: being painted over a spout of a jar or pot (Le Breton 1947, fig. 22: 7), it is identified with the a liquid jetting out of the spout, and thus to the imagery of fertility and proliferation force. There is a fairly numerous group of animals, mostly wild ones, as it seems, with birds and fish to follow (Le Breton 1947, figs. 29 and 30). This is most probably a fact of recent archaeological origin, as the excavators may be presumed to have collected sherds bearing legible or pleasing patterns, to which the animals certainly belonged. A surprise of

Djowi are the paintings of human figures (Le Breton 1947, fig. 30: 15, 16 and 17). At least some of them may relate to dancing (ibid., Nos. 15 and 17), but one clear scene of a military triumph, with a male warrior brandishing a bow and arrow and lifting his right hand in gleeful rejoicing, is present (ibid. No. 16).

Of particular interest is the fragment depicted by Louis Le Breton as the right-hand sherd of the group of two he gave us as his fig. 30: 15. This sherd shows a human figure lifting his or her hands and flanked by two creatures standing upright, with long ears and prognathic jaws; whether these are animals or humans in disguise cannot be said at present. The central figure puts his or her right hand close to the snout of the being standing on his right side. This is a scene the great time of which will wait until about five hundred years later, the age of the Susa-B seal impressions.

Association table 3 brings to the eye the differences between the painted pottery of Susa and Djowi. Again, the most conspicuous similarities include the marked occurrence of animals on jars and bowls, and of water motifs on jars. Cross images on bowls are also visible, differently from Jaffarabad. Patterns completely absent at Djowi include triangles, combs, gipar- and arc motifs.

Table 3 Association table of motifs from the pottery excavated by the former French mission at Djowi (Le Breton 1947)

	Pot	Jar	Bowl	Sun	Arc	"Ho"	Cer	Wat	Gip	Com	Arm	Ani	Cheq	Tri	Cro
Cross	0	0	3	0	0	0	0	0	0	0	0	1	0	0	0
Triangle	0	0	0	0	0	0	0	0	0	0	0	0	0	0	
Chequerb'd	0	1	1	0	0	1	0	0	0	0	0	0	0		
Animals	0	27	4	0	0	0	0	0	0	0	0	0			
Arms	0	1	0	0	0	0	0	0	0	0	0				
Combs	0	0	0	0	0	0	0	0	0	0					
Gipar	0	0	0	0	0	0	0	0	0						
Water	0	3	0	0	0	0	0	0							
Cereals	0	1	0	0	0	0	0								
"Hourglass"	2	1	3	0	0	0									
Arc	0	0	0	0	0										
"Sun"	1	0	0	0											
Bowl	0	0	9												
Jar	0	36													
Pot	3														

The **Bendebal** evidence features, much in line with materials obtained from other Susaiana sites, sherds of preponderantly geometrical ornament. Needless to say that the ancient Halaf-related patterns are again present but in some instances, they seem to have been living on vigorously and inspiring new creations of the local potters. Wittness the motif of a large lozenge, filled in by a chequerboard pattern consisting of full (dark) and latticed fields (Le Breton 1947, fig. 36: 8). The emblematic value of the chequerboard ornament is borne out by a bowl bearing a rather curious ornament – two big circles, filled in by series of similar concentric circles of a diminishing diameter, and linked together by a double broken line. The whole resembles an image of spectacles bearing, in the midst of their "glasses" and at the centres of the areas delimited by the diminishing concentric circles, one circular field with two dark and two light segments each – quite in the manner of the mark of the BMW cars of Germany. Comb depictions take on peculiar forms as well: they combine with an "hourglass" motif (Le Breton 1947, fig. 38: 19), turn up alone (ibid., fig. 39: 16) or unite with a dark-filled rhomboid (ibid., fig. 39: 22). Neither are cross motifs absent (ibid., fig. 39: 6, 11, 12). Plenty of wild animals lead a thriving life on Bendebal pottery (Le Breton 1947, fig. 40), with birds and fish to keep them company (ibid., fig. 41: 1–4, 9). One of the animal-image jars even displays the "sun" motif painted over a spout and thus associates it again with the world of liquids, standing probably for fertility and proliferation force (Le Breton 1947, fig. 41: 10, 10a). Since this device is also present at Djowi, and since the Bendebal animals appear to be wild (with russeted skin, possibly leopards or other felines), we may legitimately ask whether an allusion to the goddess Ninhursag (cf. supra) is not made here.

There are again human figures standing upright with lifted hands (ibid., fig.6 and 7), one of them being accompanied by a large and unwieldy object, possibly a part of an architecture (ibid., fig. 41: 5). A most interesting image is borne by a sherds depicted by Louis Le Breton as No. 8 in his fig. 41. Unfortunately, the upper part of the sherd is missing, but we again recognize a human body with lifted left hand, accompanied by a bulky "pedestal" on his or her right side. This could have been an "animal-feeding scene" of the same character as we know from Djowi.

Association table 4 indicated well the switching relations within the source groups of the individual sites treated here. Some of the *grandes lignes* are there all right: numerous examples of animals on jars, visible presence of water on jars. There is a much weaker representation of chequerboard patterns, combs, gipar and sun motifs. Arms, cerals and arc motifs are entirely missing from Bendebal.

Table 4 Association table of motifs from the pottery excavated by the former French mission at Bendebal (Le Breton 1947)

	Pot	Jar	Bowl	Sun	Arc	"Ho"	Cer	Wat	Gip	Com	Arm	Ani	Cheq	Tri	Cro
Cross	2	3	0	0	0	0	0	0	0	0	0	0	0	0	0
Triangle	1	0	0	0	0	0	0	0	0	0	0	0	0	0	
Chequerb'd	0	2	0	0	0	0	0	0	0	0	0	0	0		
Animals	1	28	2	1	0	0	0	0	0	0	0	0			
Arms	0	0	0	0	0	0	0	0	0	0	0				
Combs	0	2	0	0	0	0	0	0	0	0					
Gipar	1	0	0	0	0	0	0	0	0						
Water	1	4	0	0	0	0	0	0							
Cereals	0	0	0	0	0	0	0								
"Hourglass"	1	2	1	0	0	0									
Arc	0	0	0	0	0										
"Sun"	1	1	0	0											
Bowl	0	0	3												
Jar	0	44													
Pot	7														

The new excavations at **Djaffarabad** have put at our disposal a new group of pottery which presumably represent a more reliable sample of the ancient state of things than that acquired by the foregoing mission (Dollfus 1971). And, in fact, this is visible from the very beginning of the publication on.

The magnificent bowl with the dancing scene, featuring a large comb as an inset motif (Dollfus 1971, fig. 9: 1), is executed in unmistakable Susa style but depicts a scene that was never seen at Susa itself. The same goes for most of the painted pottery shown on the Figure 9, with chequerboard- and cross-patterns attesting to their affinity with the Susa examples. Much the same goes for the images in fig. 11, where the bowls with the finely drawn parallel vertical lines, interrupted by the central zone roughly between the rim and bottom of the vessel, display the degree of interrelations of the artistic world of Susa (with a file of dogs, my No. 97), and Djaffarabad (Le Breton 1947, fig. 14: 13, chequered snake). The new motifs visible in the central zones include cross- and "hourglass" emblems (Dollfus 1971, fig. 11: 4 and 6), "hourglass" only (ibid., fig. 11: 5), and an ibex head with what looks like

102

water flowing from bathroom showers, and what probably means streams of water flowing down the mountains (ibid., fig. 11: 7). The ibex god is a lord of snakes (Michalowski 1998, 244). All these icons do point in the direction of Enki, but especially Ninhursag, the "Lady of the Foothills" and wild animals. The form of comb atested to at Djaffarabad does display a character different from that of Susa (Dollfus 1971, fig. 12: 8) and seems to be related to a sign of proto-Elamite writing appearing at Tepe Yahya (but not at Susa) as the smallest unit of the ŠE system of measures (Damerow, Englund and Lamberg-Karlovsky 1989, 30). Some of the painted vessels of Djaffarabad do, in fact, look exactly like those of Susa, the case being especially that of the pots bearing the images of flocks of birds (Dollfus 1971, fig. 16: 8 and 9).

Association table 5 does again attest to the same general trends, with minor divergences. Much as at Susa, the cross icons turn up often on bowls. Water motifs often go with pots and jars Animals on pots and jars predominate at Djaffarabad (animals on jars and bowls at Susa).

Absent from the Djaffarabad icons are triangles (unlike the first group where they do appear, albeit in a trace fashion), and arms (again unlike the first group).

Table 5 Association table of motifs from the pottery excavated by the modern French mission at Jaffarabad (Dollfus 1971)

	Pot	Jar	Bowl	Sun	Arc	"Ho"	Cer	Wat	Gip	Com	Arm	Ani	Cheq	Tri	Cro
Cross	0	0	6	0	0	2	0	0	0	0	0	0	1	0	0
Triangle	0	0	0	0	0	0	0	0	0	0	0	0	0	0	
Chequerb'd	2	3	3	0	0	0	0	1	0	0	0	1	0		
Animals	9	6	2	0	0	0	0	1	0	0	0	0			
Arms	0	0	0	0	0	0	0	0	0	0	0				
Combs	0	1	1	0	0	0	0	0	0	0					
Gipar	1	0	0	0	0	0	0	0	0						
Water	5	5	0	0	0	1	0	0							
Cereals	0	1	0	0	0	0	0								
"Hourglass"	1	2	3	0	0	0									
Arc	0	1	0	0	0										
"Sun"	0	0	0	0											
Bowl	0	0	11												
Jar	0	17													
Pot	16														

The Susiana sites – conclusions

Should we have wished to postulate a genetic connection between the Susiana- and Susa pottery, we could not have desired a better result. On one hand, the Susiana masters still remembered well the art of Halaf-culture painters, and they extensively borrowed from the rich *répertoire* of this ancient and venerable culutre. On the other hands, they boldly invented new patterns and new icons to match the demands of the masters of houses who intended to fortify their social positions by extensive feasting and entertaining guests. Many patterns on tableware, from which the partaken food was supposed to be embodied by the followers who saw in it the externalization of the chiefs' benign powers and capacities, undoubtedly recalled famous deeds which such high-rank individuals wished to celebrate.

Ultimately, such ornate pots, jars and bowls went with the chiefs to their graves, when the large and prestigious site of Susa was established. The Susa masters were clearly working in the tradition of their Susiana predecessors, but, meeting a different demand, did not slavishly copy the works of their teachers. In Susa and Susiana, the style was identical; the iconography, not. Some motifs were common, and explain each other, such as military triumph scenes; some other motifs were apparently not shared because of the different character of the Susa "Walhala" (the Susiana rows of dancers with the underlying fertility symbolism, not appropriate in a cemetery setting). In general, however, it might be said that what we witness here is a) a gradual emergence of a set of signs commonly understood, which, as time went by, acquired a "canonical" form and were repeated over and over again, and b) the sufficiently firmly established patterned structures and compositional principles in which at least some of these symbols operated. The first symbolic "lexical treasure" of mankind, operating within a definable syntactical system, thus woke up into the light of day.

The air beneath the wings: conclusions

The transmission of the Halaf cultural heritage, mediated most probably via Tepe Gawra and the Jebel Hamrin sites (Breniquet 1996, 39), is likely to have assisted in the growth of a similarly structured society in Susiana. Here also the "big chiefs", the high-rank personages, considered it one of their main duties and obligations to share out their riches with the rest of their communities, transforming thus the material affluence which their offices brought them into things immaterial – support and loyalty of their followers.

One of the principal devices, by means of which this could have been achieved, was ceremonial feasting and banqueting. In the course of elaborate entertainments at the chief's table, his followers might have intended to embody the results of his efforts, likely to have been perceived as material externalizations of his chiefly virtues and talents, by partaking them as food and drink. The exclusive painted ware from which they ate their portions might have commemorated, at least in the most prominent examples and in artistic "abbreviations", the heroic deeds and memorable feats which the high-rank individuals had performed.

As time went by, some of these chiefs went to their graves accompanied by the very examples of exquisite tableware which had once been used to celebrate their achievements and which now served as repositories for the very bodies that caused these *memorabilia* to happen. This came to pass at the cemetery of Susa, established at the end of the Ubaid-culture period. Even before, however, a tendency to unify the message of art which the painted vessels conveyed, to make it consist of a definite number of "signs" of constant form and probably also content, and to display these "signs" as operating within definite and comprehensible structures, became perceptible. How can we read the message of these primeval "signs"?

First and foremost, a series of emblems outlines the *dramatis personae* of this remote period of human history. We shall now meet them in review.

Let us begin with what then, as now, is the motion force of history, its foremost actor but, at the same time, its most pitiful victim – the individual human being, here probably of high rank, symbolized, as it has been indicated at length in the foregoing chapter, by the image of **the comb**. Most of the comb images appear on bowls which presumably served as a funerary receptacle for the deceased person's most important relic – the head. The rather frequent linkage with the cross symbol is likely to commemorate those members of highly ranked groups who founded new "cities", that is, foci of life "civilized" according to the Susa patterns; such efforts would, of course, entail not only the building up of the respective habitation- and traffic structures but also finding solutions for the problems of subsistence of the new settlers, their protection, transport facilities, integration into networks of political coherence, etc. The rather prominent association of the comb symbols and animal figures is likely to symbolize an act of domination over untamed, and hence "unhumanized" and potentially dangerous uncultivated nature, most probably a record of a successful hunting expedition. The association between remains of hunted game, beakers likely to symbolize ceremonial commensality, and more solid architecture (implying the presence of high-rank personages), has been elucidated by Henry T. Wright's excavations at Tepe Farukhabad (Charvát 2002, 63).

Human individuals form groups of which the closest one, setting the stage for the initial years of life of all humans, and frequently influences their whole life, is apparently the family, symbolized in the Susa pottery by the sign that I choose to call **gipar**. These signs also occur on bowls, and associate frequently with the cross signs and animal images. Their main functions thus appear to fall in with those of the individuals, a logical fact in terms of a pre-state society where kinship relations must have played a dominant role. Unfortunately, there is no means of knowing how big these groupings were; the mutual associations of up to six gipar signs (lineage-, or clan-segment alliances?) show that at least some might have been fairly numerous, and that we probably have to reckon with extended families (lineages? clan segments?). On the other hand, images joining a couple of gipar signs with a cross cannot but arouse the suspicion that a union of two prominent families of one "city" was celebrated here ("Bella gerant alii, tu, felix Austria, nube!").

The central points, out of which the life of the Susiana and Susa communities were managed and directed, the pristine "cities", were probably represented by the symbol of the **cross**. Concentrating, in an overwhelming majority, on bowls, the cross symbols tend to occupy the central, most important point of the whole composition. Their association with combs and animal designs have already been mentioned; reminiscences of their "founding fathers" in the form of combs exist side by side with the marking of "cities" as centres of "civilized" life, surrounded by wild and unhumanized landscapes symbolized by animal figures (and, farther on, by the divine element symbolized so frequently by chequerboard patterns). Chequerboard associations of the cross icon, also quite visible, may either implore sufficient fertility and proliferation force for the inhabitants of the city and their resources, or, alternatively, place it under protection of one of the primeval gods, probably Enlil.

Finally, let us mention the rather enigmatic **triangular** symbol, standing possibly for the entire geographical unit organized according to the Susiana and Susa principles, the "civilized world". This finds also place chiefly on bowls, and tends to combine more frequently with cross-, chequerboard-, comb- and gipar symbols. In relation to the triangle, the cross symbol may refer to a central site, playing, at the time of burial of the respective vessel, the role of a "capital city". The chequerboard may again invoke supernatural blessings while the comb and gipar symbols may represent

106

the individuals and families aspiring at the highest positions within Susa society.

The individual symbols on Susa pottery do, however, also include references to activities of individuals or communities deemed to be worthy of historical commemoration. Let us now see the stage with actors at play.

Major projects of bringing agricultural land under plough, building irrigation works or changing tracts of hitherto waste land into arable are likely to be epitomized on Susa pottery by painted depictions of **cereals**. Visible chiefly on jars, they associate with animal icons, chequerboard-, "hourglass"- and cross motifs. Cereal production was clearly a "municipal" undertaking, visualized by the cross. On the other hand, it did have something in common with uncultivated landscapes: animal symbols could commemorate fertilizing tracts of waste land, or, alternatively, refer to cereal nourishment of livestock. Chequerboard and "hourglass" symbols are likely to denote the ultimate donors of agricultural wealth – personifications of fertility, such as Enlil and Ninhursag.

In the life of the Susiana and Susa communities, peaceful pursuits may have, from time to time, given way to the war cry and the clash of arms. Emblems involving **military gear**, most likely intended to celebrate war triumphs, usually consist of spears and bows and arrows, sometimes depicted in quivers, but also of fairly sophisticated halberd-like weapons with curved blades(?) set on long poles. Often borne by bowls, arm images combine more frequently with cross-, chequerboard- and comb patterns. Military valour of particularly gifted commanders has undoubtedly found appreciation here (combs), much as military dominance over "cities" (cross). As to the chequerboard patterns, these may again implore divine favour even in this kind of undertaking, or depict the abundance flowing out of successfully fought wars.

On Susa pottery, the plough and spear were joined by a pious gesture of **libation to the gods**, represented, as it seems, by the arc sign. The emblem, later to be represented as RU in Sumerian, turns up on jars. Insofar as it forms alliances at all, it links up with "hourglass"-, cereal- and animal designs. All this points to the sphere of unhumanized nature, but also fertility and, thus again, to one of the chthonic goddesses, perhaps to Ninhursag.

The inhabitants of the Susiana and Susa settlement lived in constant contact with uncultivated nature, symbolized on the painted pottery by the images of **animals**. It has been already pointed out that these are chiefly of wild species, though images of cattle herds may be present. Of the more conspicuous figures, let us notice at least the stag, an animal of Ninhursag (my No. 1), or the frequent image of ibex, an ensign of Enki. An enigmatic feature is the depiction of birds on Susa pottery. Given their abundance and variability, they are likely to convey a message of some importance. The fine images of densely spaced heads and bodies of birds flowing on water or standing in it may simply stand for large bodies of water as a landscape element. On the other hand, at least some bird images did play a symbolic role, such as a marker of one of the four cardinal points (my No. 136). We could legitimately expect the bird images to stand for the realms of the Susa high-rank individuals, like those disposed in regular compositions like the concentric circles of my No. 3 or the "four quarters" of my No. 4; there are no indications that this is actually so. The reptiles may represent the earthly or chthonic symbolization of fertility; the association of a snake and a boring instrument on one of the Susa beakers (my No. 137) finds an exact counterpart in Sumerian proto-cuneiform writing around 3000 B.C. (UŠUMGAL: Glassner 2000, 209).

Animal images are to be found mainly on jars and bowls. The most frequent associations which they make are with cross-, water-, "hourglass"-, comb- and chequerboard patterns. The cross and comb refer undoubtedly to features of "civilized" life, human individuals and "cities"; water and "hourglass" may assign the animals to the world ruled by the divine donor of water and fertility, perhaps Ninhursag, much as the chequerboard, likely to stand for the partner incarnation of fertility, perhaps Enlil. In this it is well visible how the masters of the Susa painted pottery strived to bring the untamed and wild element of uncultivated landscapes under control, albeit in a symbolic fashion.

Finally, a series of symbols present on Susa pottery probably refer to the world of the gods. This goes first and foremost for the **chequerboard**, symbolizing probably either an impersonal fertility- and proliferation force, or, alternatively, as its avatar, the god who was to become the Sumerian Enlil. Appearing primarily on bowls, the chequerboard associates with cross-, water-, animal-, cereal-, triangle- and arm symbols. The cross association undoubtedly invokes the favour of this power towards a particular "city". Water, animal and cereal icons may refer to the life-giving force of this particular supernatural agent, while the arm and triangle designs point to the sphere of "worldly domination", most appropriate for a male deity.

A number of Susa symbols related to **water** may stand for yet another representative of the primeval pantheon of Susa, that of the waters, later Sumerian Enki. With his permission and support, major projects of bringing agricultural land under plough, building irrigation works or changing tracts of hitherto waste land into arable might have taken place. Not surprisingly, the water symbols figure more prominently on jars and pots than on bowls. Their most numerous associations are those with animal icons and chequerboard patterns, followed by the "hourglass"- and cross motifs. While animals are again likely to stand for tracts of uncultivated landscape along the watercourses – or for the abundance of wild nature – , the chequerboard patterns may materialize a desire for a supernatural blessing with fertility (or a "male determinative" for this deity?). Water was, of course, essential for the foundation of "cities" and the cross-water connection is thus quite logical. On the other hand, the "hourglass" symbol may refer to the god's partner, divine provider of flowing water, most likely one of the chthonic goddesses – Ninhursag, if not Ninki (or their equivalents, of course). A predecessor of the proto-cuneiform sign RAD (ZATU No. 432, p. 264) may be seen in my illustration No. 66.

I suppose that the most decorative and ellegant **"hourglass"** motif stands for a symbol of one of the goddesses giving life to uncultivated landscapes, probably Ninhursag or Ninki. It turns up primarily on jars and associates with animal-, cereal- and water designs. All this seems to corroborate the above cited equation, as Ninhursag is a fertility-giving lady of wild animals; the stag (my No. 1) is an animal of Ninhursag. The same deity , or a related one, may hide behind the rather enigmatic **"sun"** ensign. This ornates a bowl and a jar and asociates with an arc and a triangle. Primary data are extremely limited but the function of the sign in Proto-Elamite script indicates that it could really mean something like "a given number of revolutions of the sun", "a day". Sun images placed on vessel spouts of some Susiana pots may point to a relation with flowing liquids, and thus with fertility. How far this emblem could refer to a bi-sexual deity, or to the god An, is not clear at present.

Thus the images on the Susa painted pottery usher in the individual characters of the historical drama, show them in action and refer to the higher world of the gods, donors of all life on earth. But why was it necessary to go to such pains to put the ancestors to their well-deserved rest in exquisite, painted, symbol-laden pots? Who initiated this whole process, and to what purpose?

In searching for an answer to this question, it is commendable to take into consideration the whole situation, as we know it from Susa. We have seen that the Susa cemetery was probably founded on virgin soil, at a site previously unsettled, and that a great deal of energy was spent in the proper conduct of funerary procedures. In the ancient Near Eastern cultures, cemeteries weres always held in particular esteem; even in historical periods, families tended to keep houses with

109

ancestral tombs and to sell them only in cases of dire necessity. In such cases, a special ritual for (reconciliation of?) the dead had to be performed (Durand 1989). It is somewhat difficult to see whether the Susa burial ground was a regular cemetery on flat land or a "hillock of the dead", as Roland de Mecquenem asserted. Actually, the funerary-barrow idea would fit better here, as at least the ancient Mesopotamians had definite ideas about the appropriate and desirable relations between the high and the low (Kirk 1970, 125–131, on the Etana myth). However that may have been, the cemetery was in use for a considerable period of time and the dead were laid to rest with a great deal of care (excarnation of the bodies, building of burial cists…). Three features stand out clearly:

a) the cemetery entombed physical remains od persons who are likely to have once lived as members of local highly ranked groups;

b) these persons were laid to rest together with, or even in, items of exquisitely painted pottery, bearing designs presumably recording major events of their lives;

c) such designs assumed gradually the form of a set of fixed-form signs ("lexicum") with assigned meanings, grouped into compositions according to definable structural principles ("syntax").

It would thus seem that a considerable amount of both material and spiritual energy was invested into the carrying out of the funerary obsequies. Why was this so?

In an attempt to answer this question, I shall revoke once more the eloquent ethnographic analogy of the Polynesian *kava*-drinking chief. At the very moment that he drinks from his cup, he becomes mystically united with all his chiefly ancestors as far as the founder of the genealogy, the goddess Hikuleʻo (Douaire-Marsaudon 2001, esp. pp. 11, 21–32; James 1991, 303). This, in fact, could be the very purpose for which the Susa chiefs needed their "hillock of the dead".

The whole cemetery complex could have become an huge tool for legitimization of power of the chiefs ascending to the ruler's stool. It is possible, and conceivable, that at the moment of his inthronization, every new Susa chief became mystically identical with the whole line of his deceased ancestors. This particularly sanctity-laden moment would have also entailed re-activation of all the ancestral spirits and re-enactment of all the heroic deeds and feats they had performed. (Something of this kind was normal in ancient Egypt, where every pharaoh was credited with having mystically followed all the "prescribed" stages of his life trajectory, which he had to pass as a divine being, regardless of whether he had in reality performed the deeds ascribed to him.)

But here, apparently, a shibboleth was hidden: in order to re-enact the mythical past of the Susa chiefdom properly, an intelligible record of it had to exist. In other words, every ancestor laid to rest at the Susa cemetery had to help his descendants by being interred with a pictorial "file" of the *memorabilia* of his or her life, a file that had to be constantly read and re-read, as it came to life upon every inthronization of a new incumbent of the Susa stool. This, I believe, may be the reason why the style of the Susa pottery had not changed for a long time and why it displays such a remarkable tendency to freeze the artistic expression forms into symbolic images of fixed significance ("lexical units") and to combine them according to discernible "syntactic" rules.

The proper running of the whole complex of rules regulating the succession upon the Susa stool might have been even more important than we see today. In fact, the Susa cemetery evidence implies that social status was not heritable there. The conclusions of Lewis Binford's investigations of pre-industrial burial practices show this to be the case, when children are buried in houses and adults in a cemetery, as at Susa (cited in Wright 1978, 213). The chiefly succession might thus have been quite free, and dependent on the personal qualities and achievements of all the likely candidates. Needless to say that in such circumstances, mythical and ritual observances can assume a special significance, as they would invariably provide a ground on which the succession disputes would be settled.

With the establishment of the Susa cemetery and the whole complex of activities linked to the funerary activities performed there, we thus arrive at a point in the history of mankind the importance of which is matched by very few of its kind. A decisive step towards the introduction of one of the first known scripts of history was taken. Prior to this moment, the carrier of this new recording system, painted pottery, served as a conveyor of mystical messages and embassies among the exteriors and interiors of Eneolithic chiefs and their retinues. By now, it assumed the position of a tool of permanent re-creation of the past, of a bearer of a system of signs that, having been originally proposed to provide and maintain legitimacy of a certain type of balance of social relations within a particular region of South-West Asia, were ultimately to evolve into a device of recording human speech and all the inventions of the human spirit that could be put in words.

For the first time in history, the human spirit spread its wings to soar up to empyrean heights of permanent creativity.

This happened in conjunction of two major groups of high-rank individuals whose presence now looms on the horizon of our vision. The pre-brahmanas, members of the first caste, had done their deal well: Enlil, Enki and Ninki/Ninhursag join now An, their predecessor, on the Susa painted pottery. This medium was nonetheless apparently chosen to commemorate chiefly the glory of illustrious personages who prided themselves on helping their communities also in this world – directing irrigation projects, facing phenomena of untamed and wild nature or waging wars. Leaders, organizers and officers, they constituted a group that will, in distant India and in subsequent but foreseeable human history, be known as ksatriyas, managers, administrators and commanders, join now their efforts to those of the "priestly class".

THE WATER OF LIFE

With the seal impressions on clay, datable most probably to the early stages of the Uruk-culture period, we are entering a new age at Susa. For the very first time, the imagery involving pristine highly ranked groups and their activities ceased to be concealed in funerary monuments and was publicly displayed to substantiate and justify the structurally new energy flows that characterized a crucial period of the buildup of early Western Asian statehood. Also, the frequency of the image display increased considerably and presumably acquired a certain rhythm and pattern. Let us now see how all this happened.

The archaeological summary

For the sake of clarity, let us present the basic data on the archaeological contexts, in which the sealings from Susa appeared, once more. These bits and pieces of clay turned up in strata overlying the ancient cemetery (Susa I) but unfortunately, no precise data on their mutual relations are furnished by any of the excavators (de Mecquenem 1943, 9–12). De Mecquenem found clusters of seal impressions at various spots in his trench. He noted that a quantity of them appeared by the side of two big oval-shaped and wheel-turned terra-cotta jars (ibid., 10, fig. 5: 2). He also pointed to the fact that a seal which left its impression at this findspot (ibid., 11, fig. 6: 4) appeared in Trench I at the Acropole, where a large number of such impressions rested on a plaque of fired clay close by a kiln (ibid., 11).

The Susa seal impressions seem to be contemporary with a huge mud-brick construction, not much later than the *massif funéraire* in date. This was built of individual compartments enclosed by a system of walls, perpendicularly crossing one another and filled in with clay. The only informations available on its exterior come from the southern facade, at least 80 metres long. This facade rested on a socle (basement or pedestal) some 2 metres high, superimposed by an incut around 4 metres deep, above which a revetment loomed to the height of at least 8 metres. A zone of this facade some 3 metres above the incut bore a form of architectural decoration by means of groups of four or five big clay wedges stuck in the masonry. The top part of this *haute terrasse* displayed traces of buildings interpreted as granaries, storage spaces and perhaps workshops; another complex might have played the role of a temple, of which all traces were obliterated but the form of which survived in the shape of a fragmentary model found here.

The *haute terrasse* perished in a fire and a débris layer gradually accumulated by its lowest part. Habitation buildings have been erected on top of this débris until the worn-out and derelict facade collapsed and buried the house ruins below it (Amiet 1986, 36–37).

The new excavations at the Acropole of Susa have shown that seal impressions of a similar style turned up in layer 25 of Acropole I (Amiet 1986, 37, n. 6).

At the very end of this period, the *haute terrasse* was restored once more (Acropole 2 layer 7), but after a short time it collapsed again and was not rebuilt any more (Amiet 1986, 39; a convenient stratigtraphic summary ibid. 235 fig. 3, for a general review cf. also: Carter-Stolper 1984, 112–114; Harper--Aruz-Tallon 1992, p. 27 fig. 23 and pp. 28–29; Algaze 1993, 13–18; Rova 1994, 32–40).

All this points to a considerable amount of power wielded by the contemporary high-rank personages of Susa, as well as to the essentially successful acceptance of the model of social relations which they proposed to the commoner strata. This makes it crucial to understand properly the trajectory taken by contemporary social developments. I shall try to achieve this by means of iconic analysis of the seal impressions, obviously an issue of the new trends of aperception and construction of social reality.

Iconography of the Susa seal impressions

From among all the seal impressions belonging to the traditionally defined stage of Susa B, I have chosen those which either display figural iconography, a novelty of the period, or show, in one form or another, connections with the preceding stage of Susa art. This, of course, means leaving a fair share of the non-figural (seals and) seal impressions of the same age out of my considerations here (good examples of these may be seen in Amiet 1972, Pls. 1–4, and in von Wickede 1990, Pls. 439–448 and 450–451). My conclusions concerning this material must thus be weighed with reference to this procedure. However, I see no means how to "read" any intelligible message from seal imagery that displays no connection to any of the patterns to which a meaning and significance may be assigned (on a wider interpretation of sealing practices vis-à-vis early social formations cf. now Pullen 1994, esp. pp. 38–39).

As to the common assumption that prehistoric seals must needs mean individual symbols by the exercise of which the sway of individual persons over material objects or their receptacles or storage places comes to expression, this remains to be proved. Just for the sake of comparison, the containers themselves could have been made in a way to enable the identification of the supplier of the goods, much as the bags manufactured in a particular region on the Chino-Burmese frontier, which can be tracked down to the weaver who made the respective cloth (Formoso 2001, esp. pp. 44–54). Thus I assume the sealing procedures to have had a significance which remains to be unravelled by patient research and observation of all the facts available.

The cross

Nos. 111, 114, 115, 117, 118, 121, 123, 124, 129, 130.

The numerous and, in many cases, fairly elaborate cross symbols, appearing on the Susa seal impressions, may well symbolize entities of the "civilized world", consisting of a centre and the four cardinal points. They thus seem to carry on the tradition of the cruciform emblems on Susa pottery, referring perhaps, much like the latter, to such elements of the humanized landscape as, for instance, "cities". The only difference that has been brought by the new age seems to be the emphasis laid on the protuberances of the cross patterns, with the centres, once so prominent, occupying a far less visible position. Let us realize that some of these emblems are most elaborate, and, imagining them featured in the open like "totems", or, for instance, embroidered on showy robes or shining on shields of warriors, we may at least catch a glimpse of the finery accompanying social display of that distant age of human history.

The symbolic character of the cross device comes to a full visibility in the case of my No. 123, in which the arms of the cross terminate in human faces. Here one is almost tempted to recognize an image of the "races of mankind" in what we would tend to perceive normally as a "decorative pattern".

In fact, an ethnographic parallel may help us understand such symbols. Some of the African social groupings refer to a total of thir adult men as to "masks". The eldest member of the founding lineage of the grouping in question bears the title of "father of the masks". If someone has perpetrated a particularly heinous crime against his or her kith and kin, the eldest member of the founding lineage pronounces a capital punishment, which, in local parlance, is defined as the sentenced one's having been "swallowed by the mask". After execution the criminal's house is pulled down, his family enslaved and his property given over to the lineage (Holder 1998, 86–87).

As to the functional identification of the objects bearing these seals, most of them, insofar as the sealing reverses are legible, come from mobile containers. The only exception is represented by my No. 111 which may bear an impression of a wall, and therefore belong to one of the "lock" sealings, that is, devices closing not mobile containers but immobile storage structures.

Scenes of military triumph

Nos. 126, 127.

These images do not turn up very frequently but speak up with unusual clarity. Both of them show a certal personage dressed in an elaborate skirt-like garment, bearing what is likely to depict a decorative pattern and provided possibly with a hem differentiated from the rest of the fabric – perhaps again an ornamental rendering of the lower edge of the personage's dress, traditionally credited with a special magical power (cf. the role played by the hem of a person's garment in the Old Testament). The question whether this attire might not represent a suit of reed armour rather than a textile garb must be left open. The personage's chest above waist appears to be bare.

A minor figure, standing to the left of the central personage, attends to what appears to be a quiver full of arrows in a standing position between both persons. The minor figure, who may wear a garment different from that of the chief personage (insofar that he/she is dressed at all), pulls arrows out of the quiver and breaks them under his/her foot. This is a gesture clearly meant to convey the meaning of rendering a certain set of weaponry, presumably that of a defeated enemy, harmless.

The same kind of allusion seems to be made by another diminutive figure, situated right of the chief personage. This second figure, situated lower than the chief occupant of the scene, is again dressed in a skirt-like garment and seems to be raising his/her left hand, perhaps in a gesture of acknowledgment of the supremacy of the cheif personage. Various small items of shapes that can hardly be distinguished, let alone identified, "hover" around the *dramatis personae* in the image fields. The object close to the "worshipper" figure may perhaps be explained as an item of tribute brought to the chief personality in recognition of his victory, but I do not believe we can identify such components of the image with any certainty.

A feature that may be important is represented by the form of the tips of the arrows broken under the "servant"'s foot. This is likely to have displayed a cutting edge turned towards the target at which the arrows were aimed. In other words, the tips of the arrows, rendered harmelss on the orders of the chief personage, possessed a trapezoidal form, such as that used in ritual contexts under tholos LXVII at Halaf-culture Yarimtepe II (cited in Charvát 2002, 90) and at Shamsuddin Tannira (Miller-Bergman-Azoury 1982). This strongly implies a ritual context for the whole scene.

The inside surface of No. 126 is illegible; that of No. 127 seems to have preserved traces of a pottery vessel that once bore the sealing.

"Master of animals"

Nos. 113, 116, 119?, 120?, 125?, 128, 131.

This is the case related to the famous "dompteur" or "maître des animaux" which coined a denomination of a certain iconic type, specific for the glyptics of this period. I do believe, however, that this, admittedly very important, icon merits a fresh examination.

In our sealings, the central place is invariably occupied by a dominant personage, dressed in a skirt-like garment displaying a pattern of zigzag lines parallel to one another. In some instances, the lower edge of this garment is again provided with a visible hem, enhancing the function of this magically potent component of human attire. Above the waist, some of these personages display a bare chest, like the "triumphant commander" above. In other cases, they wear two sets of double bands, cords or strings, crossing on the chest within an oval or circular object which may possibly depict a knot or a coil, or, alternatively, a device to hold the bands in place (a clasp or brooch of some kind). Their faces are hidden behind what appears to be a mask of a cylindrical shape with vertical ribbing, topped in some instances by a plumage of long, thin and flexible leaves, feathers or objects of a similar kind, The personage may hold either a short stick or rod, or, alternatively, a larger oval object in his/her left hand.

The rest of the image field displaying such personages would invariably be filled with sets of parallel wavy lines, which may symbolize streams of water, as well as with filling motifs, frequently depicting such creatures of the earth as lizards or other reptiles.

The three problematic sealings, those of my Nos. 119, 120 and 125, do show what appear to be images of quadrupeds and other bigger animals (ostriches? birds?). Nevertheless, the manner of depiction of these beings is so peculiar that we suspect rather showing of animal likenesses made by human hands, like figures cut out of wood, bone or other pliable materials, than the portrayal of actual living beings. In this connection it may be of importance that in my No. 120, a human(?) personage, possibly again wearing a disguise, is touching one of these images with a stick, such as that held by at least one major personage of this kind (my No. 113).

Taking into account the characteristics of the central personages of this group, we cannot fail to observe the close relations between some of the elements employed in these cases and components of images displayed by the painted pottery of Susa. The patterns borne by their skirts, for instance, may well be related to the earlier images of water, of ears of corn, or, alternatively, of the plaited work made of reed (my gipar sign of the Susa pottery). The very strange "masks", bearing, in some instances, the plumage of feathers or leaves at the top, may again allude to the imagery of trees (as embodiments of life force?). All these references may point towards the semantic field of fertility, procreation- and proliferation capacity.

As to the "sacred threads" crossed on the persons' chests, we may perhaps see in them elements of an attire required for the cultically proper, and thus efficient, performance of a ritual depicted by these icons. It is worth reminding that ritual has been defined as "an abstraction whose meaning is defined by social context" (Leach 1999 [1968], 176), a "medium of communication", as well as "social communication", "power" and "belief" (Leach 1999 [1968], 180–181).

The streams of water flowing around the chief officiants of our cult, much as the strange lizards and other reptiles crawling towards them, may, then, refer to the cultically desirable outcome of the performance of the ritual in the act of which the chief personages are portrayed. If this was meant to secure fertility and procreation capacity, then we understand not only the streams of life-giving water, gushing forth at the officiants' command, but also the images of the creatures of the earth, traditionally interpreted as symbols of chthonic deities who convey fertility and life-giving forces. This symbolism may well apply here.

Here we will also do well to recall that some painted-pottery images from the Susiana sites (Djowi and possibly Bendebal) do actually show similar scenes in which the central human figure touches the mouths of the animals. In other words, he is providing food to them, not rendering himself their master by holding them in a dominant position.

This icon must have sunk so deep in the memory of the high-rank Susa individuals that as late as the Late Uruk period, seal images with the "dompteur" tend to be typical for the Susa glyptic art (Rova 1994, 154).

All the sealings have once closed portable containers, the only exception being No. 119 which may come from a "lock", this time a wall peg wound around by a cord fastened to a door. This is the second case when an immobile structure could be closed by a sealing on clay, documented among the Susa sealings.

Hand in armpit

Nos. 108, 109, 110, 112, 122?, 132?.

This scene, documenting for us the very core of contemporary statehood ideology, merits a particular attention.

The key character of the image is again represented by a dominant personage situated at the centre of the icon field. He (or, less likely, she) wears the kind of skirt that we know already from the "master of animals" figure, with the parallel horizontal zigzag lines and terminating in a prominent hem. The personage is naked from the waist up. On his head he wears a kind of high rounded cap with an pointed top, or tiara, terminating, in its topmost part, in a feather or streamer of some kind. He wields in his left hand a most interesting object of an elongated form, displaying, along one side, a series of short parallel points or "teeth" protruding perpendicularly from the long handle, the whole being reminiscent of something like a huge toothbrush.

This personage lifts his left hand and another, minor person approaches him from the left side. This second participant lifts his right hand and lays it into the armpit of the central personage. The minor participant has also donned a wavy-lined hemmed skirt, at least in one case with a prominent waistband. Again, where the minor participant's head has survived to na extent showing him at least to some detail, he demonstrably wears a beard and must thus be (or impersonate?) a male (a good photograph in Amiet 1972, Pl. 50 No. 231).

As to the filling motifs, one of the most prominent ones is the rayed sun disc shining from the blazing sky above the tiara of the central personage. This is shown in all cases where the upper part of the sealing survives, and is particularly well visible in the photographs published by Pierre Amiet (1972, Pl. 50, No. 231), as well as by Prudence Harper, Joan Aruz and Françoise Tallon (1992, 43).

In addition to this, the central personage is approached by a third participant in the rite. This celebrant lifts his cup, presumably to acclaim the action going on in the centre of the scene, by both hands. Incidentally, this cup takes the form of a protocuneiform sign that could be read variantly as a particular form of NI, GAR or NINDA and which is attested to in finds from Early Uruk strata at Susa (de Mecquenem 1943, 14, fig. 10 : 3). Unlike the first two persons, the celebrant does not wear a skirt and it is not clear whether he is dressed at all, though at least in one case he boasts a waistbelt. However, the depiction of a beard shows him to be a male as well.

The device appearing between the "big man" and his follower takes the form of a horned and hooded snake, equal to the protocuneiform sign BU = $GID_2 = SU_{13}$ or possibly MU (ZATU No. 56, p. 181, cf. also Steinkeller 1995, 699). Its function here is difficult to discern. How far it might represent a symbol of a deity supervising – and approving – the whole procedure, as seems to be implied by some snake depictions on the painted pottery of Susa (cf. supra), must be decided by further research.

What we may witness here seems to be a scene portraying a fairly complex ceremony. As I have already demonstrated, a host of pre-literate and pre-state societies see in human hair the expression and excrescence of the "innermost human self". Armpit hair is commonly considered to be the most concentrated form of such protuberance of the nature of a particular human being. We may therefore presume that the minor person, laying his hand on the central personage's armpit, is depicted in the act of imbuing himself with the inner nature, *mana* of the "big man", presumably in a ritual of a major social significance.

We shall probably not miss the point if we see in this scene a transmission of the legitimation to rule the given community. This could be understood either horizontally – the central personage may legitimize executive organs who will represent him in those parts of his realms where he cannot be present in person. Another possibility is the vertical transmission of power – surrendenring his throne, the paramount may transfer his mission to rule to his successor in office.

The participation of the third celebrant was obviously of consequence as well. Much in line with the *kava*-drinking ceremony of the Tonga island chiefs, cited so often here, that ceremony could not be considered fully accomplished unless the central rite was acclaimed and approved by other participants, playing their role at the solemn-commensality table which constituted an intersection point of a system of coordinates, with reference to which the ceremony acquired sense, as well. It may be speculated whether the banquet really contributed to the full consumation of the ceremony or whether it enabled the participants to (re-)assume their acknowledged roles within a social system that had to endure a change. At any rate, the participation of a table society was obviously considered crucial for the complete unfolding of the ceremony in question.

Here we have a final and clear proof of the social role of ostentative commensality in the preparatory stages of the emergence of pristine statehood in the ancient Near East. From the Halaf culture on, we have been handling only source material constituted by the exquisite vessels themselves. The Susa sealings bring the first unequivocal evidence of the role of ceremonial banquets for the socially constitutive ceremonies of the late prehistoric age.

A most intriguing question is represented by two features of the scene: image of the sun and the "saw"-like instrument in the hand of the central personage. Any cuneiformist will, of course, instantly recognize the parallel to Akkadian-period cylinder-seal images of Šamaš, god of the sun, wielding his "saw" (or key?) with which he opens his way through the wild mountains of the east. The Akkadian name of this emblem of Šamaš, *šaššaru* (CAD Š II, 174–175, cf. esp. under d) on p. 175) does not exclude the interpretation of "key", and the existence of the "Egyptian lock", which was opened with a large toothed key of this type, is attested to from late 4th millennium B. C. (cf. the literature cited in Charvát 1992). A similar instrument appears, in association with a human figure, on one of the Late Uruk seal impressions from Arslantepe (von Wickede 1990, Pl. 400).

The problem, of course, is to know how far such a parallel can be drawn at all. In fact, we have witnessed the appearance of the "sun" on the painted pottery of Susa, and I have suggested that this icon combines the notions of "a given period of time, a number of revolutions of the sun" with that of fertility. We may even speculate how far the sun image may refer to the god

An, who could well confirm the validity of the undertaking depicted by the seal image by his authority. It would again be tempting to associate these ideas with our central figure, on whom an appropriate regnal period, filled in with fertility and abundance showered on him and his realms by the great gods, might have been conferred by the seal image. Alternatively, a "key" to such well-being and bliss may be seen in the instrument which he wields. The link with the sun god need not have been fully defined at this period of time, as we shall presently see.

Libation scenes

Nos. 133, 134.

Although we possess but two examples of this interesting scene, its relevance to early social developments is by no means diminished by this fact. Pierre Amiet apparently believed that this scene is identical to that of the military triumph, as his drawn reconstruction shows (*apud* von Wickede 1990, Pl. 464). However, being not entirely certain that this is actually so, I prefer to treat the theme in a separate fashion.

The chief protagonist is a personage of whose body the surviving examples show only the part above the waist, showing him to wear a waistbelt. His chest again appears to be bare. We cannot but guess whether his face is hidden under a mask, or whether the prominently figured nose represents just an artistic convention to depict facial features. The observer's eye is caught by the high cylindrical cap, slightly tapering downwards and covering the head of this personage. A beak-shaped configuration, somewhat reminiscent of that of the *deshret*, the red crown of Lower Egypt, protrudes from the front part of this cap or tiara, and a feather or a streamer again flows from its top part. The personage holds a conical cup, and, in the other case, a conical bowl in his raised hands.

On his left side, this "big man" is accompanied by a minor character, appearing to act as an attendant. Unfortunately, only in one case has the upper half of a depiction of the whole scene survived to an extent allowing at least a rough idea of the outlook of this assistant figure. He also apparently displays a bare chest and may wear a waistbelt. The most prominent feature associated with him is the high oval-shaped object that he bears on his head, pointed at the upper end. The attendant of No. 133 lifts his left hand while No. 134, which has preserved only the high oval-shaped cap(?), does not show any traces of the possible figuration of such a gesture. It is thus most difficult to say whether the attendant raises his hand in a greeting, or whether he simply helps to maintain the object on his head in position.

As to the filling motifs, they cannot be identified with any reasonable amount of certainty.

Unfortunately, the reverses of these two sealings are illegible to such an extent that save for cord traces they do not allow any determination of the surfaces to which they had once adhered.

Conspicuous absences as against the Susa painted pottery

In making comparisons with the iconography of the earlier painted pottery of Susa, we must be aware of certain differences blurring our vision of the problems. The chief factor which must be taken into consideration is, of course, the quantitative difference; we have much fewer seal impressions than painted pots. For this reason we shall do best to limit ourselves to a simple presence-absence count.

Of the first three major motifs, only the cross has been taken over by the seal impressions, the triangle and the chequerboard remaining outside the scope of the decorative elements employed. This, of course, does not mean that both motifs were forgotten. The chequerboard re-appeared in the protocuneiform script while triangular signs had been taken on by Proto-Elamite script (cf. supra).

As to the motifs of animals, arms and combs, only the scenes of military triumph withstood the onslaught of time, to re-surface in the seal impressions. Animals may be symbolically present in the "master of animals" compositions while the disappearance of the combs is puzzling. It might be argued that having usually been long worn on the body, the seals became so permeated with the invisible component of their bearees' personalities that no further references to their own human individualities were deemed necessary. Something of this kind is suggested by a sealing from the Iranian site of Tepe Sabz, consisting clearly of multiple impressions of a long bead which must have been worn in a necklace (von Wickede 1990, 215 and Pl. 486). How far this reasoning corresponds to reality is open to question, and will be discussed below.

The absence of gipar-, water- and cereal motifs is notable and may perhaps be explained with reference to the "master of animals" icon, which may have served as an overall designation of fertility symbolism.

Finally, of the "hourglass", arc and "sun" triad only the sun remained above the horizon of seal impressions, perhaps retaining its symbolical meaning alluded to in the earlier painted pots, as we have already seen.

Out of this demonstration it follows that though the *répertoire* of the Susa seal impressions is demonstrably limited in comparison with that of the preceding painted pottery, its semantic contents have remained largely stable and without more marked impoverishment. The "civilizing" undertakings, probably establishment of "cities", symbolized by the cross icons, are still there, much as the scenes of military triumph. A host of emblems concerned with fertility and procreation force have apparently been replaced by the iconic *cliché* of the "master of animals" composition. A number of devices known from painted pottery probably "went into hiding". Some of them could have become secondary and complementary components playing an auxiliary role in more richly structured compositions like, for instance, the sun icon within the "hand in armpit" scheme. Other configurations sank below the horizon but lived on with the help of other (perishable-matter?) carriers, only to re-appear when the need for them was felt (chequerboard, triangle). This might be the case of files of long-necked birds so popular on Susa painted pottery. One example re-appears in times of the Late Uruk period, on a seal impression from the Syrian site of Jebel Aruda (Rova 1994, p. 309, No. 31 Tav. 2).

Why is it especially these motifs that re-appear in the Susa seal impressions? Ethnology can again be of assistance here. The inhabitants of highland Burma on the Chinese border denote, as the highest category of possession, the property of the "hunch-eaters". These persons are so named because they enjoy the privilege of demanding a hunch from every game killed during a hunting expedition. Anyone can become a "hunch-eater", provided that

– he inherited the title,
– he established a brand-new village in a clearing in the forest,
– he conquered this right by means of armed violence, or
– he married the daughter of an original "hunch-eater" who had had no sons.

This gives a fairly instructive overview of possibilities of interpretation of the cross motifs (foundation of a new village), military-triumph scenes (self-evident) and "hand in armpit" icons (inheritance of the title).

There does, however, exist one notable exception to this continuation of the four broad avenues of the painted-pottery semantics of Susa – those of the *oecumene*, *anoecumene*, military triumphs and human individualities. The world of the Susa seal impressions knows the *oecumene*, *anoecumene*, and war-conflict tales. The human individual, however, has by now ceased to be imprecated directly.

It may be that the whole seal impression was perceived as a stamp impressed into, and "enlivening", hitherto inactive matter by the exercise of human individuality, indeed, as "offspring" of the seal-bearer. Among the prehistoric seals from Susa, Pierre Amiet has depicted an example carved in the form of two human beings in close embrace. The sealing surface, occupying the lower, flat side of the seal, bears an image of a small human figure, the lower half of which is depicted as a cylindrical configuration. I cannot get rid of the impression that an image of a baby wrapped in diapers was intended (incidentally, this would make our image the most ancient reference to keeping babies in diapers known to me: Amiet 1972, Pl. 58 No. 414, SB 5539). This idea seems to have lived on until the Neo-Assyrian times (Winter 2000, 82). In this particular instance, the message is clear. When two humans embrace, they give life to a baby – in reality, but also metaphorically, in the seal form; impressing a seal in soft clay produces "offspring", much as a real embrace.

Nevertheless, this absence of addressing the individual by the Susa seal impressions is conspicuous. Here the central theme is not the individual prowess of a cultivator, shepherd, hunter, chief or warrior. The Susa seal impressions address im- or rather supra-personal forces – forces beyond the capacities of individuals, forces filling their bodies, forces communicated by individuals to other individuals, but forces entirely beyond individual acquisition, appropriation or management. We witness a major, and indeed, a fundamental change: birth of the state idea. Much as in other parts of the world, the state is here a correlate of a certain state of the human mind. Only when humans realize that, regardless of the standing and status of every single member of a given group – regardless of whether they be wives, husbands, uncles, grandsons, granddaughters, cousins, in-laws or whatever – , they all possess one universal, unique human quality common to all of them, and present in all of them, only then can they form and establish, on their own free will, a true state. The state is no kingdom of God on earth; only the gods, elevated high above the ordinary human craving, suffering and toil, can rule impeccably and immaculately in their own divine realms. Fate ordained the humans to live on earth and to imitate, imperfectly and with blunt and clumsy tools, the work of the gods which they had perceived ever since the Halaf-culture age. If living humans could not hope to achieve the perfection of divine kingdoms, all they could do was to build more or less passable imitations on earth.

In fact, this process is visualized by the Susa seal impressions; the universality of the substantial human quality, taken on in different accidental forms by different individuals of the human species according to the particular role they play in society, but uniting all of them in the breathtaking drama of the composite human existence, for the successful staging of which the proper acting of all the *dramatis personae* must be required, emanates from these humble figurations on bits of low clay. Let us now see how this universal "humaneness" was depicted and perhaps felt and lived in fourth-millennium Western Asia.

The chiefly *mana*: filling the body

The "hand in armpit" scenes show clearly that by Early Uruk time, the human body began to be viewed, at least in some cases, as filled in by special and presumably sacred substance (*mana*) that might have been essentially identical with the innermost human nature of the personage concerned. This substance could have been transferred to other humans by touching the excrescence of the "innermost human nature" of the chief carrier of this *mana*, i.e. his armpit hair. It has been demonstrated that human hair may stand for the royalty of kings, the divinity of gods, the fertility of crops, the power of sorcerers and the *mana* of heroic warriors (Leach 1999 [1958], 236), and one – or more – of these cases may very well apply to our Susa images. Indeed, what happens here may consitute one of very distant precursors to an Assyrian royal rite in which the king's hair- and fingernail clippings, deposited in a bottle, are buried at the empire's frontier to guard its subjects from evil (George 1997, 70).

The fact that the transfer takes place among men with chests bared down to their waists may be taken as evidence that this ritual belonged to those transferring the idealized form of virility among men of chiefly rank, in the course of which muscle display might have found its place (Douaire-Marsaudon 2001, 7, 12–13). This may be the origin of the ribbed chests of some of the figures of a similar kind from seal impressions excavated at the Ubaid-culture site of Değirmentepe on the upper course of the Euphrates. These "X-ray snapshots" may, in fact, show the virile musculature of the high-rank males depicted by such icons (von Wickede 1990, Pls. 362–367).

The bare chests of the protagonists link these scenes with those employing the libation motif, as well as at least with a part of the "master of animals" figures.

126

It is interesting to observe that the only really good parallels for the "hand in armpit" scene come from Uruk- and Jemdet Nasr-age cylinder seals (Rova 1994). Unfortunately, most of them have sustained considerable damage and none of the scenes have survived in entirety. Yet, at least two of the relevant images involve a minor human being reaching out his/her hands towards the armpit of a much bigger figure, who may well be imprecated for protection and favour. The former of these comes from a Susa bulla, the latter had once decorated a seal which left its impression on one of the Jemdet Nasr tablets (Rova 1994, Tav. 21 No. 392, and Tav. 51 No. 851). The last case, an impression on a bulla from Susa, is not very clear but it may well convey the message of a military triumph: a person seated on the floor (a captive among other captives?) reaches out his/her hand towards the armpit of another human figure lifting his hands in jubilation (Rova 1994, Tav. 20 No. 359). An interesting detail may be observed in another sealing from Choga Mish, where a horned animal, presumably an ibex of mouflon, puts his/her muzzle into the armpit of a human who caresses the animal's head (Rova 1994, Tav. 5 No. 79). This scene is quite realistic, as will undoubtedly be conceded by all who had an opportunity to deal with friendly and inquisitive long-muzzled animals who frequently probe the identity of those who face them in this manner.

Ethnological parallels bear out that a contact of hands or by hand on body usually convey positive feelings such as joy, friendliness and the like, provided they take place among equals. When two interlocutors agree in a village of the Ibo tribe of Nigeria, each of them slightly knocks the clenched fist of the other (Green 1964, 184). Touching by hands, or pressing by a right hand against one's chest, expresses mutual joy of a meeting between two friends (Basden 1966, 163, 165). The chieftain's neck is caressed by hand as a gesture of affectionate respect (Hanna 1976, 92). Alternatively, the Ibo chiefs' bodies cannot be touched by ordinary men and women who may be defiled by menstrual blood or sexual intercourse, and even their food must be prepared by virgins of both sexes (Henderson 1970, 230). The hand may serve both as a symbol of the protection of the kinship group to which a particular individual belongs and, alternatively, as a symbol of subordination of a slave who is "a hand of" or "in the hand of" his master (Holder 1998, 78–79).

On the other hand, Oceanic societies display different and much more elaborate manners of manifesting respect to a chief or of diffusion of his power. In the Tonga islands, a chief is venerated by touching his feet with one's hands or, in the case of one's own chief, by putting one's own head into contact with his feet (Gifford 1929, 118). Among the Tikopia, an elder-to-be crawls on his four legs and arms to his chief, pressing his nose to the chief's knee. The chief then takes two leaves which he has passed close to a fire, twists them and binds them around the appointee's neck, reciting an imprecation to the gods to accept the new elder in peace (Firth 1970, 58).

In more recent social formations, transfers of property or paramountcy over inanimate or animate entities came to be symbolized by other means, including various craft products, charged with emanations of personalities who make use of them. These may be personal clothes which, when spread over such an object, imply that the owner of the clothes claims property over that which is covered by it. One of the wives of Zimrilim of Mari refers to her husband's "posing the hem of his garment" over her (Lafont 1989). In other cases, human identity is expressed by means of the lower parts of feet which may be impressed into clay to give the person a new identity (Joannès 1989). The same custom lies presumably at the root of the symbolization of holding of sway over something or somebody by transfer of a shoe, such as the transfer of the biblical Ruth to Boaz in a medieval European manuscript illustrating a scene from the Old Testament (Kocher 1992, 112 Abb. 172).

The nature of the *mana*, filling the bodies of pre-state chiefs, has been surveyed, with comprehensiveness and sobriety characteristic of the Chinese thinkers, by authors of the following text, datable perhaps into Late Zhou period (10th–9th centuries B. C.), well worth citing here in full:

"Anciently, humans and spirits did not intermingle. At that time there were certain persons who were so perspicacious, single-minded, and reverential that their understanding enabled them to make meaningful collation of what lies above and below, and their insight to illumine what is distant and profound. Therefore the spirits would descend into them.

The possessors of such powers were, if men, called xi *(shaman), and, if women,* wu *(shamaness).*

Those who supervised the positions of the spirits at the ceremonies, made the vases (used to) present victims, and appropriate clothes, made the descendants of the past saints glorious, knew the (sacred) names of mountains and rivers, the principal ancestors, (dealt with) all the affairs relative to the ancestral temple, (were in charge of) the difference between father and son (in the ritual), the enforcement of respect, the proper order of ceremonies, the principles of respect and justice, the proper physical behaviour, the control of fidelity and trust, offerings and purifications and manifested respect to the luminous deities, were the zhu *(invocators) officers.*

Those who established family and personal names, who knew what plant should be cultivated for each season, the colour (of the hairs of) sacrificial animals, the different kinds of jade and textile, the different colours of (ritual) clothes, the (proper) quantity of (ritual) vessels, the rules (concerning) the order of ancestral tablets, the proper positions during sacrifices, mounds and swept soil (for sacrifices), deities of above and below, the origin of the clans and abided by the ancient rules were the zong *officers.*

Therefore, there were officers for Heaven, Earth, the spirits and the different things, who were called the five officers, who ruled their own domain (of competence) and did not intermingle (with each other's domain). So the people were trustful, the spirits had a luminous virtue and the people and spirits had their own realm. There was respect and no untoward familiarity. As a consequence, the spirits sent down blessing on the people, and accepted from them their offerings. There were no natural calamities" (Boileau 2002, 357).

Though, of course, this text is to be situated within the religious discourse of the religious position of the early Chinese states, it records with remarkable accuracy all that the high-rank groups of the incipient state bodies considered to be of crucial importance. We could wish for no better illumination of what the foremost personages of ancient times themselves thought, and we can only regret that the Sumerians have not summarized, in such a convenient fashion, their earliest ideas of the substances they called *me*.

For the complete success of this, much as any other ritual, it was clearly of importance that the participants do perform the required gestures properly. The significance of this point will be brought out by a detail from the burial customs of the Seleucid-Parthian Mesopotamia. Some of the funerary female statuettes display a gesture so important that the bodies themselves were deposited in the same attitude (Karvouen-Kannas 1995, 50). This is certainly rather unusual for us, but it helps us to understand the nature of what was deemed appropriate and fitting for ancient ritual, where even human bodies had to conform to pre-concieved ideas.

The chiefly mana: acting by drinking

At the edge of the "hand in armpit", we see an image of a third participant who raises his goblet. He may be doing this either as a sign of greeting, acclaiming or approval of the central scene, or with the aim to achieve a transformation of his own personal status, in the spirit of the *kava*-drinking ceremony in which the participating chiefs become mystically united with their own ancestors (cf. supra).

It is somewhat difficult to guess which of these two is the right interpretation. Data from – admittedly much later – cuneiform texts show that common eating and drinking from a cup established a particular status of associates, who were not expected to show ill-will towards one another, among banqueters who had eaten and drunk together (CAD K s.v. *kāsu* 253–256, esp. p. 254). In much the same vein, Dominique Charpin refers to an Old Babylonian Mari text describing an action of a vassal who drank from his overlord's cup in sign of subordination to him, but who, when turned into an enemy of his former liege, terminated his former obligation symbolically by defecating into the cup which he had once raised in recognition of his vassalage (Charpin 1990, 81).

These facts point rather in favour of the first interpretation alternative: the third participant may be there simply to acknowledge the new superior who has received sanction from the former paramount, and to conclude peace with him at the banquet table.

The fact that the transfer of the chiefly status was here regularly accompanied by the approval of "people" (in reality, perhaps the retinue of the old paramount who thus acclaimed their allegiance to his successor in office) does show that consent of those ruled over with a change in a leading social position was by now at least formally required.

The chiefly mana: acting by libation

Finally a third activity type by which the "big men" turn up in the Susa seal impressions is the libation, either by cup or by bowl. Though the bare chests of the protagonists link the libation rite with that denoted here as "hand in armpit", as well as with a part of the "master of animals" scenes, the ceremonial perquisites seem to be different. This pertains first and foremost to the chief personage's tiara, which no longer looks round and pointed upwards, buth rather assumes a cylindrical form, wider at the top and tapering towards the wearer's head. With the oval object borne by the chief personage's attendant on his head, we do not have any certainty as to whether this refers to the rounded and pointed cap of the "hand in armpit" protagonist, or whether this might possibly be a depiction of a jar containing the liquid used by the chief personage for the libation.

Cuneiform sources, offering rather rich data on libation (Akkadian *naqû*, CAD N 1, 336–341) say explicitly that libations were offered to the spirits of dead persons, including royal ancestors of the initiator of the ceremony ("libation for the spirits of the kings, my predecessors" – CAD N 1 p. 357). The other adressees of libation were customarily the Mesopotamian gods. Libations, involving in some cases animal sacrifice, might have been performed before the assembled family of the initiator (ibid. p. 339), and sometimes, in a general manner, offered "in the direction of all four winds" (ibid. p. 339).

To whom exactly the Susa libation was adressed will be investigated further.

The new masters of time and space

In comparing the patterns borne by the earlier Susa painted pottery and those carved on the later seals from the same site, one feature, of a rather functional than artistic character, commands our attention instantly. The former represent a variant of a more or less permanent, indeed, "eternal" carrier, a painted image laid with its possessor to rest in a huge funerary monument, with the intention of incarnating for ever the heroic and memorable deeds which he or she had accomplished. As against this, the later seal impressions come from matrices designed to produce, in a repeated fashion, icons that found their way into everyday-life routine, though in this particular case we would probably better prefer the term "seasonal" to that of "everyday-life". That the seals were used to mark commodities which travelled to their destinations, where the goods were unpacked and the seal impressions discarded, in mobile containers is attested to by the impressions of the seal carriers on the back sides of the sealings. The weight of this conclusion is enhanced by the fact that the archaeological find contexts of our sealings, insofar as described in an intelligible manner in the excavators' reports, may be described as those linked with settlement activities, the sealings having probably been discarded and left in ordinary rubbish strata (cf. supra).

A rather important conclusion follows out of this observation: during the Early Uruk period, seals were used at Susa in a repeated fashion, on occasions articulating the calendrical sequence of public events with a certain degree of regularity. The material supplies which they visualize for us thus kept coming in at a steady pace, and we can hardly escape the conclusion that these seal impressions bear out before us a systemized and orderly form of redistribution of the surplus collected from contributors to the system (who might or might not have been the producers of the goods thus delivered themselves), in other worlds, an embryonic form of taxation, or of something that was very near to it.

In addition to this observation, let us take notice of another fact. Though between terminal Ubaid and Early Uruk the functions of the icon carriers did undergo a transformation at Susa, the semantics of the images remained, by and large, nearly the same. We have observed above that those categories of visual signs referring to the *anoecumene*, the *oecumene* and to military triumphs are present both in the painted pottery and in the seal images there. The only category that changed its contents is that of the individual human personages: as against single individuals, referred to probably by means of the comb image at the earlier age, the later epoch featured individuals as carriers of a particular mission, to whom the fulfilling of a certain number of tasks in the interest of the whole community was entrusted.

This observation helps us to understand the nature of the public events alluded to by the seal images. In fact, the high-rank individuals of Susa clearly dared to manipulate all entities of the whole wide world surrounding their communities – first and foremost, those of their "civilized" world, the *oecumene*, represented both by the cruciform signs and by the scenes of military triumph. They did nonetheless claim supremacy even over the "uncivilized", unhumanized and therefore wild and potentially dangerous outer world, the *anoecumene*, visualized by the "master of animals" motif. In this we can measure the scale and magnitude of ideational concepts and constructs proposed by the chief personages of Susa, which pertained to the entire world known to them, both "civilized" and "uncivilized". We thus no longer wonder how the members of highly ranked groups came to the conclusion that instead of handling the visible world in a variety of ways, it might have been more expedient to distill its essential base into a system of signs, encapsulating the immaterial and therefore eternal substances of all the components of the human and natural environment, and "trapping" them thus to be manipulated at will. The first step in this direction has been made by the set of visual signs encoding the messages of the painted pottery of Susa. Now, the historically first form of script as a set of intelligible symbols, conveying messages by being combined into sequences ordered according to commonly understood and universally acknowledged syntactical rules, emerged. Quite in line with the practical and down-to-earth spirit of the day, it is likely to have been employed for the registration of material deliveries for which (im?-)material compensations were due. Let us see how this happened.

The emergence of true script

Step One: Collection of sealed items

The "big chiefs" of Susa, the activities of whom pertained to impressing the seal matrices in soft and pliable carrier substances, must have made it their first and foremost task to collect contributions to socially approved, and centrally organized, public events in sealed containers. Many of these have come to light during archaeological excavations of Mesopotamian sites (Ferioli, Fiandra, Fissore and Frangipane 1994). The fact that they tend to turn up in clusters implies that prior to their archaeological deposition, they have been treated together in the course of one, single and well-defined procedure within the given social context. The current opinion is in favour of keeping these seal impressions as evidence for the unsealing process in "archives before writing".

I wish to point out that I still do believe the high-rank individuals registered these contributions in true writing, the traces of which have not come down to us simply because they could not survive the long deposition in unfavourable soil conditions, having been made of perishable materials (cf. Glassner 2000, 148–149, and Charvát 2002, 152–153).

An interesting corollary to this assumption can be built up by considering texts written in historical periods (the Neo-Babylonian period) on such transitory vehicles as boards of organic materials (wood, bone, wax: MacGinnis 2002). These instances include not only records of running transactions, but, together with registers or commercial documents, literary and scientific texts as well as ritual dispositions. Examples of this kind show well that entire worlds of learning could be lost if the script carriers did not survive into modern times.

Step Two: Registering the sealed deliveries

I have already pointed out that in my vision, the decisive step towards the invention of writing had come through in the preceding, Susa A phase, in the Final Ubaid age. The canonization of motifs appearing on the painted pottery of Susa and the recurring patterns of their association resulted in the emergence of a set of intelligible signs, forming associations according to recognizable rules, in fact, of the first lexicum and the first syntax of history, here pertaining to the visual forms of expression.

It may be assumed that the script of the Early Uruk period, by means of which the lists of sealed deliveries were registered, differed from this earlier sign system in having found a much more frequent, but also much simpler and less elaborate employment. Having been used for the regular recording of exchange of material- against possibly other goods, Early Uruk script differed from its terminal Ubaid predecessor, the Susa painted pottery, in three aspects:

   a) it did not glorify the dead ancestors but help living communities,
   b) it was not designed for not re-enactment of the mythical past but, as we shall see, for (the release of fertility? for) the present,
   c) it was not resorted to not once in a regnal period of a given chief but at regular intervals (annually? seasonally?).

As to the use of script at pre-Late Uruk Susa, the evidence is rather meagre but it does exist. In addition to the results of analysis of the painted pottery found at our site and the connections between its individual artistic components and signs of later proto-cuneiform and Proto-Elamite scripts (cf. supra), a clearcut testimony is presented by tokens found in the local Early Uruk strata and bearing incised signs (de Mecquenem 1943, 14, fig. 10: 1–3). The last example (No. 3) bears a sign that would be read NI or I_3 in proto-cuneiform. Here it is of relevance that the sign approximates the depiction of a bowl or goblet raised by a minor personage participating in the "hand in armpit" scene (cf. supra). If the token bearing the NI sign really symbolizes its bearer's participation in the power-transfer ceremony, we may perhaps see in it a symbol of a material contribution towards the costs of such a festivity, in exchange for which the donor could hope for an (im?-)material compensation.

In actual fact, the existence of a true script at Early Uruk Susa is borne out by the occurrence of – admittedly – no more than two signs, incised on contemporary writing carriers (Amiet 1972, 68–69, on tablet No. 474, vol I p. 85, depicted on Pl. 62 in vol. II and another tablet ibid. No. 604, p. 97, photo vol. II Pl. 76; similarly Algaze 1993, 17).

Let us also notice the occurrence of incised signs akin to Late Uruk script in Middle Uruk strata at Tell Brak (Oates-Oates 1993, 172–173 and p. 195 Fig. 53: 51, 55, 56, 60 and 61). One of these incised marks (Oates-Oates 1993, 195 Fig. 53: 51) is identical to a Late Uruk sign (ZATU No. 737 p. 329).

Chronologically, the Susa seal impressions belong to a period identical to layer 25 of the new Acropole excavations, dating to terminal Ubaid or Early Uruk (Amiet 1986, 37 n. 6).

It is a question how far the written registration of sealed contributions could have entailed expressed supremacy over the donors who supplied the abovementioned contributions. Above all, the Mesopotamians considered the script to have been revealed by the gods from whom all the wisdom had come (Glassner 1999, 24–26). The ingenious interpretation of the "Enmerkar and the lord of Aratta" tale, proposed by Jean-Jacques Glassner (2002, 37–39), sees the decisive turning point in the moment when the paramount of Aratta perceives the written message of Enmerkar "nailed in" by a wedge. Glassner believes that this alludes to the early Mesopotamian customs of driving a wedge into a house wall as a sign of taking over that house as a property, and that by having read the message, the lord of Aratta has, in fact, caused the "driving-in of a wedge" that made him Enmerkar's subordinate. However, it can also be argued that the author of the tale had in mind a "wedge" as symbol for writing ("un signe polysémique" – Glassner 2000, 35). This would mean that the paramount of Aratta saw himself subdued by Enmerkar's power in view of the fact that his domain was registered by the written word of the Uruk lord. That cuneiform writing, together with the Sumerian language and civilization, shall ultimately prevail all over the world, which, submitting to Enki, the patron of both, shall reap her reward in peace, harmony, welfare and joy is an idea also present within "Enmerkar and the lord of Aratta" as the "spell of Nudimmud" (Vanstiphout 1994, esp. pp.152–154).

In fact, all this could pertain to a situation similar to that which we view now: registering of sealed contributions from a donor agency could mean that this donor agency considered itself subordinated to their adressee, the receptor agency of the sealed goods. That, however, is a mere hypothesis.

However all that may have been, it seems that by the Early Uruk times, contemporary thinkers set their minds on a much more down-to-earth, practical manner of manipulating the script than their prececessors of the terminal Ubaid age.

That the early Western Asiatic scripts, the invention and introduction of which I dare to date into Early Uruk, may be just examples of how the human need of communication is commonly treated in certain, well-defined social contexts, may be shown by citing a hitherto neglected but most eloquent parallel to the proto-cuneiform script. This can teach us a lesson worth remebering about how early – but, in fact, any – communication-sign systems may work. The device in question is the sign language, used in monasteries of some reformed orders of the (Roman) Catholic world since the Middle Ages up to this very day (Bruce 2001; Quay 2001). This was probably introduced in Late Carolingian times (first half of 10th century A. D.) in Benedictine abbeys of strict observance where talking was considered a sin to be evaded and supplanted, if possible, by the sign language learned during the noviciate by the new brothers-to-be. Sign language, taken over by such reformed monastic orders as the Cistercians, outlived the virtual extinction of true regular observance in the 16th and 17th centuries and is used to this day in Trappist monasteries all over the world.

Trappist sign language possesses singular structural characteristics that are remarkably similar to the proto-cuneiform script. In the medieval parlance, the individual signs were referred to rather as *"notae"*, each of which was assigned a definite semantic value, then as *"signa"*, being thus put one semantic level higher (*quas puto grammatici digitorum et oculorum notas vocare voluerunt*, Bruce 2001, 197). Sign inventories, preserved in medieval manuscripts, number from 118 to 216 signs. This "manual and ocular" language, consisting essentially of substantives (Quay 2001, 212), had few signs for verbs or abstract notions, and no signs whatsoever for pronouns, prepositions, conjunctions and appropriative adjectives. Denotations of time and syntax were also missing (Bruce 2001, 199–200). Some of the signs were composed and used as determinatives: the difference between the signs for "thread" and "needle" rested in hitting the palm of one's hand with a clenched first in the case of the latter sign, in order to indicate hardness and thus the iron of which needles are made. The most interesting thing was the great flexibility of this system: when Cistercians took it over from the Benedictines, they felt free to introduce new signs for new facts of their life (lay-brothers, or *conversi*, for instance: Bruce 2001, 204–205). The communication set underwent a complete re-shuffling in the 17th century with the advent of Trappists who observed much stricter rules and allowed themselves only a very moderate diet, refusing meat, fish and eggs. It was thus necessary to drop a series of medieval sign which lost their relevance, but to introduce new signs for leafy vegetables which supplanted foods permitted in the Middle Ages (Bruce 2001, 207).

The parallels between this and the protocuneiform writing, both in character and structure and in flexibility of use over prolonged periods of time, are self-evident.

Monastic sign language possesses some tremendous advantages which visualize for us singular attractions offered by early Oriental writing. First and foremost, it can be developed further quite individually in two ways: 1) by expansion of the semantics of existing signs, and 2) by introduction of new signs. It can be learned at a young age (monastic noviciate), regardless of the mother tongue of the student, as the signs refer to entities readily visible and comprehensible in his or her well-defined environment, structured by firm rules resting on a coherent cultural pattern underlying the acitivites of all participating individuals (Quay 2001, 216–217).

The manner in which the sign language is handled in living Trappist monasteries bears a fascinating resemblance to proto-cuneiform writing. The vocabulary used in St. Joseph's monastery at Spencer, Massachusetts, consisted of 627 signs including names of 16 saints, 81 individual monks and 15 Cistercian monasteries. Just for the sake of examples, let us take up the manner of denoting nationalities: the Netherlands are referred to by a composition of signs for HOUSE + ARRANGE + CORN + WATER, while Ireland by signs meaning either GREEN or POTATO + EAT. The denomination of Poland shows the phonetic side of sign language: it is done by movements of the right hand as if holding a piece of textile. To a native English speaker, this associates instantly with "polish" (Quay 2001, 217–220). Even here, however, flexible polysemy can be introduced into this system: Russia was referred to at St. Joseph's by the original Trappist sign for the colour RED and this very sign received a meaning of "Communist" in Japan (Quay 2001, 220). The device can function regardless of particular languages spoken in the area of its use: monks of Chinese and Japanese Trappist monasteries used the existing signs, which they had all learnt in the noviciate, to express particular features of their own world (Quay 2001, 221–228). This adaptation, however, reveals profound differences in the perception of the nature of some essential entities of the world. In the United States, names for individual monks in the sign language, for instance, were composed either of professions and occupations, or of references to some particular and identifying feature of the individual named. On the other hand, particular surnames of the individual kinship groupings from which the monks were descended served for the definition of the signs in the Far East (Quay 2001, 228).

It is thus clear that one of the archetypal functions of the human soul is the creation of communication systems that may not be bound to language, but that may employ a variety of various signs, among which the visually conveyed signs are not the least important. In a condition where a limited group of initiates share a coherent, well-defined and tightly organized cultural pattern, underlying sets of their activities, systems of signs by which entities of this neatly arranged, visible and predictable world may emerge which possess the same characteristics over millennia. These characteristics can illuminate each other in a most instructive manner, regardless of whether their inventors and bearers could even have been in contact (chances are that they could not).

Some of the systems that functioned in the history of medieval Europe and are still alive within the cultured world may thus give us fascinating insights into the creation of the earliest scripts of Western Asia.

Of course, sign language has a disadvantage as well: is is forgotten only too easily, and apparently is bound to a rather strictly defined social environment requiring two characteristics: 1) tight social organization, and 2) a coherent and well-defined underlying cultural pattern. Once these two conditions are not present – as, for instance, in Mesopotamia of the Roman world –, there is no need to bother with the cumbersome signs and they fall into oblivion.

Step Three: Unsealing the goods
and
Step Four: their ceremonial consumption

But back to prehistoric Western Asia: up to now, the departure point of this procedure, the consumption of the unsealed deliveries during a ceremonial banquet, has been documented in two cases only: first, at Susa itself, where a group of seal impressions has turned up together with two big storage jars, visualizing thus one of the possible forms of linkage of these items (cf. supra). The other and much clearer case has been documented recently at Arslantepe in Eastern Anatolia. The Italian excavation team, directed by Marcella Frangipane, has unearthed in the layer Arslantepe VII a Middle Uruk "temple" building 29 with ample finds of sealings on clay and pottery vessels ("Çoba bowls") clearly serving for the consumption of foodstuffs (Frangipane 2002; Greaves-Helwing 2003, 78). The problem, of course, is to know the nature of the rite involving this ceremonial consumption of the delivered goods.

The sources offer us only one direct hint: a person clearly raising his cup in celebration of the new paramount is present in the "hand in armpit" scene. Interpreting this fact in a broad fashion, we could say that the ceremonial consumption was related to a "filling" of the participants with an immaterial substance generated on the occasion of a ritual performed either prior to the banquet or in its course.

One of such instances which seems to offer a likely candidate is the provision of fertility and proliferation force to the participants of this festive meal, or, alternatively, to the communities which they might have represented. In this respect it seems to be of relevance that the earlier stages of the Uruk culture are likely to have witnessed the introduction of grape wine as a beverage, as is attested to both by analysis of pottery-vessel deposits and by a single grape pip excavated at Susa itself (McGovern et al. 1997, 14–16). The intoxicating properties of wine-drinking must have produced in the banqueters an impression of having been possessed by a substance of supernatural character and power.

If this hypothesis is valid, we could imagine a ritual going on in two, or even three steps:

a) the chief officiant, or the president and organizer of the banquet, could at first address a libation to the great gods, in whom all fertility and proliferation forces were incumbent. Having obtained a favourable answer to his plea, he could then proceed to

b) distribute the magic-charged beverage to the participants, inviting them to draw on the store of its supernatural strength. That the libating chiefs and other high-rank individuals of the Early Uruk age could use special receptacles for this purpose is borne out by the numerous finds of spouted vessels which turned up the in the archaeological contexts of the period. Some of these utensils show an exquisite artistic finish implying that their function was really out of the ordinary. At Tepe Gawra, a nearly complete pot with an elongated spout imitating the bed of a rocky stream with pebble deposits came forth from stratum XIA (that with the "Round House"), accompanied by fragments of other spouts of this kind (Bache 1936, 7 Fig. 2 and p. 8, cf. also Tobler 1950, 152–153, Pl. CXLI: 342);

c) the banquet donor could then proceed to carry out a fertility-infusing ceremony on behalf of the inanimate denizens of the animal world, with a purpose of securing proliferation of livestock and other living possessions kept by the beneficiaries of the ceremony. This step could be referred to by the seals bearing the "master of animals" scene.

We could well hypothesize how far members of the the Early Uruk highly ranked groups put themselves in the place of the original water- and fertility god Enki, who is described in the "Enki and the World Order" as having produced, by his mighty ejaculation, the river Euphrates flowing down from the mountains into the plains (Bottéro-Kramer 1993, ll. 253–256, pp. 173–174; Vanstiphout 1997, 120).

1) collection of sealed items
2) opening and consumption of contents of sealed deliveries during a banquet
3) spell by libation
4) spell by drinking

Conclusions

Thus, in fact, with the developments taking place during the Early Uruk age, all the three essential groups necessary for proper functioning of any state society are well established, or rather, well discernible in our field of vision. The pre-brahmanas and pre-ksatriyas are now joined by the third estate, whom the more history-immersed readers of this book have already guessed will be called pre-vaisyas. These men and women proposed, as the chief concern of humanity, neither service to the gods nor heroic feats and exploits, but toilsome and patient creation of material goods catering for the everyday needs of both rank and file of human society. One of the later pointed tongues advocating their cause put the matter bluntly: "Whoever has caused that two ears of corn grew where previously only one had sprouted, has done more for mankind than all the politicians put together". If the toothed object with long handle, held by the major figure of the "hand in armpit" ceremony, does indeed represent a key for a pegged-bar lock, then the rulers of this age could choose no better symbol as an emblem under which to gather their followers. They apparently saw bounty and abundance of all things comestible and useful, which can be brought under the keys of the storage rooms, as their greatest contribution to the welfare of their respective communities.

THE GOOD MOTHER EARTH

We have now seen how the values of the third estate of human society made a progress in the prestige which they had enjoyed at Susa. We have witnessed the gradual shifting of the social balance towards those social strata that were concerned with production of material goods and thus held fertility, fecundity and the proliferation force in the greatest esteem. We have become aware of how the discharge of this vital form of energy became the concern of two formations in the social life of high-rank groups of Early Uruk – the Lords Spiritual, imprecating the gods for access to fertility, and the Lords Temporal, securing the social balance necessary for full enjoyment of the outcome of the nature's multiplication capacity. Let us now see how this trend worked on the eastern neighbour of Susa and Susiana situated in the alluvial plains along the twin rivers that were to give to this other civilization its name, Ubaid-culture Mesopotamia.

Absence of naturalistic motifs on painted pottery

The first glimpse of Ubaid-culture pottery permits an instantaneous observation of a fact which almost springs to the eye. Ubaid-age tableware from Mesopotamia failed to become a carrier of the exquisite decoration displayed by the cups, bowls and jars of terminal-Ubaid Susa. Though the site of Eridu in the extreme south of present-day Iraq has brought forth, in its layers XIII–VIII, a well-excavated and well-documented series of Ubaid- and early to middle Uruk-age pottery (Safar, Mustafa and Lloyd 1981, 154–172, 178–193), none of this shows the abundance of either the ornamental or the figural decoration borne so proudly by the products of the eastern potters. Though the Eridu vessels undoubtedly served as tableware, as is shown most eloquently by the numerous flagons and spouted vessels, their surface is articulated by ornament of an abstract kind, pleasing to the eye but hardly susceptible to iconic analysis. Only in some cases do the Eridu finds attest to the presence of an aesthetically more accomplished decoration, albeit of a very specific nature likely to imitate receptacles of organic matters, most probably of plaited work from reeds, twigs or similar materials (e. g. Safar. Mustafa and Lloyd 1981, 178–179 on Fig. 82, or 182–183 on Fig. 84). How far this may indicate a difference in cooking- and table manners, with preference for either dry or piecemeal comestibles, served at the chiefly tables of Ubaid-age Mesopotamia, as against the cuisine of Susa, where cooked foods might have been served in the exquisitely decorated table sets, must remain a matter of further research.

There is one single Eridu item that may possibly bring to mind a link to Susa: one of the exquisite painted bottles, from an Ubaid settlement by the Late-Ubaid Eridu cemetery, bears in its uppermost part a lattice-decoration circle disposed among four tubular lugs, quite in the Uruk-culture manner. Below this, however, there is another concentric zone in which "hourglass" metopes define three segments filled in by "palmette" motifs (Safar, Mustafa and Lloyd 1981, p. 15 and Fig. 78: 16 on p. 166, and also the enlarged illustration on p. 167). Any triangular motifs are a great rarity in Ubaid-culture pottery. Nevertheless, one single pattern is too little to go by.

In Ubaid-culture Mesopotamia we thus have to proceed without the most welcome aid of images borne by painted pottery which had been so eloquent at Susa. This must on no account be interpreted as a testimony of the lower degree of cultural development attained by the Mesopotamian bearers of the Ubaid culture. It simply means that the populations of Mesopotamia entrusted their socially and spiritually relevant messages to other kinds of carriers than painted pottery, and that in that point their etiquette differed from that of the Susa chiefs.

What were the material forms, which the emanations of the traditional Near Eastern culture assumed in Ubaid-age Mesopotamia, must then be investigated by an independent analysis.

Cones of burnt clay: *monumenta temporis acti*

An archaeological medium observable in early Mesopotamia, and likely to confer a spiritual message, is represented by the frequently occurring cones made of burnt clay with head parts dipped in colour. Having been stuck into soft mud plaster, such terra-cotta cones displayed their coloured parts out of which sophisticated ornaments could have been composed. At this moment, it is rather the colour composition of the relevant schemes than the ornamental motifs as such that will be of interest to us. The cone heads invariably display white, red and black colours and thus carry through the ages the message of the Halaf-culture triad of the same colours, borne by painted pottery, personal jewellery, colouring agents and the grinding stones used for their pulverization and found deposited at Arpachiyah (Charvát 2002, 92–94). The three colours occurred together at Ubaid-culture Gawra (layer XVI, Charvát 2002, 50); the decoration by means of terra-cotta cones multiplies beyond all measure on the cultic buildings of Late-Uruk precinct of Eanna, showing thus the relevance of the message of the three colours to early Sumerian religious life and presumably heralding the cult of the sky god An, of whom we have already heard in the first chapter. In the Eanna deep trench, mosaic cones turn up for the first time in layer XIIa, that is, in Early Uruk (Charvát 2002, 99). Middle Uruk examples have turned up at the Syrian site of Tell Sheikh Hassan (Boese 1995, 60, 212ff., 224 Abb. 10, layers 6–7).

Now let us dwell for a while on another object which is also likely to carry a spiritual message of the Uruk age. At Sheikh Hassan, the finds of the terra-cotta cones occurred in contexts from which one of the ubiquitous "eye idols" have come forth as well (Boese 1995, 60). This kind of device, found throughout the Sumerian and Sumerian-influenced world from SW Iran to Anatolia (Boese 1995, 212), has long evaded any attempts at interpretation and it is indeed difficult to try to decode the message which it conveys. Nevertheless, a certain clue is offered by the new excavations at the Syrian site of Umm Qseir.

In a Late Uruk pit investigated at this site, an "eye idol" was lying on the top of a gypsum vessel which, in its turn, occupied the interior of a small conical bowl made of lead (Hole-Johnson 1986–1987, 183, 207 Fig. 16). The rarity of this composition makes it likely to have possessed a special significance, related perhaps to an attempt to "humanize" the site, previously not belonging to the Late Uruk *oecumene* and thus presumably in need of integration into the "human civilization".

The two vessels, standing possibly, with their hollow interiors, as symbols for bodies of liquids, may be presumed to refer to the Abzu, the body of sweet water concealed within the earth (gypsum), and to another of the watery abodes, for instance, to the outer and lower cosmic ocean encompassing the earth in its midst (lead) (cf. Horowitz 1998, 314 on the *lalgar* : *apsu* duality, 334–347, esp. pp. 341–342, 344 and 346 with Ea's cella on the upper surface of the Apsu; on the latter cf. also Vanstiphout 1997, 121). It might indeed be legitimately asked whether the "eye idol" does not constitute a material incarnation of aa symbol hidden in the interior of the shrine of Enki (and Nanše), which, in *Enki and the World Order*, receives the form of a "maze" or "[knot of] threads" (Vanstiphout 1997, 121). A symbol of Enki, one of the chief gods of Mesopotamia – if not of *the* god of Late-Uruk Sumer – , executed in a material extracted from, and processed in, a country very much alien to that of the origin of Sumerian culture, would indeed constitute a very eloquent symbol of integration of the new land into the realms where Mesopotamian civilization reigned supreme. Here it may even be speculated that the lead of the lower bowl may refer to a land called in later Mesopotamian texts Anaku, of which it seems to be clear that it is one of the lands across (neighbouring on) the Upper Sea, i.e. situated within the Mediterranean area. It has been variously identified as Cyprus, Greece, Anatolia and even Spain (Horowitz 1998, 87–88).

Indeed, in a flight of fancy we could perceive in this deposit a respectful gesture adressed to all three supreme divinities of Mesopotamia. The whole cavity, if viewed literally as "bur, bùr, bùru, *burû*" = pit, hole, well, equivalent to one of the names of heaven (Horowitz 1998, 232), could refer to An, while its filling, again literally "*šupuk [šamê]*" (Horowitz 1998, 239–241), would then incarnate the competence sphere of some celestial god, possibly Enlil as in *Enuma Eliš* (Horowitz 1998, 247). Enki's realms would then be situated at the base of the whole composition. (Of course, it must not be neglected that "bùr, bùru, *haštu*" can also mean either land or the underworld: Horowitz 1998, 285). Needless to say that this breakneck attempt has been included only as a note of caution not to omit considerations, pertaining to the ideational world of ancient Mesopotamia, from purely archaeological considerations.

In this case the "eye idol", dominating the two watery bodies, would stand for the fertility god Enki. In fact, we do perceive features of symbolic behaviour linked to Enki in the earliest cuneiform texts, as I shall proceed to demonstrate. Again, such an interpretation does not contradict the data obtained by means of analysis of cylinder-seal imagery, in which the "eye idols" figure profusely in contexts frequently alluding to fertility and proliferation force. Whatever the proper interpretation of the "eye idols", the terra-cotta cones hark back to the white-red-black triad proposed in Halaf-age Arpachiyah and carried out the Ubaid age at least by the residents of Tepe Gawra.

144

Something brand new: binarity in architecture

Another factor likely to give evidence of spiritual constructs of Ubaid-age Mesopotamia, representing, in this respect, an innovation worth dwelling upon is the duality, or rather binarity, well visible in contemporary architectural creations.

From the Ubaid period down to Late Uruk, a whole series of Near Eastern buildings yielded evidence for, on one hand, pairs of niches displayed by the front walls of the central halls of such buildings, and, on the other, sometimes even pairs of entrances by which such structures could have been entered.

This phenomenon is present at Eridu temple VI (Safar, Mustafa and Lloyd 1981, Fig. 10 on p. 61). At Uruk itself the feature turns up, after the "Kalksteintempel" of layer V (Charvát 2002, 102), in Temple C of layer Uruk IVd-IVb (Charvát 2002, 104). Significantly, one single central niche ornates the front sanctuary wall in Temple D of layer Uruk IVa (Charvát 2002, 104).

Another instance of the two-niche layout has come up at Late-Uruk Grai Resh (Charvát 2002, 108). In the case of Tepe Gawra, the first symmetrical pairs of entrances belonged to the Layer-XV building (Forest 1983, Pl. 8 p. 172, building 27), with pairs of niches in walls of structures which came up in layers XIII and XII (Charvát 2002, 50; Forest 1983, Pl. 11 p. 175, "pièce blanche"). One single niche in the front wall is displayed by the "temple" in Layer XI (Forest 1983, Pl. 13 on p. 177, "temple") while paired entrances do still appear in buildings of layers IX and VIII (Forest 1983, Pl. 35 p. 199: Temple Ouest VIII and two buildings under the heading "Temple IX"). A two-niche disposition is visible in the "Northern temple" of layer VIIIC (Charvát 2002, 112; Forest 1983, Pl. 25 on p. 189, "Sanctuaire nord").

A particular version of the same device has recently been documented at the Syrian site of Tell Sheikh Hassan, a Middle-Uruk fortified town on the Euphrates (Boese 1995). A "bent-axis approach" building of layer 6 boasts in its inner (NE) frontal wall a low podium, flanked on both sides by two buttresses and two niches (Boese 1995, 166–167, Abb. 4–5). A matching pair of niches may be found in the opposite, SW wall, while a rectangular flat hearth is situated in the midst of the "aisle". At Tell Sheikh Hassan, layer 6 has been dated to the Middle Uruk period, equal approximately to Eanna IX–VI, or roughly 3600–3300 B.C. (Boese 1995, 188).

Here it may well be of interest to take into consideration the earliest form of the proto-cuneiform sign ALAN, meaning "statue", "idol" or something of that kind (ZATU No. 25 p. 173). The binarity, clearly visible in its construction resembling a pair of pillars which may be supplemented by a low podium in front of them, may ultimately stem from the same ideational sphere as that reflcted by the twin recesses in front walls of exquisite buildings.

These architectural devices give us a precious testimony of the feature that we shall meet in the cultic life of Late Uruk, as mirrored by the earliest cuneiform texts. There, we witness the holding of a ceremony referred to as NA_2, performed by the "pontifical couple" of Late Uruk, the male EN and the female NIN (cf. infra).

It seems likely that this binarity, observable as one of the constitutive principles of socially relevant architectural decorations of the Ubaid- and Uruk cultures of Mesopotamia, harks back to the participation of both a male and a female partner in the sacred rite, required for the proper holding of the NA_2 ceremony, and thus to a spiritual construct that differed from that obscrvablc at Early-Uruk Susa.

The cylinder seal and its significance

What, however, represented a truly fundamental invention was undoubtedly the cylinder seal, invented and introduced perhaps some time during the Middle Uruk culture or at the end of this phase (Uruk Eanna VII). In addition to its technological advantages, the cylinder seal represents a nearly perfect materialization of the Sumerian perception of the spatiotemporal structure of the world (cf, Glassner 1993, as well as Glassner 2000a, esp. pp. 193–202). The matching is so conspicuous that we may be tempted to see in this construct of the immediately pre-state age a manifestation of a "major leap", when a whole bundle of changes transformed, at a relatively speedy pace, essentials of (also) the mental apparatus used by human beings until then over a very long period of time, reaching perhaps as far back as the beginnings of Neolithic (in terms of Fernand Braudel's "longue durée").

Having the faculty of being endlessly rotated along a wet and pliable surface, it represents symbolically, but also quite realistically, the circularity of time. Being capable of producing an infinite linear arrangement of images, it stands for the linearity of time. Being endowed with the capacity to impress images in the wet clay or any soft matter, and thus to create a new form of materiality, it may not only function within a coordinate system of a different order than time, such as that of space, but it can actively create spatiotemporal reality, either visible or invisible. At this stage of development of the human mind, practical operations involving the human environment tend to be

146

performed both in actual fact and "magically", (also) by means of images; one approach is a prerequisite of the other. And, indeed, in view of the fact that cylinder seals were obviously used to close deliveries of agricultural surplus to the high-rank sites, their impressions also "produced plenty" and the seals were, in a certain sense, correlates of the cycles of natural fertility. In this aspect they elaborated on the tradition present at Susa as early as the preceding stage of the Uruk culture when a seal, showing an embracing couple from above and what appears to represent a depiction of a child borne by the sealing surface below, clearly alludes to parallelism between any fruit-bearing activity and the sealing procedure (cf. supra).

The cylinder seal, this symbolic-cum-functional artifact, must have represented a powerful tool with the aid of which the prehistoric leaders convinced their followers that they were capable of creating a new world order. What came after was just a repetition of the original creative act, a solidification and clarification of a notion which had existed ever since the beginning of the Sumerian civilization. No wonder that modern scholars are fascinated by the "Eigenbegrifflichkeit" of the Mesopotamian culture (recently e. g. Selz 1999, 511–512). They invariably observe that nearly all the creative acts have already been performed by the anonymous members of late-fourth-millenium inventors. Trapped in the results of the enormous spiritual effort of their ancestors, the Sumerians, Babylonians and Assyrians contented themselves with the conservation of the cultural heritage which they took over from them. There was only one way to bring more perfection to a system of this kind: to abandon it altogether and to build something radically different. That, however, had to wait for the Hellenistic times.

A lucky chance has offered us a possibility to witness the emergence of this basic time concept in its material incarnation (the cylinder seal) in the middle Uruk cultural stage, at a moment just preceding in time the creation of one of the world's first literate civilizations. The rotation of the cylinder seal stands for the circular/cyclical time; the linear extension of the image impressed by the seal represents the linear orientation, the "vector" of time. The cylinder seal's faculty of making an impression in the pliable surface stood for the basic unity of time and space; and the fact that supplies marked by the cylinder seals brought plenty to foremost households indicated the filling capacity, or "fruition" of time. How far the development of this perception of time reflected notions developed in the preceding, prehistoric age, or how far did it represent a deep-reaching transformation of the mental apparatus of bearers of the Mesopotamian civilization, must be determined by future research.

147

Questions involving practical issues of functioning of the cylinder seals and especially differences among the "schematic", simpler and less demanding from the artistic point of view, and "naturalistic", frequently attaining a very high level of sculptor's art, have been debated over and over again, but unfortunately, no totally convincing solution has been proposed. The author of the last summary treatment of Late Uruk- and Jemdet Nasr-age seals, Elena Rova (1994, 53–69, 183, 262–270), sums up the source informations available at this moment. It may be said in general that both the individual components of the seal images, and the compositions which they help to build up, are deliberately chosen and constructed. However, no fixed semantic symbol sets which would attest to the existence of a precisely formulating "pictorial language" can be observed. Most of the seals and seal impressions have turned up either in sacral ("temple")- or settlement contexts and only four are known from graves dated to the end of the Jemdet Nasr age (Uruk, Fara and two at Ur: Rova 1994, 53–56).

The "schematic" seals turn up in all types of sites and mainly in settlement contexts, and have left impressions only rarely. In cases where these survived, they tend to bear traces of door-closing devices, "locks". The depictions borne by them display a high degree of uniformity and artistic homogeneity. They do seem to reflect, in a simplified form, the imagery of the "naturalistic" seals and no substantial chronological distance from the latter may thus be expected. Their iconography displays some peculiar features: they lack depictions of war, "heraldic" animal compositions and the "Mann im Netzrock" image. As against this, they do feature what may be female figures at large.

As against this, impressions of "naturalistic" seals, featuring sacral motifs, "heraldic" animal compositions, the "Mann im Netzrock", war scenes, or themes particular to the city of Uruk, do appear on mobile goods. "Bullae", stemming frequently from settlement-find contexts, usually associate with the earliest cylinder-seal types involving depictions of arts and crafts, animals and some other scenes ("Mann im Netzrock", war), and are thus to be expected chiefly at Susiana, less so in Syria and least frequently in Sumer. "Olives" or plum-shaped tags, on the contrary, do not particularly favour animal scenes, and are found in Iran and Syria rather more frequently than in Sumer. No females show up on "naturalistic" seals.

Regional variation, relevant from the historical point of view, is observable in Late Uruk/Jemdet Nasr seal imagery. Sacral scenes and war motifs predominate in Sumer and Uruk, while icons involving economic and subsistence activities constitute a "trade mark" of SW Iran and Susa. Syrian images hover "in between" Sumer and Susiana, while Anatolian examples display a degree of iconic and stylistic liberty. An interesting phenomenon is constituted by the high proportion of the "animals and ladders" motif at Jebel Aruda, in which an assumption of the site's involvement in animal husbandry or even hunting activities may not be entirely erroneous. At Habuba Kabira, the pots and symbols show well the site's dependence on provisioning from the downstream centres (Rova 1994, pp. 156–160).

Immovable storage space might thus have been secured by impressions of the "schematic" seals more or less everywhere; these would have been employed by the less numerous local store managers, who would presumably have no problem or recognizing one another's seal. The sealing and unsealing of the storage space would have occurred at a fairly rapid pace and the relevant seal impressions would thus have had less chance to survive.

As against this, deliveries from the centre(s) to the periphery of the Late Uruk world might have been denoted by central-administration seals manufactured by the cream of contemporary artists. Such portable icons, referring perhaps to the particular instances, from which the delivered goods resulted, by means of their depictions (as seems to be the case with tablets: Rova 1994, p. 60 n. 212), would have not only closed actual packages of goods (baskets, bales, pots, sacks, etc.), but also their symbolic representations ("tokens" in bullae). The central administration might have required the actual submitting of such sealings, attesting to the actual delivery of the goods in question, during periodical controls of the economy of the peripheral plants and this could have contributed to better preservation of archaeological samples of such practices.

What thus does rise in front of our eyes is a concept of a large unified area consisting of self-supporting economic units, the managers of which took care to control the access to community goods deposited in singular storage facilites by means of closing their doors with sealed devices. In addition to this, the major centres did collect their shares in the resources stapled by each of the individual communities. They put this through by means of a series of public events (war, ritual), in the course of which a part of community goods was assigned to the focal points and insitutions of public life. The central institutions a) had a particular form of cylinder seal ("naturalistic" ones) of a fairly high artistic merit made, probably in organic materials (wood, bone or the like); b) claimed a share of community goods, falling to them by common consent, which was subsequently packed in movable containers marked off by impressions of such "naturalistic" seals, in the course of public events deemed to be of capital importance, and transported these to their own central-place premises; c) finally, goods so redistributed were consumed either by the personnel of such central institutions, or by anone to whom the representatives of the central offices assigned the privilege to participate in consummation of such goods. It might legitimately be asked whether the "naturalistic" seals do not visualize for us either the beginnings of the NI+RU fund, known from the Jemdet Nasr texts (Charvát 1997, 15–18) or those of the GA+ZATU 753 goods circuit (Charvát 1997, 51–52).

If this hypothesis applies, a very interesting outline of internal composition of the Late Uruk corporate polity emerges. The centralization, achieved by political practice, power factors and religious consideration would not have put on the top of Late Uruk hierarchy a single one but two centres, those of Sumer (religious and military matters) and Susiana (economic provisioning). If such dichotomy of basic social activities really existed, it gives a very high credit to the Susiana section of Late Uruk polity. This was not only allowed to keep her own regional identity, but even entrusted with a task of considerable importance, that of management of the economic life of a major part of the Late Uruk territory. I would find such an assumption rather difficult to reconcile with the idea of brutal conquest of Susiana by Sumerian forces.

So what kind of eternity did the bearers of the Late Uruk culture impress into the soft and pliable materials, creating thus a new reality to their liking? This question must be answered with reference to the iconography of the earliest cylinder seals, which has recently been most conveniently summarized, at a fully sufficient quantity of 970 examples, by Elena Rova (1994).

In order to keep our research at the nexcessary methodical-unity level, let us resort to the fourfold sequence which we have established already at Susa: the *anoecumene*, *oecumene*, war scenes and, in this particular instance, rituals as the last category.

Late Uruk/Jemdet Nasr seal imagery: the *anoecumene*

We cannot fail to observe that the image group that we encounter most frequently on Late Uruk seals draws its inspiration from the *anoecumene*, the world of wildlife uninhabited by any denizens of the human sphere. Depictions of animals of most diverse kinds make up 315 items from the total number of 970, that is, 32.47% of the total. The kinds of beings shown include birds, reptiles, fish and also insects with the particularly popular scorpions and spiders; in the last case, we may speculate how far the spider images could denote, by way of a pictorial analogy, supplies of woven textiles. That they could also serve as emblems or idols is indicated by a seal (Rova 1994, No. 952 Tav. 57), in which spider likenesses are interspersed with images of crouching human figures raising their hands (on links between spiders and weaving, symbolized by the goddess Uttu, cf. Vanstiphout 1990). A seal found in Jemdet Nasr-age layers at Ur associates what seems to be a depiction of weaving activities with that of a spider (Legrain 1951, Pl. 2 No. 31). In many instances the animals are arranged into "heraldically" symetrical groups, pointing thus to the very likely conclusion that the animal images served as symbols or carriers of messages difficult to decode today. Mythical animals such as the griffin did not fail to appear among the *menagerie* rampant on Late Uruk seals (Rova 1994, p. 89).

In some instances the symbolical role of the animal depiction clearly flows out of the accompanying images. They may appear accompanied by a likeness of the KUR sign (Rova 1994, p. 95, No. 592, Tav. 34, ibid. No. 852 Tav. 51?), by divine symbols (MUŠ$_3$ = INANNA, Rova 1994, 608, Tav. 35, or the single, doubled or trebled loop twins on an upright rod, Rova 1994, No. 678 Tav. 40; ibid. No. 724 Tav. 42; ibid. No. 867 Tav. 52, cf. also ibid. p. 99), by reed-hut or similar icons (Rova 1994, No. 621, Tav. 36) or by a picture of an object that can be either and ear of corn or a pitchfork for winnowing grain (Rova 1994, 616, Tav. 36).

A particularly interesting icon is represented by the creatures displaying artificially prolonged necks, or, alternatively, tails which may be skilfully arranged into symmetrical interlace patterns pleasing to the eye (Rova 1994, p. 88). In some instances the animal images are interspersed with rosette motifs; what these could stand for is indicated by the seal No. 557 (Rova 1994, Tav. 31), displaying a band of "heraldically" arranged animals with two border zones divided into rectangular compartments filled in by alternating rosettes and the arc images clearly related to those of the painted pottery of Susa. Here the animal file may be "consecrated" to the god An, as the rosette may incarnate the divine aspect of the plant world (Rova 1994, 95).

The simple animal representations are closely followed by groups combining the animal images with various other icons. Animal depictions involving, in one or another form, a kind of ornament consisting of two long parallel lines linked by a series of short perpendicual strokes ("ladders"), amount to 68 instances, i.e. 7.01% of the total (cf. also Rova 1994, Fig. 3 on p. 152–153, "animali e scale"). In these instances the animals may be accompanied by depictions of humans or of pots, including those more or less close to the proto-cuneiform sign GA (ZATU No. 159 p. 203: e.g. Rova 1994, No. 64 Tav. 4; ibid. No. 595 Tav. 34; ibid. No. 609 Tav. 35). Scenes of wild animals attacking tame ones combined with this sign (Rova 1994, No. 208 Tav. 11) imply that (deliveries stemming from) a kind of refuge for animals kept in the open, a provisional corral or pen, may be referred to by such images. Such an enclosure, together with the shepherd's shelter, or boolley, does actually appear in one instance (Rova 1994, No. 405 Tav. 22, cf. also ibid., pp. 92–93). One seal (Rova 1994, No. 962 Tav. 58) combines such penned animals with an "eye idol", indicating thus a logical connection with the idea of bounty and fertility.

The category of "animals and pots", showing them accompanied with vessels and pots of diverse kinds, is attested to by 64 instances, equal to 6.60% of the total. The GA containers are again present (Rova 1994, No. 574 Tav. 32; ibid. No. 590 Tav. 33; ibid. No. 595 Tav. 34; ibid. No. 609 Tav. 35; ibid. No. 633 Tav. 37; ibid. No. 713 Tav. 41, with a griffin). In some instances such animals turn up in the association with pots overflowing with long and tasselled materials, most probably textiles (Rova 1994, No. 3 Tav. 1; ibid. No. 594 Tav. 34; ibid. No. 639 Tav. 37; ibid. pp. 102–103). The message of these icons, probably showing the animals as sources of revenue, is demonstrated by a seal in which heraldically arranged animals display handled and netted pots instead of heads (Rova 1994, No. 132 Tav. 8). The same idea may lie behind a rather enigmatic image of spiders combined again with handled and netted pots (Rova 1994, No. 135 Tav. 8). An emblematic interpretation difficult to explain links pots with images of birds of prey (vultures? Rova 1994, No. 222 Tav. 12). A particular seal links spider images with pots and "eye idols" (Rova 1994, No. 589 Tav. 33) and a very strange image presents an association of snakes with handled pots (Rova 1994, No. 620 Tav. 36). A most peculiar instance is represented by a seal in which two "personalized" human-headed ships carrying pots drink by means of long and pliable tubes from a common pot (Rova 1994, p. 93–94 and 331, No. 966 Tav. 58, from a Choga Mish settlement context). Humans show up here and there in such combined scenes.

The symbolic role of animal images is borne out by the next category, that of animals combined with geometrical patterns, numbering 15 examples (= 1.55% of the total). In most cases these associate with interlace patterns and a particularly famous motif is that of two intertwined snakes, the bodies of which make up a decorative zone consisting of round fields ("caduceus": Rova 1994, No. 172 and 175 on Tav. 10, and possibly also ibid. No. 766 on Tav.

46). As we shall see when discussing the "spread-legged female" icon, such associations may allude to the female aspect of procreative force.

Animal hunt- and animal-contest scenes are a rarity in the Late Uruk/Jemdet Nasr seal imagery. Animal-contest icons account for 10 examples (= 1.03% of the total). In two cases they involve animal-cum-"ladder" depictions and they might thus refer to actual attacks of wild beasts of prey on penned animals. Hunting scenes appear in 11 cases (= 1.13% of the total; Rova 1994, p. 72–73). In two cases they involve rosettes (Rova 1994, No. 291 Tav. 16; ibid. No.900 Tav. 54). A "sacred hunt" in a montane valley, where a naked hunter leads a file of equally naked standard-bearers, seem to be alluded to by one of the seal cylinders from Uruk (Rova 1994, 95, No. 777 Tav. 47; ibid. p. 327). Let us notice that archaeological sites amply attesting to Late Uruk hunts *en masse* do exist (Hole-Johnson 1986–1987, 177–179: Umm Qseir, 74% of bone from hunted animals such as gazelle, onager or aurochs).

Taken altogether, scenes depicting wildlife account for 483 seal images out of the total of 970, that is, for nearly 49.79% of all the icons. This respectable number is nevertheless to be viewed in the light of the probably symbolic character of the animal depictions. To what extent they can be understood as referring to supplies delivered by the "outer receptors" of the Late Uruk economic system, apparently frequently located in uninhabited landscapes and involving various segments of animals husbandry such as livestock-keeping or hunting, must be investigated by further research. The sheer numerical quantity of the motifs involving various forms of wildlife does nevetheless shed sufficient light on the "frontier spirit" of bearers of the Late Uruk culture who certainly did not fear advancing farther and farther into regions unknown before their times.

Late Uruk/Jemdet Nasr seal imagery: the *oecumene*

Let us now proceed to the other major divisions of the early images, that of the *oecumene*, or land inhabited by people. First and foremost, I shall refer to a category of images which, in fact, would probably belong to the preceding category, from which it differs by combining the animal images with those of human beings, a proper sign of the "civilized" or "humanized" land tracts. Such images turn up in 80 instances (= 8.25% of the total). Most of them involve images of humans protecting animals or catering to their needs, and are thus likely to refer to shepherding- or other animal-production activities. Only some icons do differ from this general scheme, especially those of the man clutching symmetrically two animals by his hands, the "maître" or "dompteur des animaux" (Rova 1994, No. 118 Tav. 7; ibid. 268 and 278 Tav. 15; ibid. No. 286 Tav. 16; ibid. No. 640 Tav. 37; cf. also ibid. p.70). Such an icon of a man holding a pair of enormous snakes (Rova 1994, No. 735 Tav. 43) shows the symbolic character of the action taken; in fact, the rather friendly gestures of some animals treated in this way (Rova 1994, No. 118 Tav. 7) do allow the question how far a taming process is being involved and whether it is rather not that the human being, who infuses a form of energy into the animals by contact of his or her hands. Something of this kind is also suggested by the scenes in which the bearded and kilted individual ("Mann im Netzrock", Rova 1994, p. 71), commonly understood as EN, feeds the animals under the shade of a symbol of Inanna (Rova 1994, No. 782 Tav. 47; cf. also ibid. p. 99). A mythical allusion links a naked human offering-bearer with rosettes, intertwined snakes, a couple of ibexes and a file of lion(?)-headed birds (Rova 1994, No. 838 Tav. 50).

A rather strange depiction links a human bearer of a handled pot with pairs of intertwined-neck beings, which may thus be denoted as an emblem of a particular population group (supplying deliveries to the Late Uruk corporate polity? Rova 1994, No. 653 Tav. 38; ibid. No. 719 Tav. 47). One of the seals show veneration of what appear to be big scorpion idols (Rova 1994, No. 961 Tav. 58).

The second most numerous category of seal images of this period pertains to depictions of files of human beings, either walking/standing or sitting. These amount to 178 items (= 18.35% of the total).

The processions of walking figures frequently carry various objects such as pots (presumably with supplies), textiles (Rova 1994, No. 326 Tav. 18; ibid. No. 619 Tav. 36), or, alternatively, symbols, emblems or staffs (of office?). In some instances, such conveyors may be denoted as demons by possessing parts of animal bodies (Rova 1994, No. 370 Tav. 20, with GA containers; ibid. p. 89). The symbols carried by them may sometimes include "eye idols" (Rova 1994, No. 423 Tav. 23).

The seated persons, frequently located among pots or other utensils or objects of uncertain form and function usually raise their hands. Again, "eye idols" may feature among the objects, in between which they are seated (Rova 1994, No. 434 Tav. 24; ibid. No. 444, 445 and 446 Tav. 24; ibid. No. 783 Tav. 47; ibid. No. 797 Tav. 48; ibid. No. 805 Tav. 48; ibid. No. 826 Tav. 49, held in hands; ibid. Nos. 878 and 879 Tav. 53; ibid. No. 931 Tav. 56; ibid. No. 950 Tav. 57), aside of spider figures (Rova 1994, No. 430 Tav. 23; No. 435 Tav. 24).

The supplies presented by the seated persons may sometimes be "denoted" by peculiar emblems like the side-looped staffs (Rova 1994, No. 86 Tav. 5). This particular "label" of a supplier community, may be equated with the sign URI_3, standing for the city of Ur (ZATU No. 595 p. 306; cf. Rova 1994, p. 98). One of the particularly interesting images associate an "eye idol" with sitting humans who touch it with their hands (Rova 1994, No. 967 Tav. 58).

Some of the pots associated with these scenes assume a form close to the GA sign (Rova 1994, No. 588 Tav. 33; ibid. No. 645 Tav. 38; No. 796 Tav. 48; ibid. p. 106), but sometimes an UKKIN pot may be surmised (ZATU No. 580 p. 302; Rova 1994, No. 431 Tav. 23; No. 449 Tav. 25; ibid. Nos. 798 and 800 Tav. 48; ibid. No. 880 Tav. 53; ibid. No. 941 Tav. 57; ibid. p. 108). A file of naked standing cup-bearers is interspersed by intertwined-neck animals (Rova 1994, No. 651 Tav. 38). One of these images may show a file of dancing figures (Rova 1994, No. 889 Tav. 53). We may even witness true "tax-delivery" scenes in which a file of seated persons who appear to be purveyors of textiles face another seated figure who may be a scribe, registering their deliveries in writing (Rova 1994, No. 110 Tav. 7).

The Late Uruk/Jemdet Nasr *oecumene*: human toil and its outcome

The next category, embodying in actual fact the transformation work of bearers of Late Uruk culture, may be termed "humans at work". It is represented by 50 seal images, equating 5.15% of the total. These scenes appeal to us by the depictions of all kinds of everyday human toil which made the inhospitable landscapes of Mesopotamia into flowering gardens pleasant to behold. Most diverse kinds of work are represented: agricultural enterprise such as tilling the fields by means of hoes (Rova 1994, No. 311 Tav. 17) but also ploughs or rather ards (Rova 1994, No. 674 Tav. 40, lower field). Threshing and winnowing the grain is also present (Rova 1994, No. 70 Tav. 4; the identification of the threshing sledge is borne out by winnowing pitchforks carried by the participants), much as the ensuing tying of the sacks full of provisions (Rova 1994, No. 346 Tav. 19; ibid. p. 109).

Animal husbandry and care of the living resources may be featured by scenes appearing to represent dairy activities (Rova 1994, No. 2 Tav. 1, occurrence of "ladders"; perhaps also ibid. No. 52 Tav. 3, with a lovely image of a thornbush-enclosed cattle-pen; ibid. No. 80 Tav. 5; ibid. No. 105 Tav. 6; ibid. No. 131 Tav. 8; ibid. No. 762 Tav. 45).

Neither have the Late Uruk-age seal cutters omitted arts and crafts of the period (Rova 1994, pp. 73–74). Among the depictions of the relevant activities feature such occupations as possibly brick-firing (Rova 1994, No. 674 Tav. 40, upper field), perhaps rope-making (Rova 1994, No. 362 Tav. 20), work with textiles (Rova 1994, Nos. 331, 332 and 333, Tav. 18) and the well-known depictions of weavers' looms (Rova 1994 No. 106 Tav. 6; Nos. 364, 365, 366 and 367 in Tav. 20; ibid. No. 413 Tav. 23; cf. also ibid. p. 111).

The bringing of provisions resulting from the toil of the Late Uruk communities constitutes a particular iconographical theme, in the case of which we may be pretty certain that the authors wishes to perpetuate such scenes "from here to eternity". The cases in point include 19 examples, amounting to 1.96% of the total. The deliveries may be brought to what appears to be an architectural complex (Rova 1994, No. 567 Tav. 32; ibid. No. 650 Tav. 38; ibid. No. 665 Tav. 39; ibid. No. 722 Tav. 47; ibid. No. 750 Tav. 44; ibid. No. 751 Tav. 45, the last three with an emblem with three superimposed double loops on a rod, cf. Rova 1994, p. 99). In some cases divine symbols, such as that of Inanna, are involved (Rova 1994, No. 604 Tav. 34, Nos. 604, 605 and 606 on Tav. 35; cf. also ibid. p. 99); for Nos. 605 and 606 it may legitimately be asked whether the instruments held by the participants aside of the divine symbols do not represent winnowing pitches, and whether the scene might be interpreted as thanksgiving for a plentiful harvest.

A number of seal images the themes of which may be subsumed under the heading "subsistence" does outline a sub-category of this iconographic field. It consists of 13 cases, making up 1,34% of the total number. Most of these depictions usher in the well-known dome-shaped granary constructions, shown in the process of being filled with comestibles or other products (Rova 1994, p. 92, Nos. 349, 350, 351, 352, 353, 354 on Tav. 19). The variety of substances stored in such facilities is borne out by proto-cuneiform signs of the MAH series in which the contents are indicated by particular signs (ZATU Nos. 341–351, pp. 241–243). Other structures may be used for this purpose as well (ibid. No. 356 on Tav. 19; 359 Tav. 20 where the character of the structure is unclear). Some of the scenes may pertain to final food processing (baking? Rova 1994, No. 360 Tav. 20). Feeding animals may be considered a special case of this sub-category (Rova 1994, No. 403 Tav. 22). Two images, showing human figures reaching up to the branches of trees and carrying small recipients in the other hands (Rova 1994, Nos. 421 and 422 on Tav. 23) may allude either to picking fruit in orchards or, alternatively, to artificial fructification (pollination) of date-palm trees.

As we shall repeatedly encounter the boat scenes, it may be useful to take a closer look at them even now. Although there are only two of them (0.21% of the total), they constitute quite well-defined contexts of Late Uruk social activities. In addition to those moments about which we shall hear more below and which may point towards cultic activities, both these "civilian" scenes, include discharging of a boat cargo (Rova 1994 No. 312 Tav. 17) and what may be a landing of a booty-laden boat, returning from a fishing trip (Rova 1994 No. 655 Tav. 38; cf. also Rova 1994, p. 93).

A particular group of images worth considering apart displays depictions of inanimate objects as the fruit of human efforts, whatever form they may assume. It consists of 53 icons, representing 5.46% of the total (cf. also Rova 1994, 110–114). Insofar as intelligible objects are featured, which may not always be the case (cf., for instance, Rova 1994 No. 16 Tav. 1), they invariably include pots, frequently large storage jars (Rova 1994 No. 859 Tav. 52; in general ibid. pp. 102–109), serving as transport containers for other materials, e g. textiles (Rova 1994 Nos. 25 and 26 Tav. 2; ibid. Nos. 46 and 47 Tav. 3; ibid. Nos. 323 and 324 Tav. 18; ibid. No. 638 Tav. 37; ibid. pp. 102–103). Some of such pots may bear designation by means of various emblems such as the intertwined-neck monster (Rova 1994 No 46 Tav. 3). In other cases tableware items turn up, such as the UKKIN pots (Rova 1994 Nos 910 and 912 on Tav. 55). Other pot types may be accompanied by textiles, including even a complete weaving loom, and by hides or furs (Rova 1994 Nos. 113 and 114 Tav. 7). A seal displaying netted pots, netted pots with textiles and stone containers (Rova 1994 No 320 Tav. 17) has been described as typical of the periphery of the Late Uruk *oecumene;* its impressions are known both from Uruk and from the "colonies" but a cylinder seal bearing it has never occurred at the capital (Pittman 1994a, 182, 191 Fig. 14a). Likenesses of objects made of perishable material such as reeds are especially welcome to the archaeologist (Rova 1994 No. 613 Tav. 36). Pictures of stone vessels are nonetheless also present (Rova 1994 Nos. 969 and 970 on Tav. 59).

The objects depicted may sometimes be interspersed with emblems (Rova 1994 No. 386 Tav. 21, perhaps URI_3 ?, ZATU No. 595 p. 306). Some of the emblems command a great deal of our attention, such as a U-shaped object with inward-turned side loops on the vertical arms (Rova 1994 Nos. 623, 624, 625 and 626 on Tav. 36). Could this be an empty ship? The heaped-up big basket-like containers may be accompanied by stone vessels and a symbol of Inanna (Rova 1994 No. 612 Tav. 35).

An interesting icon combines a "ladder" pattern with textiles (Rova 1994 No. 415 Tav. 23) and another links two "eye idols" with ear-shaped devices, presumably handles to be hooked up into nets for carrying heavy loads in them (Rova 1994 Nos. 424 and 425 Tav. 23). Objects likely to be identified as "eye idols" feature among the things depicted fairly frequently (Rova 1994 No. 465 Tav. 25; ibid. Nos. 468, 469 and 470 Tav. 26; ibid. No. 663 Tav. 39; ibid. Nos. 792 and 795 on Tav. 48; ibid. No. 886 Tav. 53; ibid. Nos. 924, 926, 927 and 935 on Tav. 56; ibid. No. 951 Tav. 57; ibid. No. 968 Tav. 59).

Sometimes the images display whole structures such as reed huts topped by emblems in the form of staffs bearing two pairs of double loops (Rova 1994 No. 658 Tav. 38; ibid. No. 679 Tav. 40; cf. also ibid. p. 99). A special case is constituted by a *tableau* of a montane landscape with the blazing sun above (Rova 1994 No. 705 Tav. 41). This may, indeed, be the very first case in which a landscape is viewed as an object of esthetic pleasure, not as a set of symbolical devices to be operated for a definite purpose. Or is this the sun of An? A lonely example of a rosette may, in fact, point in the latter direction (Rova 1994 No. 754 Tav. 45), as for Elena Rova, the rosette is the incarnation of the divine aspect of the plant world (Rova 1994, 95; on star icons ibid. p. 116).

Late Uruk/Jemdet Nasr seal imagery: *si vis pacem, para bellum*

The "civilizing" or rather integrating efforts of the Late Uruk corporate polity sometimes took in aim not only uncultivated landscapes but neighbourhoods already well settled. Scenes from the ensuing wars then constituted inspiration for the seal-cutters who depicted them on the fine stone surfaces. Altogether we register 20 such icons, amounting to 2.06% of the total. Battles were fought in sight of forts, and in their depictions the superiority of the Late Uruk military machine, commanded by our old acquaintance, the "Mann im Netzrock", is apparently celebrated (Rova 1994 No. 387 Tav. 21).

The rather strange tactics of bow-shooting depicted in this scene, where the "Mann im Netzrock" aims his arrows at the lower body parts or even buttocks of his naked enemies rather than at the vital organs of their anatomy, evoke the question whether a deprecative assessment of the enemy is not expressed here in a symbolic manner. Bowmen shooting their arrows at naked *derrières* of other humans turn up in marginal paintings of medieval Europe, where the baring of a human bottom has been interpreted as a socially offensive act, defying openly "decency", accepted social norms and commonly esteemed values (Camille 2000, 150–156, esp. p. 151). We may therefore ask whether the naked enemies of our seal are also not denoted as getting a just punishment which they had deserved for their behaviour, considered provocative and anti-social – that is, for an armed action against the Late Uruk corporate polity.

Some of these fortresses appear nonetheless to have been stormed – or capitulated on their own – , as captives are subsequently taken out of them (Rova 1994 No. 83 Tav. 5; cf. also ibid., p. 93). Among the various troop detachments of the Late Uruk army, bow-armed infantry must have occupied a prominent sight (Rova 1994 No. 375 on Tav. 20; ibid. Nos. 378, 379 and 380 on Tav. 21; ibid. p. 72). One of their most formidable weapons must have been the reflex bow (Rova 1994, 96, No. 379 on Tav. 21).

In the Late Uruk world, files of prisoners-of-war must have been a frequent sight (Rova 1994, p. 97, Nos. 373, 374 on Tav. 20 and perhaps 376 on Tav. 21; ibid. Nos. 391 and 393 on Tav. 21; ibid. p. 72). At least some of these prisoners must have served in the official subjugation ritual, in which the "Mann im Netzrock" played a key part (Rova 1994 No. 560 Tav. 31; ibid. No. 566 Tav. 32; ibid. No. 637 Tav. 37). In other scenes of this kind, however, the prisoners are led before a personage that is as bald, beardless and naked as his assistants who wield weapons above the bound captives (Rova 1994 No. 637 Tav. 37; ibid. No. 712 Tav. 41). Some of such victory icons combine the prisoner theme with images of symbolic entities who presumably demonstrate the superiority of the civilization which they represent. This is the case of human-headed birds who nibble at the prisoners' heads (Rova 1994 No. 715 on Tav. 42). Alternatively, the "spread-legged woman", to whom we have already referred to (Rova 1994 No. 761 on Tav. 45), presides over the enslavement of naked prisoners.

The final outcome of any war waged by the Late Uruk corporate polity is depicted with remarkable frankness on a contemporary cylinder seal (Rova 1994, p. 326, No. 749 Tav. 44). Here a conqueror with a "big stick", bald-headed and beardless but dressed in a knee-length skirt, accepts the capitulation of a group of bald, beardless and naked personages who present both a symbolic token of subservience (the man kneeling in front of the "general") and bring provisions which may well constitute a tribute. This sealing from Uruk – Eanna III has once closed a pot and thus may well announce a contribution collected from a subdued enemy.

Late Uruk/Jemdet Nasr seal imagery: *Diis manibus*

One of the potentially most productive ways and means how to approach the spiritual world of the Late Uruk *brahmanas* is to investigate the depictions of the structures in which the worship of deities of the day presumably took place – the Late Uruk temples and shrines (cf. also Rova 1994, p. 91). These are represented by 39 cases, on other words, 4.02% of the total. In some instances, the seal surface displays hardly more than an elaborate facade of an architectural structure, which, of course, need not represent exclusively a religious establishment (Rova 1994, No. 36 Tav. 2; ibid. No. 37 Tav. 3). Such cases as, for instance, Rova 1994, No. 568 on Tav. 32, do nonetheless strongly allude to the proto-cuneiform sign E_2 (ZATU No. 129 p. 196), likely to depict a buttressed facade of a building, of which the upper part and ceiling consists of ornamented cornice(-s, outside) and of superimposed layers of various materials (inside, thus *contra* Glassner 2000, 200).

Statues as idols are sometimes shown within such structures (Rova 1994 No. 646 Tav. 38). I have interpreted the very strange scene in which a human-shaped idol(?) shoots arrows at what appears as both art representations of wild pigs and the actual animals (Rova 1994, No. 53 Tav. 3) as an expression of asserting Late Uruk-culture supremacy over human groups symbolized by the pig symbols (Charvát 1994) and I still do not know of any more fitting explanation. One of the rather well-known images (Rova 1994 No. 955 Tav. 58) supplies a linkage among a "temple" facade, a human (female?) face, an emblem of the staff with a side loop (URI_3 ?, ZATU No. 595 p. 306) and rosettes.

In most cases human figures are shown to bring various kinds of objects to such "shrines", including potted or bagged goods, textiles and various emblems. Animal herds sometimes approach the facades (Rova 1994, No. 610 Tav. 35), and even hides of hunted animals may be referred to (Rova 1994, No. 314 Tav. 17; ibid. Nos. 400 and 401 on Tav. 22). In one instance (Rova 1994 No. 343 Tav. 19), the three rows of triangular configurations situated behind the animal approaching a "temple" facade may denote some kind of product but another possibility to be considered is a reference to foreign lands, KUR. In such a case the bringing of foreign cattle to the temple could allude either to tribute exacted from foreign lands, or, alternatively, to a contractual obligation on behalf of the temple, the personnel of which could be "hired" to care for other peoples' livestock. The centralized organization of animal transhumance may be referred to in proto-cuneiform texts by the instances of

UKKIN, "assembly", of animals (Charvát 1997, 45). The "temple" attendance of mythical creatures is borne out by a seal (Rova 1994, No. 383 Tav. 21) in which a griffin appears amoung various objects depicted in front of a facade. In fact, one of the images (Rova 1994, No. 929 Tav. 56) bears such a strong resemblance to the medieval image of a pelican feeding his offspring on the blood of its chest that at least the existence of a bird-shaped idol must be surmised here. The (ritual?) feeding of animals on leafy branches or bushes in blossom take sometimes place in front of a "temple" facade (Rova 1994, Nos. 918 and 920 on Tav. 55).

The contributions of those approaching the "temples" may be taken over by personages confronting them before the "temple" and thus presumably belonging to its personnel. These may be depicted as a bald and beardless character, dressed in an ankle-length skirt and assisted by a naked, bald and beardless attendant (Rova 1994, No. 722 Tav. 42).

The Late Uruk and Jemdet Nasr seals abound in the depictions of individuals or "worshipful companies", presumably doing homage to the deities of the day (Rova 1994, p. 73). Altogether, these amount to 22 items, standing for 2.27% of the total. In some instances it is not clear whether the act takes place indoors or under the open sky, such as the impressive scene of sitting worshippers raising their hands in the salute of a series of "eye idols" (Rova 1994, No. 24 Tav. 2).

Targets of such practices are constituted by emblems like the "eye idols" (Rova 1994 No. 51 Tav. 3; ibid. No. 363 Tav. 20), symbols of Inanna, occurring virtually only at Uruk-Eanna (Rova 1994, p. 99), maces (? Rova 1994 No. 530 Tav. 29, where the "mace" may be mounted on a kind of podium; possibly also ibid. No. 949 Tav. 57) or side-looped staffs (URI_3?, ZATU No. 595 p. 306; Rova 1994 No. 40 Tav. 3, where the emblems stands behind the worhsipper's back). An interesting instance links the veneration of "eye idols" with a major figure placed by the side of a bush- or tree motif. How far this may provide a connection of the "eye idols" with vegetation deities must be investigated (Rova 1994 No. 905 Tav. 55).

We also have scenes in which divine likenesses (statues?) may be venerated, such as an instance in which the human worshipper seems to touch a statue with hands (Rova 1994 No. 890 Tav. 53, cf. infra on the TAK_4.ALAN ceremony). Sometimes it is nonetheless difficult to guess who is adoring whom (Rova 1994 No. 884 Tav. 53).

In other cases the addressees of the veneration may be whole architectural complexes, temples, at which the believers worship together with the "Mann im Netzrock" (Rova 1994 Nos. 648 and 649 on Tav. 38). Here the worship may be accompanied with bringing of provisions or offerings (Rova 1994 No. 767 Tav. 46). Sometimes such activities involve people coming both on foot and by boat to demonstrate their respect of a certain temple (Rova 1994 No. 901 Tav. 54). Such a shrine-worshipping scene may entirely take place in a boat (Rova 1994 No. 666 Tav. 39).We also do have examples of cult scenes in which the worshippers carry emblems, presumably those identifying their communities (Rova 1994, p. 328, No. 818 Tav. 49).

A particularly delightful scene takes us to the vicinity of a temple denoted by the side-looped staffs (URI$_3$?, ZATU No. 595 p. 306). The end tassels of a banner flying over its roof are skilfully plaited into an accomplished braid by a figure in an ankle-length skirt who, to my eye, looks like a female. She is accompanied by two naked, bald and beardless companions, one of whom is leading an animal(?) on a lash while the other raises a cup in a toast.Both of them walk in a "garden of Eden", adjacent to the temple, with animals and plants (Rova 1994, pp. 72 and 327, No. 768 Tav. 46). This impression of a seal, which once secured a pot mouth, turned up in a secondary temple context datable to Uruk-Eanna IV (Rova 1994, p. 327). Could the head-cloth of the lady employed in front of the temple be identified as a (symbolic?) veil? If yes, the dame may be identified as a bride and her participation in some kind of a nuptial (or nuptial-like) rite could be surmised (on the veil symbol cf. Van Der Toorn 1995).

Together with two big basket-like objects, possibly symbolizing a plentiful harvest, an altar very like that carried by the "Mann im Netzrock" in a boat (cf. infra, Rova 1994 No. 602 Tav. 34) is being adored by another "Mann im Netzrock", wielding an ear of corn or a winnowing pitchfork (Rova 1994 No. 786 Tav. 47).

Some of the scenes of ritual feeding of animals by the "Mann im Netzrock" may fall in with the general character of worship activities in view of the symbol of Inanna which may be present (Rova 1994 No. 603 Tav. 34, cf. also ibid. p. 99).

A true "altar" resing on the back of a bull or cow and provided with a twin symbol of Inanna seems to be worshipped by a "Mann im Netzrock" in a boat propelled by two naked, bald and beardless rowers. The chequerboard field with intervening "butterfly" motifs, situated behind the "Mann im Netzrock"'s back, may enhance the fertility-discharge character of the whole scene (Rova 1994 No. 602 Tav. 34). The combination of a simplified chequerboard form with an "hourglass" or "butterfly" motif, accompanying an erotic scene in one of the archaic Ur seal impressions (Legrain 1936, Nos. 239, 368), refers to the fertility symbolism inherent in such images. We may also see a connection between a "temple" facade and a boat, manned, unfortunately, by rowers only (Rova 1994 No. 654 Tav. 38).

One of the most complex but also most incomprehensible scenes, presumably involving worship, takes place in a boat (Rova 1994 No. 82 Tav. 5). It is unfortunately far from clear what exactly is the big personage, presumably the "Mann im Netzrock", surrounded by smaller persons standing and squatting, one clutching a standard, and an animal figure, doing.

An icon occurring repeatedly within the sphere of Late Uruk/Jemdet Nasr seal imagery, with presumably cultic connotations, is represented by whom I choose to name "a spread-legged female" (Rova 1994, p. 71). This is a human personage shown in a frontal view, sitting with outstretched arms and legs spread widely apart. The figure has no beard and at least in one instance she seems to display female genital parts (Rova 1994 No. 307 Tav. 17). In all the five instances of her occurrence (0.52% of the total) she is accompanied by animals but various interesting details may be observed. Aside of two images too fragmentary to be considered (Rova 1994 Nos. 306 and 307 on Tav. 17), she is once happily settled among a herd of animals, to whom she extends her hands, holding in one of them a rosette quite in the "Mann im Netzrock" manner. Another small human figure, squatting in her presence, seems to hold a big spouted pot, thus alluding to the idea of abundance, bounty and thus probably fertility (Rova 1994 No. 305 Tav. 17). Her favourite company, a herd of animals, might be supplemented by snakes, arranged in artfully coiled guilloche patterns and licking affectionately her knees; these creatures of the earth do not discomfort her in any visible way (Rova 1994 No. 728 Tav. 42). These ellegant guilloche patterns link our wanton lady with the much more appropriately dressed, considerate and socially acceptable dame who plaits the ends of a temple banner into a tasteful braid (Rova 1994 No. 768 Tav. 46). Nevertheless, a company of two rather hilarious naked male companions of the well-mannered lady in the last-cited instance does point to the fertility character of the scene, making the fecundity connotations of our "spread-legged female" rather likely. In the earlier Middle Ages of Europe, prominent display of female genital parts (in architecture, for instance) is supposed to have stood for warm welcome and protection (Camille 2000, 154–156).

The last instance when she appears is curious but very instructive. The upper register of a contemporary seal (Rova 1994 No.761 Tav. 45) shows her with her usual company, horned quadrupeds (ibexes?) while the lower register of the same seal displays bound captives denoted each by his respective emblem. In this instance the "spread-legged female" is likely to stand for a symbol – I feel almost tempted to say "ensign" – under which aggressive wars are waged by the Late Uruk corporate polity, and under which captives from such wars lose their liberty and are enslaved to serve the victors. This, I think, is the first instance where we can speak about a true symbol, the relationship of which towards a certain action is coded exclusively in cultural terms and has nothing to do whatsoever with the entities depicted.

A particular instance of cultic activities is represented by feasting and music which are also alluded to in Late Uruk/Jemdet Nasr seal imagery. We have six related icons (0.62% of the total, cf. also Rova 1994, p. 113). A certain festive occassion involves a double file of humans equipped with emblems, arms and carrying a prominent personage in a palanquin (Rova 1994 No. 382 Tav. 21). A solemn occasion is undountedly shown on a seal, bearing an image of a socially prominent personage, a theme otherwise very rare in Late Uruk art. This "big chief", who may be a female, is sitting on a low stool and enjoys a drink poured out for her from a spouted flagon held by a naked attendant, standing in front of her. Another naked attendant stands behind her and displays a banner – or refreshes her with a fan (Rova 1994, p. 325, No. 685 Tav. 40). The scene ornates a cylinder seal of light red limestone, found in a secondary temple context at Uruk-Eanna IV (Rova 1994, p. 325). A rare moment of intimity is caught in a scene in which two persons, probably a man and a woman, drink a toast from the same cup (Rova 1994 No. 701 Tav. 41).

A scene in which vessels are handled, presumably in preparation for a feast expressedly denoted by the EZEN sign (ZATU No. 150 p. 201), is accompanied by a band playing music on a harp, with clappers and other percussion instruments (Rova 1994 No. 81 Tav. 5). Two other "Orpheus-related" instances link harp music with animals (Rova 1994, Nos. 256 and 257 on Tav. 14). Elena Rova has noticed that images of musicians frequently accompany those of craftsmen and craftwomen (1994, p. 77, in general ibid., pp. 75–77). This is a most peculiar phenomenon requiring explanation. Two solutions may be proposed at the moment: a) this is an artistic or rather locational convention, alike unto the medieval depictions of smiths and musicians alluding to citations from the Scriptures; b) the link between the two is causal, proposing that the provisions of materials treated by artisans flow freely in consequence of fertility rituals, a component of which has always been the music (Charvát 1997, 85).

Finally we should not forget epigraphical creations such as the "City--league seal" (Rova 1994 No. 841 Tav. 51). On the City League, probably a confederation of successor communities to the Late Uruk corporate polity, visualizing – and symbolizing – its coherence by an exchange flow of token volumes of various commodities, cf. Charvát 1997, *passim* (cf. the register on p. 98), and Matthews 1993, 34–38.

Let us now show the results obtained in tabellary form.

Anoecumene seal images

animals	315	32.47%
animals and "ladders"	68	7.01%
animals and pots	64	6.60%
animals and geometrical patterns	15	1.55%
animal contest	10	1.03%
hunting scenes	11	1.13%
wildlife total	**483**	**49.79%**

Oecumene seal images

files of humans, either walking/standing or sitting	178	18.35%
animals and humans	80	8.25%
humans at work	50	5.15%
bringing of provisions	19	1.96%
subsistence	13	1.34%
boat scenes	2	0.21%
inanimate manufactured objects	53	5.46%
Oecumene **total**	**395**	**40.72%**

War scenes in seal images

war (battles, captives, tribute)	**20**	**2.06%**

Ritual scenes in seal images

temples and shrines	39	4.02%
"worshipful companies"	22	2.27%
"spread-legged female"	5	0.52%
feasting and music	6	0.62%
Ritual total	**72**	**7.42%**

The general-motif analysis should not hide the fact that regional variation, relevant from the historical point of view, is observable in Late Uruk/Jemdet Nasr seal imagery. Sacral scenes and war motifs predominate in Sumer and Uruk, while icons involving economic and subsistence activities constitute a "trade mark" of SW Iran and Susa. Syrian images are quite close to Sumer while Anatolian examples display a degree of iconic and stylistic liberty. An interesting phenomenon is constituted by the high representation of the "animals and ladders" motif at Jebel Aruda in which an assumption of the site's involvement in animal husbandry or even hunting activities may not be entirely erroneous. At Habuba Kabira, the pots and symbols show well the site's dependence on provisioning from the downstream centres (Rova 1994, pp. 156–160).

Late Uruk/Jemdet Nasr society: highlights from the written sources

The historical phase of Near Eastern cultures datable between c. 3500 and 3200 B.C. boasts a comparative advantage that places it into a situation unique in the history of mankind. For the first time ever, the rays of light emanating from written sources illuminate the horizon of our vision and, joining the voice of archaeological objects and contexts speaking out of the darkness of prehistory, add a brand-new dimension to the early phases of human history, however sparsely and in a disjunct fashion. The time has thus come to grasp this chance and to see how do the first written sources portray the society that created them. Here I present, in an abbreviated fashion, the conclusions of the work I have submitted six years ago (Charvát 1997; more recently cf also Michalowski 1997 and Supplément 2002).

As to social structures, the lowermost level accessible by means of the written sources is the "household", *oikos*, represented by the Sumerian expression É, meaning literally "house", but signifying doubtlessly both the material incarnation of this notion, i. e. a building protecting its inhabitants from the elements, and the coherent and structured human group living together in a singular accommodation facility. There are indications that some É were sedentary while other were nomadic but hardly anything beyond this simple observation may be asserted with at least a shade of probability. Among the humans plying their trades within the É, the documents name a great variety of individual occupations and professions, a part of which must have been carried out by adult married men, the LÚ, and adult married women,

MÚRUB. In one way or another, the highest social groupings on which the earliest documents of Mesopotamia shed light may thus be characterized as age groups or age sets. Any knowledge pertaining to their internal principles of organization and the role played within them by various forms of kinship is denied to us due to the silence of the sources

The individual É, displaying great flexibility both in economic occupations exercised in them and in their spatial locations, are likely to have clustered around regional settlement foci, likely to be represented by the AB or EŠ$_3$, structures probably identical with the "terraced temples", as is indicated by the sign they are referred to in writing. This sign probably depicts a generally rectangular or cubic building standing on a basement or pedestal in the shape of a low truncated pyramid or cone. A series of functionally differentiated É, comprising workshops, storage facilities, habitation buildings but also shrines, oscillated around the AB. It is very difficult to define any functions of the communities referred to in conventional cuneiform as "cities", URU; the sign does exist but the functions of such settlements do in no way imply anything out of the ordinary. They probably played no distinct role as a particular category of human communities; on the other hand, roles of the individual cities, represented in the written sources by their place names, are well discernible (for the city of Uruk cf. Charvát 1993).

Somewhere at this level we may situate two categories of Sumerian political life which must have played rather visible roles but about which we know miserably little. The LUGAL, "big men", must have assumed a middle-status role somewhere between the ordinary LÚ and the highest offices of EN and NIN. Appearing for the first time in rather inconspicuous roles in texts of Jemdet Nasr age, they might have played the roles of representatives of their communities, or "speakers" of the respective age groups. At any rate, at least some degree of involvement of the LUGAL in cultic matters muts be assumed in view of the later developments, about which I shall speak in the following chapter.

Even more elusive is the role of the "assembly", UKKIN (ZATU No. 580 p. 302), appearing quite frequently in the texts (and, as we have just seen, also in cylinder-seal images). Who gathered where and for what purpose is not immediately clear, though the assemblies must have convened rather often. At any rate, they do introduce into the whole system an element of democracy, however "primitive", somewhat difficult to reconcile with a commonly held belief that these early state bodies of the Near East were characterized by "Oriental despotism". The easily acceptable idea of the assembly as that of the "labour force" or even "assembly of young men" (*un + kin: Selz 1998, 291, 301–312, 317–319, 326) strenghtens further my assumption that the highest social-organization unit visible in the proto-cuneiform texts is represented by the above-named age grades or age sets. Special provisioning sources, visualized possibly by seal impressions which once closed spouted vessels, might have been available to officials of the assembly (= the UKKIN sign, Rova 1994, p. 65–66).

The direction of the most important affairs within the particular nucleated regional groupings of Late Uruk settlement enclaves probably incumbed on the bearers of their highest offices, those of EN and NIN, the primordial "pontifical" couple, who figure most prominently in the earliest written texts of Mesopotamia. In what manner did they perform their functions, and what was the foundation of their power, is not imminent from the texts which register no more than tranfers of property, in most cases comestibles, on the occasions of particular moments in the life of Sumerian cities of the period. For this reason, any reconstruction of the activities of EN and NIN must be considered tentative and must be always checked against evidence of other sources and contexts. In view of the nature of the earliest cuneiform texts, representing either registers of commodity deliveries or disbursements, or auxiliary word lists, it is extremely unlikely that we shall ever lay our hands on documents directly describing the functions of this twin office; all we can go by is the circumstantial evidence offered by the texts, coupled with the testimony of the Sumerian language and of later cuneiform sources.

The EN and NIN probably performed together a ceremony which appears in the texts as NA_2. This took place in a special building (É) and at appointed times (U_4). The texts do nowhere specify the character of this ceremony but in view of the sense of the Sumerian verb NA_2 (to sleep, to sleep repeatedly, to have sexual intercourse repeatedly, CAD N 1, 204–206), it seems to have constituted a predecessor, or an early form of, the "sacred marriage", representing a cultic "triggering off" of fertility and the procreation force conveyed by the divinities, its ultimate and sole possessors ("Inanna's Descent into the Underworld"; cf., in general, Hurowitz 1992, esp. pp. 45–46 with n. 1, p. 58 and 60–61). I assume here a compatibility with rites based on the commonly held conviction that *human fertility and natural fertility are strictly interrelated,* (Kirk 1970, 98; cf. pp. 91–98) much as in the Sumerian hymn of "Enki and Ninhursag". At least in one case the ceremony links up with the name of a grain deity, and this might show how it was intended to result in the stimulation of natural fertility to produce abundance and bounty (Charvát 1997, 10–12, 27–28, 57–58). In addition to this, later Sumerian sources designate the god Enlil as the "EN who lets grain grow forth" (Weadock 1975, 102). A ritual of this kind may be depicted on the, alas, now stolen Uruk Vase (Selz 2000, 30–32).

The fertility activated by means of the NA_2 ceremony seems to have been "kept in store" by the EN and NIN. It could have even been distributed to all those interested by the EN, who is attested to have travelled outside his residence both by land and by water, perhaps carrying with himself the sacred symbols (Charvát 1997, 58, cf. also Charvát 1995). Some of the seal images seem to refer directly to such activities (Rova 1994, Nos. 602 Tav. 34, No. 666 Tav. 39). Journeys of divine statues, which may constitute a later version of such pursuits, are attested to from Ur III times (Zettler 1992, 105 on the voyages of Inanna's statue and of Ninlil's barge).

However, the activation of fertility by means of the NA_2 ceremony was but a first step in the long and colourful series of ceremonies and cultic obligations of the EN and NIN. Most of these took place in order to make the fertility, rendered accessible by the NA_2 ceremony, accessible to the widest possible circles of consumers.

The É in which the "lie-in" took place apparently included a room with a statue (ALAN) which, in the progress of the ceremony, became permeated with the highly desirable life-giving force. In its turn, this object then became a target for another particular ceremony by means of which the visitors to this sacred area received their share of fertility, namely the TAK_4.ALAN, "touching of the statue" (Charvát 1997, 11–12, 28, 58). This ceremony may be depicted upon a cylinder seal found in a Jemdet Nasr-aged stratigraphical context at Ur (Legrain 1951, No. 30, p. 11 and Pl. 2, and Rova 1994, No. 890 Tav. 53). In historical times, one of the relevant translations may be "to anoint" (Frayne 1997, pp. 253–254 on ki-šu-tag).

Another tactile ceremony included that of "touching the heaven and earth", TAK_4.AN.KI, which was sometimes performed for the sake of a given community, such as Eridu, as is indicated by the phrase NUN.TAK_4.KI (Charvát 1997, 17 n. 128, an observation by R. Matthews). This ceremony might have been intended to bring to full swing the fertility of arable soil, resulting in abundant harvests. The complexity of the local agriculture, especially of field management involving irrigation, is well attested to by historical and ethnographic evidence from the pre-modern Near East (e. g. Lambton 1953, esp. pp. 148–149, 173, 312, 319 and 363).

One of the most interesting ceremonies of this kind is likely to have represented the "charging" of female beings of all kinds by fertility and life-giving force. This has probably been referred to by the phrase TAK$_4$. SAL AMA NIN, attested to in Late Uruk texts (Charvát 1997, 11, 85). The idea apparently lives on until the later Sumerian literature; in particular, we find it in "Enki and the World Order", where Enki is credited with evoking fertility in female domestic animals by the touch of his divine hand ("Enki and the World Order" ll. 53–55, Bottéro-Kramer 1993, 167).

This is, in all brevity, a sketch of Late Uruk society as it may be culled from the earliest proto-cuneiform texts. It is plain to see that in this early time, we still cannot speak about theocracy or about profane government, and only with hesitation about "clerocracy". Rather, the power wielded by the "pontifical couple", EN and NIN, rested on a fragile base made up both by their prestige and by the tenacity of beliefs in their functions, shared by wide population strata. We find here a particular version of the duality of the crucial idea upon which all public life of these early times was built, that of fertility and propagation force. The ultimate guardians of fertility were the gods who had to be invoked and worshipped in order to allow the mortals to draw on the store of fertility in their possession. Alternatively, however, special qualification, or a special ritual, must have been required even from the denizens of the earth to discharge the fecundity and procreation force and to bring it to full fruition. of As a form of public administration, this system could only function as long as it kept its credibility at a high level, existing in a "believe" order. Once it was discovered that it had acquired a "make-believe" character, the base of its power was gone.

Sumer and Susiana in Late Uruk: conquest or cohabitation?

This seemingly marginal question is, in fact, of a high relevance, insofar as I have been assuming an overall unity of social and cultural developments along the eastern arm of the "Fertile Crescent" from about 5500 B.C. down to the age that I am commenting upon now – that is, to terminal fourth millennium of the pre-Christian era. Protoliterate Sumer and Susiana, the twin components of the Western Asiatic "cradle of civilization" do, in fact, constitute in this perspective the last two links of a chain of predecessor communities, who had toiled towards the common purpose for centuries before in the darkness of prehistory. With the pictorial evidence being now by far more numerous than that of the Early Uruk age, and, before all, in view of the now existing written sources, a unique opportunity to investigate the character of their links and interconnections now lies ahead of us.

Can any assessment of relationships between the two historical regions – Sumer and Susiana – be put forward? Is there any reason to believe that both of them might have shared a common spiritual culture, and, essentially, strived for the same goal, albeit pursuing different paths, as I ahve imagined before for the Halaf- and Ubaid-culture communities? Or is their mutual relationship to be envisaged as a hierarchical subordination of one to another, as an annexation of subdued Susiana by victorious Sumer?

We have already seen that in the Late Uruk period, Susiana did play a rather significant role. According to the testimony of the seal images, the lords of this Western Iranian region could have acted as economic managers to most of the Late Uruk corporate polity. There does seem, however, to have been more than that.

The existence of war motifs in the imagery of Susa- and Choga Mish seals shows that some decisions of a purely political character – and a decision to wage war undoubtedly belongs to this sphere – could well have been taken by governors of the eastern province of the Late Uruk corporate polity themselves (Rova 1994, p. 265).

Most interesting information is furnished by the sphere of spiritual and religious constructs. First and foremost, let us notice that the icon of the "dompteur" or "maître des animaux", Master of animals, carved into Early-Uruk seal matrices from Susa, does survive into Late Uruk times, and turns up typically in the Susa seal imagery of that age (Rova 1994, pp. 70 and 154). This shows that the old ritual persisted at Late Uruk Susa, with only the pictorial medium changed.

In the preceding chapter I have already drawn my readers' attention to the fact that the original Early Uruk script of Susa lived on until this period of time, albeit the evidence for this is very thin. In this aspect, then, the bearers of Susiana spiritual culture kept control over their cultural heritage as well, and apparently, nothing prevented them from retaining their own identity as a cultural unit. The Late-Uruk managers of Susa did take over the cylinder seal, which, as I have already argued, must have constituted a very powerful and persuasive tool of magical domination of both the visible and the invisible world. In addition to this, they also borrowed from Sumer the idea of the numerical denotation by special script signs, though in a modified form. They apparently introduced a purely decimal system, without Sumerian parallels (Damerow, Englund and Lamberg-Karlovsky 1989, 21; also Carter-Stolper 1984, 6).

The common symbolism of both literate cultures of the Late Uruk age is particularly well shown by finds from Susa likely to date from the Early to Middle Uruk (de Mecquenem 1943, 14–16, fig. 12). The richly furnished graves of children have yielded one a necklace composed of three cross-shaped pendants, the antecedents of which reach as far back as the painted pottery of Susa I (ibid., fig. 12: 4). The other, even more interesting necklace, comprised, among beads of carnelian, lapis lazuli, mother-of-pearl, quartz, other minerals and *Dentalia* shells, seven silver pendants in the form of three-plus-two drop-shaped configurations. These fivefold symbols could well represent a variant of the proto-cuneiform sign EZEN, attested to from early Mesopotamia (ZATU No. 150 p. 201, with a variant i = ezen sub No. 259, p. 223). The central piece of this necklace, comprising a threefold "columned architecture" of copper and silver with two ranges of rock-crystal beads and two tiny bird figures on top could well indicate the divinity which the necklace bearer honored, could we but read its message (de Mecquenem 1943, 15, fig. 12: 5).

These two interments show the full compatibility of the symbolic sphere of Sumerian and Susiana cultures of the Late Uruk age. At the risk of a too far-fetched assumption, I would propose to see in them evidence for an – admittedly – very nasty procedure of a building sacrifice, carried out in the course of an "inaugurating ceremony" (EZEN) for the establishment of a human settlement (cross-shaped pendants).

Thus Susiana not only retained its economic capacities, political freedom and spiritual "profile" under the sway of Western, Sumerian culture. Susiana appears to have been treated rather as an ally, friend and helper, than as a conquered and subdued province. The managers of Susiana grasped the opportuntiy to extend their activities over most of the realms of the Late Uruk corporate polity. They also borrowed the cylinder seal for directing the currents of goods flow, but pondered over the numerical systems which they saw in use by their neighbours and improved them as they took them over. Above all, however, they retained both some of their rituals and their own script. They managed to preserve their identity, though, of course, they also extensively borrowed from other spheres of Sumerian material culture (the bevelled-rim bowls, as one instance for many). Mutuality seems to have been the slogan of the day, rather than subordination or domination. A readiness to respect the other, to borrow from him and to work together on the improvement of devices of common utility is apparent from the source material. This, in fact, does, as I believe, confirm my hypothesis of the enchainment of efforts of preceding communities and their high-rank personages, who seem to have exhibited precisely the virtues I have just been commenting upon.

It is, of course, not excluded that this "cohabitation" of Sumer and Susiana might have been facilitated by the duality or rather binarity, apparent in Sumerain culture ever since the Late Ubaid times (cf. supra). Perceiving in the NA_2 ceremony, performed by EN and NIN, a condition necessary for bringing the fertility of all beings to full swing, the Sumerians could conceptualize in the same fashion to co-existence between both provinces of the Late Uruk corporate polity, for instance, as a cohabitation of husband and wife in a common nuclear family.

Conclusion

In the time which had immediately preceded the creation of one of the world's first state and literate society, the Mesopotamian plains played host to communities which were somehow different from that of its eastern neighbour at the foot of the Iranian mountains. There seems to have been far less competition, far less ostentatious ceremonies and much more straightforward, down-to-earth modes of both division of material goods and of social and religious ritual.

This may nonetheless be a view erroneously overlooking factors which left no traces in the archaeological record. Continuity with the preceding period and its cults must certainly be seen in the white-red-black triad surviving from Halaf times down to the Late Uruk temples, very likely to have carried from the hoary antiquity the message of the god An who was to assume the supreme position within the Sumerian pantheon.

On the other hand, the idea of fertility and its securing soon occupied the central place in thoughts and beliefs of both the ancient inhabitants of the lower Mesopotamian plains which were to become the historical alnd of Sumer, and bearers of the Uruk culture in all the remaining parts of the Fertile Crescent area. Soon a concept emerged according to which the gods, ultimate possessors and keepers of fertility, can be imprecated to make their stores of the life-giving force accessible to humans, provided the proper rituals were enacted. This ritual was centered on the NA_2 ceremony, an early form of the "sacred marriage" performed by a couple of a priest and a priestess who were to bear the titles of EN and NIN in the city of Uruk of the final fourth millennium B.C.. The emergence of this ceremony, and thus the entire "thought package" that accompanied it, may be dated in the Late Ubaid period when the binarity principle finds reflection in the architectural layout of the foremost buildings of the day (Tepe Gawra XIII).

The discharge of fertility apparently opened access to all the secrets and treasures of the world, as is shown by the invention and introduction of the cylinder seal. Managing it skilfully by their expert hands, the Uruk wizards were able to create a parallel spatiotemporal context consisting of images, and thus presumably of the same nature as the really existing universe. The pivot actions and desirable procedures could thus be repeatedly re-enacted to the profit of all those who embraced this spiritual attitude and accepted this belief. The Late Uruk chiefly class thus acquired the power both to "ignite the engine" of the substance of natural proliferation, and to determine the particularities of the accidental component processes to obtain the desired results (for one of the most recent overviews of archaeologically documented Uruk-age economy cf. Emberling – McDonald 2001, esp. pp. 22–30).

This extremely simple, but powerful and persuasive spirirtual construct did result in a deep-reaching transformation of human attitude to the world. As against the earlier pictorial evidence, interference in the uncultivated world and its transformation into consumable goods now constituted the central theme of Late Uruk socially relevant imagery, being represented by more than 90% of all the relevant images. Icons relevant to ritual and to war, once so prominent in the pictorial record, now play a distinctly minor role. The chief concern of the Uruk-culture sphere was obviously productivity – opening of natural resources and their exploitation for the benefit of the entire community acknowledging the supremacy of the Uruk corporate polity. Late Uruk cylinder-seal imagery seems to be telling the following message: "We know how to bring the natural world to fruition for our benefit. We worship our gods, chiefly Enki, and they reward us with abundance and bounty. All we have to do is to master the hitherto uncultivated areas, the resources of which lay open to us thanks to our expert knowledge and religious obedience, and to bring the harvests and goods home".

This essentially theocratic model of public power resulted in the building of a most peculiar social structure, in which the relevance and prestige of each individual was obviously a function of his or her distance from the ultimate source of fertility infused into the world by ritual action. The chief couple of EN and NIN were responsible not only for the release of fertility, but also for its conveyance to all the member communities of the Uruk corporate polity. Fertility had to find various means and ways towards its ultimate consumers: acting both through inanimate (ALAN) and animate (SAL NIN AMA) carriers, it travelled through the regional centres, AB or EŠ$_3$, which passed it on to the singular human groupings, the É. Within them, the household heads (LÚ) and managers (MURUB$_2$) disposed of this divine gift. The age groups or age sets, to which all individual humans belonged, deliberated upon, and decided about, their own affairs in assemblies (UKKIN), in which the "speakers" of the age group of adult married men, the LUGAL, could enjoy particular esteem. In this process, the Sumerian inventors of the Late Uruk age cooperated peacefully with the Susiana centre which reatined its identity under the Sumerian "mask", both sides exchanging their goods and know-how and working actively on improvement of the tools with which they built their own world.

AND LO! THERE SPRANG A WORLD

With the end of the Jemdet Nasr period, we are leaving the pure theocracy or rather clerocracy, as I have remarked before. The Early Dynastic period, covering, in absolute dates, roughly the time between c. 3000 and 2334 B. C., ushered in perhaps the most fascinating act of the birth of the state in the ancient Near East – emergence of a secular government in a *milieu* permeated with the odour of sanctity and with concern for the chief entity eagerly sought by all the inabitants of Sumer and Susiana – fertility and procreative force. Let us now pass in review one of the possible ways in which this might have happened.

EN and NIN: The uneasy way from two deities to one

The main fertility-releasing ceremony of Late Uruk Sumerian realms, that of NA_2, involved two human participants of opposite sex, the male EN and female NIN. This is likely to have arisen out of the situation of the city of Uruk where two deities, An and Inanna, incarnated by EN and NIN, were venerated. Let us now lay aside the question how this ceremony was established as a primary moment in the cultic life of the entire Sumer. Two possible explanations come to mind:

a) the whole ideational scheme came to light at Uruk and it was found to be so persuasive (or the power of the Uruk centre too overwhelming?) that the other Sumerian centres, who possessed their own EN and NIN (Charvát 1997, 55–56, 85) simply imitated the Uruk model. The second possibility is that

b) due to the prestige of Uruk, the ceremonies carried out outside the capital city were only considered valid after the enactment of the chief action by the Uruk "pontifical" couple, somewhat in the manner of Aquinas's "actus purus". We also do not know whether the Uruk EN and

NIN acted as substitutes for the respective deities, or whether the god and goddess did descend, in a temporary fashion, upon their earthly servants on this particular occasion.

So far, so good for Uruk. But cities in which only one deity was venerated faced a problem. The gender of the municipal divinity determined the sex of the EN: where the city worshiped a god, the EN was female, like at Ur. If the chief cult concentrated on a female deity, the EN remained a man (cf. Weadock 1975, 101–102).

But herein lied the main difficulty. An EN, married to his or her local deity, could not well act in the NA$_2$ ceremony, as it was unthinkable that he or she copulated legitimately with someone else than his or her divine spouse (Weadock 1975, 101, on Eanedu, daughter of Kudurmabuk: úr! nam-en-šè kù-ge-eš-e túm-ma, "a lap fit for *entu*-hood on account of its purity"). For this reason, the crucial position is now that of the NIN, who ushers in a new partner of a male sex, with whom she performs the NA$_2$ act for the benefit of the whole community. This is the moment when the third key figure in the Early Dynastic power play enters the scene: he is no other than the LUGAL, the title of whom will, in later periods, be translated as "king". The manner in which this might have happened shall constitute the target of the following investigation.

EN.SAL – the female EN

In fact, the hypothesis just emitted should, in theory be mirrored by the occurrence of the term EN.SAL in contemporary sources. It could be surmised that outside Uruk, in the other cities of the early Sumerian corporate polity, some of the EN could have been of female sex from the very beginning of recorded history. I have put this proposition to a test, using the texts which I have probed for my study of the textual evidence for the emergence of the Sumerian state (Charvát 1997).

The results were not exactly disappointing. First and foremost, there are just two occurrences of a term that could possibly be related to a female EN in Late Uruk- and Jemdet Nasr-age texts from Uruk. One is the text W 9656ex (= ATU 349, all texts now republished in Englund-Boehmer 1994), a large list recording the allotments of "bulls" (GU$_4$). This term obviously relates to "heads of cattle" in general, as the herd is, in accordance with good breeding practice, divided among the bulls cows and calves. One of the recipients was

EN B SAL. It is thus clear that the EN.SAL represents here an institution, receiving from the central administration office heads of cattle, most probably as sources of traction force.

The other has now been re-published as MSVO 4, 80 (Englund-Matthews 1996). It is an account text (list of rationed objects?), excavated at Tell Asmar, but with sign forms and combinations common in Uruk-III levels of Uruk and coming possibly from Uruk herself (Englund-Matthews 1996, 29). Line 1 in reverse col. I is read SAL? EN_C. The importance of this text is altogether unclear, but its occurrence rather far from its presumed place of origin carries a certain amount of interest.

References to EN.SAL turn up somewhat more frequently in the texts from Jemdet Nasr. In fact, the very first re-published text (MSVO 1, 1) carries this sign group in its col. 00201a (MSVO 1 = Englund-Grégoire-Matthews 1991, 39). The subscript to this text, ENGAR AB NI+RU, show that EN.SAL is one of the agencies which receive arable soil for cultivation here. The same conclusion may hold for a group of other documents, starting with text MSVO 1, 2. This has a subscript of AB NI+RU, GÁNA …, where EN.SAL also figures in col. 00105a. Text MSVO 1, 3, containing a reference to EN.SAL at col. 00101a, carries a summary GÁNA KI. ŠAGAN while text MSVO 1, 5, mentioning EN.SAL in col. 00102a, is denoted as GÁNA.HI.LAGAB. These texts pertain presumably to distribution of arable soil of various quality (Charvát 1997, 12–13, 59–60; Neumann 1996, 26).

A rather interesting information is provided by text MSVO 1, 77, unfortunately, heavily damaged and falling into the category of cereal--procession texts (Neumann 1996, 26). This text displays two references to EN.SAL: col. 00202, in which nothing else remains, and col. 00203 giving EN.SAL TAK_4.A. This may be a reference to the TAK_4 ceremony which, in Jemdet Nasr times, could also pertain to water (Charvát 1997, 65).

It is not quite clear how far SAL.EN are referred to in the extensive text MSVO 1, 212, which seems to summarize goods associated with (consumed by?) slave-girls. If yes, this would make the EN.SAL recipient of labour force, much as of that of arable soil before. The same goes for text MSVO 1, 214 with the somewhat enigmatic subscript NIMGIR SAG+MA; is this food for the personnel of the "herald"? Labour hands are definitely referred to in text MSVO 1, 218, summarized as DUB.ENGAR.AB, referring to SAL.EN.TE in co. 00101b1a (on this group of texts cf. also Neumann 1996, 26).

Two other texts, in which the EN and SAL signs associate, W 17879, AE and W 24047, link them with signs for GURUŠ (EN-A SAL GURUŠ, W 17879, AE) and ERIM (PA EN SAL ERIM, W 24047). We know of texts in which SAL.GURUŠ (W 20274,57) and SAL.ERIM (W 9579, cb = ATU 74) occur as independent, self-standing groups, so the above cited texts are likely to pertain to categories of the latter kind. Finally, there is the text W 9579 with mere two lines, linking 6 EN SAL GA_2+SUKUD and 5 SAL GA_2+SUKUD. Out of this it follows that the SAL represent here a classificatory term specifying working hands (?) of female sex, of which some belong to EN while others do not.

The source data on this category of official are thus rather scanty but one thing seems to be clear: the EN.SAL, not occurring very frequently in texts of Uruk origin, docs figure visibly in texts of other provenances, especially in those from the northern site of Jemdet Nasr. In the latter documents she appears as a denomination for fully-fledged Sumerian office, provided with all appurtenances obligatory for the organs of central institutions, including access to arable soil, to shares in grain harvests and to the disponible labour hands. Her participation in the TAK_4.A ceremony is possible.

In short, the EN.SAL seems to have been ushered into official circles of non-Uruk institutions at the end of the fourth pre-Christian millennium. How far is it a coincidence that her co-functionary, LUGAL, who was to assume the highest office in later times, also appears no earlier than the Jemdet Nasr-age texts, must be investigated in the future (Charvát 1997, 77–78). The EN.SAL does, however, probably represent a subsequent adjustment of the original ceremonial buildup centered upon the EN and NIN.

The Kish tradition: *homo sum, nihil humani a me alienum puto*

The chief deity of Kish in our period of time is Inanna (Glassner 2000, 324). Zababa was added to the local pantheon at a moment between the periods of the texts of Fara and Abu Salabikh (Charvát 2002, 168). It may thus be surmised that the local EN was a male, who had to furnish his NIN with a partner for the NA_2 ceremony. Is there any means of knowing how did he proceed in this uneasy task?

In fact, there seems to be. Of course, authentic written sources fail to drop but a single line upon this crucial moment in the life of the early Sumerian state. Nevertheless, a text recorded considerably later – in the early second millennium B. C. – describes the core of the procedure with such clarity and in a manner so absolutely identical with the proposition advanced above, that we must suspect it to have conserved a tradition of venerable age. This is the famous and well-known "Gilgamesh and the Land of the Living", the relevant texts of which have been published some thirteen years ago in a most meritorious way by Dietz Otto Edzard (Edzard 1990; Edzard 1991; Edzard 1993; cf. also Steiner 1996, all references courtesy Blahoslav Hruška). Let us now see where the data supplied by this epic do fit into our reconstruction of events at the onset of the third pre-Christian millennium.

The epic begins with the *en* Gilgamesh, who wants to "inscribe his name", presumably into the memory of successor generations by some heroic feat. This already does give us a few clues: the *en* title would, in normal later usage, be linked to Uruk but with Inanna as chief deity of Kish, it is by no means excluded that it refers to Gilgamesh's offical residence in the north. Again, the *en* title appears here rather as a honorific epithet without any real, precisely defined contents of the function, which shows us that we are fairly far away from the Late Uruk EN who carried out a well-defined cultic role.

That the EN became at one moment dissociated from NIN, his companion of yore, who need not have authomatically assumed the charge of an Early Dynastic "queen", is borne out by evidence from Ebla. At that city, the spouse of EN, the ruler, bears the title of *mâliktum* while the NIN id virtually invisible (Pomponio – Biga 1989, 90).

Wishing to leave a memory of himself, Gilgamesh decides upon an exploit well in the tradition of high-rank personages of prehistoric and protohistoric Mesopotamia. He intends to lead an expedition towards the northwest, along the Euphrates river, to the Cedar Forest to fell those noble trees in order to carry them downstream to his native city. We have seen that as early as the Halaf-culture period, foremost representatives of Mesopotamian societies did carry out expeditions, in the course of which they massacred game (and presumably also felled trees), in order to bring more nad more lands into the orbit of "humanized" and "civilized" sphere of the world. Gilgamesh challenges those more adventurous spirits from among the inhabitants of his city who have no kin affiliations to go with him as his retinue, the chief among these being his faithful retainer and friend, Enkidu, who, as we shall see, is to play a fatal role.

The party, including Gilgamesh,, Enkidu and fifty other men soon arrive at their destination, proceeding immediately to fell the cedars of the Forest. This is the moment when they first encounter a "being from the outer world", Humbaba, guardian of the forest. Humbaba strikes Gilgamesh unconscious by hitting him with a ray emitted out of his awe-inspiring halo. Hours and days pass but Gilgamesh has still not recovered his senses, which greatly worries his retinue and especially Enkidu.

Awakening finally from what he deems to have been deep sleep, Gilgamesh asks a question the purpose of which is not immediately clear but which, as I believe, represents a keystone of the whole plot: "**Am I a god or a human being?**".

God or no god, first things first. Gilgamesh now addresses Humbaba and tries a (seemingly) friendly approach. It is worth noticing that Gilgamesh wants Humbaba to become his relative, giving him a spouse who is either Gilgamesh's nin_9 sister, or nin, which, in the light of what has been already argued, be best left untranslated. (The two terms are of course, homophonous: Edzard 1991, 211–213 on ll. 139 and 143 of the text, and cf. also Edzard 1987–1990.)

Gilgamesh does in fact, exactly what I have presumed the Early Dynastic EN of female deities to have done: deprived of the possibility to carry out the NA_2 procedure themselves, they had, as legitimate partners of the NIN, to provide them with their counterparts in this duty (husbands). In actual fact, Gilgamesh is offering Humbaba to make him his peer, one of the highest representatives of early Sumerian society of Gilgamesh's native city. Even more instructive however, is the name of the lady which Gilgamesh is offering as spouse: she is called *Enmebaragesi* and links thus this current of the Gilgamesh tradition with the city of Kish and her ruler called *Mebara(ge)si*, dated to the ED II – ED III transition (Edzard 1993, 42 note 56 on text line 139). And finally, just to round up the whole argument, the name of the lady speaks in no equivocal terms about her essential function: "En = divine powers fill in the throne dais" gives *verbatim* the social relevance of her function (Vanstiphout 2002, 260 n. 4; for another rendering that seems less likely to me, cf. Alberti 1990). She is the carrier of divine confirmation of legitimity of her partner, regardles of whether he be a lord spiritual or a lord temporal. Much as in other cultures, the Sumerian lady offered in marriage to Humbaba is a status transmitter, conferring highest prestige on her partner in marriage. In fact, there may exist an illustration showing the EN and NIN sitting upon a dais or podium and facing a major figure who might well be a deity (Legrain 1951, pp. 10–11, Pl. 2 No. 24; Rova 1994 No. 884 on Tav. 53).

Thus the story of "Gilgamesh and the Land of the Living" outlines the nature of the EN and NIN titles in a manner matching fairly well our knowledge of the nature of these functions at the beginning of Sumerian history:

a) the foundation of the EN function must be sought in the sphere of divinity, of which she (or he) is a herald, conveyor and champion, and

b) an integral component of the NIN function is the conveying of divine blessings, likely to have been acquired by contact with the EN, upon any of her partners.

The plot also falls in very much with my earlier assumption about the relations between the EN and NIN in the Early Dynastic period. Unable to "act as husbands of NIN" (i.e. carry out the NA_2 ceremony with them) in cities with single divinities, to whom they were supposed to be married, the EN (here Gilgamesh) had to find partners, with whom the NIN could fulfil their cultic obligations for the purpose of common good.

But now back to our story. Humbaba reacts positively to Gilgamesh' s ouvertures; indeed, he were a fool if he turned down an offer to become a equal to a man of supreme valour and might. Alas, now it transpires that the whole thing was a mean fraud from the very beginning on. Pretending to clinch the deal with a gesture of friendship, Gilgamesh attacts Humbaba physically, manhandles him and before the unsuspecting creature can raise a finger, Gilgamesh binds him and makes him his captive. Humbaba, falling into tears, asks Gilgamesh to set him free and, indeed, the chief hero feels is moved by compassion. At this moment, Enkidu, Gilgamesh's retainer, steps in and reminds his lord that all pity laid aside, Humbaba is still an enemy and that it might not be advisable to release him. Humbaba seems now to have entirely taken over the role of a high-ranking Sumerian personage: speaking to Enkidu in a haughty and offhand manner, he turns down his words as coming from someone who, short of disposing of independent means of subsistence, must earn his daily bread as a hireling, very near to a slave. This so enrages Enkidu that he kills the poor Humbaba, cutting off his head.

A curious turn in the story takes now the two heroes – Gilgamesh and Enkidu, carrying Humbaba's head with them in a bag – to Nippur, where they address the chief god Enlil, telling him the whole story. The Cedar Forest and Gilgamesh's entourage all vanish from the text, which brings out their distinctly minor importance in the plot. Gilgamesh and Enkidu bring a testimony of their deed, laying Humbaba's head before Enlil. The disconcerted Enlil rebukes both heroes for their deed, telling them that they have killed their equal and peer, someone who should have sat with them, eaten bread and drunk water with them as their companion.

And now, as I believe, comes the answer to the question Gilgamesh has asked when he recovered from the shock of the first meeting with Humbaba.

What does Enlil in fact say is this: "You, Gilgamesh, have killed someone who was equal to you. God or no god, man or no man, your life will one day end, much as Humbaba's has already ended. **You are most definitely not an immortal god**".

This pragmatic and realistic conclusion has been masterfully elaborated upon some six hundred years later by Sin-leqe-uninni, author of the Standard Version of the Gilgamesh epic, who recast Gilgamesh's hard-won knowledge as a universal human problem of the fear of death. Nevertheless, Enlil's answer must be seen as a very relevant dictum in the debate about the nature of the new ruling-class members of the incipient Early Dynastic period. The Uruk-Kish tradition does, in fact, rest on the assumption that however mighty and powerful the new prominent personages might be, they are certainly not of divine origin and their power is thus of a different kind than that of the Late Uruk EN and NIN. In "Gilgamesh and the Land of the Living", Gilgamesh is credited with the *en* title. Nevertheless, we have shown how this is a mere empty shell of an ancient denomination, which must now be filled in by new contents. The whole story does nonetheless bring out the moral that if the newcomers to power and glory wish to "make a name", they have to admit the fact that they are not of divine origin. All they can hope for is that their exploits and feats will win divine approval, and that tehy will be remebered by their communities.

This attitude, rather close to some of the heroic epics of early medieval Europe (Beowulf, Nibelungenlied), did apparently result in the emergence of a distinctly aristocratic culture of cultivated courtly centres, in which the gentlemen indulged in such noble pursuits as hunting or war, while the ladies graced by their presence the sumptuous banquets and courtly entertainments of music, dance and heroic poetry. Indeed, in this manner might the Sumerian "Heroic Age" have been born. In later times, the paragon of such culture would undoubtedly be the royal court of Agade, the capital of the Akkadian empire.

The Ur tradition: *rex divus, rex divitiarum*

The LUGAL of Ur in written documents

In the texts of archaic Ur, commonly dated into ED I, that is, roughly to the 29th–28th centuries B. C., the LUGAL assume a position representing a visible social advance as against the Jemdet Nasr times (Charvát 1997,

184

77–78). Reigning over their own "economic sector" (ibid., 78), the LUGAL of the archaic city of Ur had established their power on foundations beyond the grasp of human sensory organs. The focus of their competence sphere rested in their ability to secure abundance and bounty to their community (Charvát 1997, 79). The very exercise of the LUGAL office, putting their persons at the head of most of the establishments of the city of Ur, represented in itself an asset of community life. Quite in the Homeric manner, **welfare and plenty** flowing from the LUGAL to their subjects were perceived as a function of their personal virtues and praiseworthy qualities, including the prowess in military matters (Charvát 1997, 79). This Ur argument established a tradition that remained with the world of mesopotamian ideas right down to the Neo-Assyrian period of the seventh pre-Christian century (Assurbanipal: Weippert 2002, 30). The Sumerian city of Ur is thus one of the very first examples of the sovereignty system in which

the metaphor of the sacred marriage of king and goddess, and the notion of the king's righteousness that made the world fruitful, were elaborately articulated in the vernacular literature [of medieval Ireland, P. Ch.] *and skilfully integrated with Christian concepts of kingship by a learned clergy* (Ó Corráin 1995, 46).

Blood kinship with the LUGAL of archaic Ur – or its socially approved artificial emulation, e. g. by adoption – carried such an amount of prestige that it conferred names (or, altenatieveIy, elevated social status) on people (Charvát 1997, 78). In view of the results of my investigations which I shall proceed to present, the fact that the essence of the LUGAL function is identical to the lion-headed eagle Anzu is interesting (Charvát 1997, 80 note 894, text UET II: 128, personal name Lugal-anzu). The charge of Anzu, an emblem of one of the early weather gods (Ninurta? Ningirsu? cf. Wiggermann 1992, 152, 156–157, 159–162; id. 1996, 219 note 144) implies, without all doubt, a rather eloquent parallel with activities of the early LUGAL, perhaps also perceived as the enlivening power of rain bringing fertility to the land. Statues or emblems of the LUGAL did exist (Charvát 1997, 80).

It is a question how far the association of the archaic Ur LUGAL with the NIN, a title associated with a series of divinities in one of the Ur texts of the period, might have been instrumental in this spectacular ascent of the LUGAL (Charvát 1997, 86 note 946). The NIN might have transmitted the sanctity of their office, heavily charged with divinity (cf. the *nin Enmebaragesi* of "Gilgamesh and the Land of the Living"), upon the LUGAL as their partners. This seems to be indicated by the theophorous NIN names of archaic Ur (Charvát 1997, 86–87).

The archaic Ur seal imagery

The source base for assessment of developments within early Mesopotamian statehood owes much of its abundance and quality to the archaeological investigations conducted at Ur in a masterly fashion by Leonard Woolley (later Sir Leonard Woolley) in the years 1922–1934.

The cemetery excavations, which gained Woolley his fame through the discovery of the "royal tombs", also entailed exploration of the strata of mostly settlement rubbish, dumped at various points of history both underneath the grave layers and over them. In between the "Royal cemetery" and burials of Sargonid age belong the Seal Impression Strata (SIS) 1 and 2, numbered from top to bottom; stratum SIS 3 was probably no more than a segment of SIS 2. Below the "Royal cemetery" stretched successive superimposed layers designed as SIS 4 to 8, generally assumed to date into Early Dynastic I, say, into the 29th–28th pre-Christian centuries (L. Woolley, in Legrain 1936, pp. vii-viii; Charvát 2002, 171; cf. also Reade 2001, 15–29). On the seal impressions from these strata I shall now focus, attempting to tie them into the overall sequence of iconic sources for the emergence of early Mesopotamian statehood.

It is apparent at first sight that the seal-impression imagery of archaic Ur does differ to a significant degree from that of the Late Uruk – Jemdet Nasr times. The two most numerous categories make up more than the entire half of all the surviving seal impressions: "other motifs" (36.41%) and *oecumene* scenes (24.46%) (cf. the tabulation below).

The preponderance of the "other" category

is, of course, caused by the great number of impressions of the "city-league seal" (on this cf. Charvát 1997, *passim*, esp. the register on p. 98, and Matthews 1993, 34–38). Yet, even this is a significant fact: while there had been no need for any tokens of coherence of the Uruk corporate polity, the unity of which obviously showed no cracks, things were different by the start of the Early Dynastic period. The circuit of goods exchanged as tokens of alliance had to manifest the ties between member communities of a confederation, declaring itself by this means an heir to the past glory of Late Uruk times. It may be of importance that in one instance, the entity referred to by a "city-league seal" is personified by a human face on the seal butt (Legrain 1936 No. 426).

The assessment of rosette patterns appearing on impressions of archaic Ur seals (on the Late Uruk – Jemdet Nasr rosette as symbol of the divine aspect of the plant world cf. Rova 1994, 95) is hampered by the fact that all designs, in which this distinctive element occurs, have been listed under this heading regardless of whether they do figure in other image categories or not. The overall number of examples is thus exaggerated and artificial, but it does show both the frequency of the motif and its associations very well. The rosette frequently figures in animal compositions in which whole creatures or only their heads (Legrain 1936 No. 277) may be seen. Particularly popular settings feature scorpions (Legrain 1936 Nos. 260, 269, 272, 273 and 382), and lizards, frogs and snakes may also be present (Legrain 1936 Nos. 281, 283). An archaic seal in the shape of a bull displays scorpions in the sealing surface, which is likely to give additional support to the association of the scorpion image with fertility (Legrain 1936, Pl. I No. 12bis). Vegetation-pattern seals also included rosette designs (Legrain 1936, 278). It marks as emblem icons in which human beings both protect animals (Legrain 1936 Nos 241, 253, 254, 256 and 257) and hunt them (Legrain 1936 Nos. 306, 380?). Something in between the two may be indicated by situations in which rosettes denote animal husbandry- (Legrain 1936 Nos. 315, 317) and dairy scenes (Legrain 1936 Nos. 346, 351). The great, and nearly universal role, played by rosette patterns in objects from the Ur "royal cemetery" seems to be heralded by the occurrence of the motif on seals of archaic Ur. In the latter, they feature in war scenes in which the enemy bodies may sometimes be neatly arranged into ellegant swastika patterns (Legrain 1936 Nos. 286, 393?). Other categories of icons labelled by rosettes include banquet scenes (Legrain 1936 No.382) and, most significantly, an erotic composition, by which a generally positive connotation of the rosette, evoking doubtlessly the sphere of fertility and procreation force, may be visualized (Legrain 1936 No. 368). Indeed, a rosette accompanies a depiction of a file of humans bringing offerings (Legrain 1936 No. 378) in what appears to be a nearly "official-emblem" position. The same kind of connotation may be meant by the display of rosettes on "city-league seals" (Legrain 1936 Nos. 404, 417, 424, 427, 439, 445, 446, 447, 449, 456, 459, 464, 465 and probably also 469). All this provides an interesting parallel to the much earlier rosette patterns displayed by the exquisite Halaf-culture pottery creations in central positions.

The geometrical compositions, greatly fashionable after c. 3000 B.C., have unfortunately so far eluded any attempt at decoding the messages which may be hidden behind the complexities of their patterning (Pittman 1994b).

In the case of the swastika patterns, an aim at the symbolism of the four corners of the world (Wiggermann 1996) is likely to hit the target. A problem is nonetheless constituted by the identification of the particular social body to which this image refers. Combinations with birds pecking at animal heads (Legrain 1936 No. 274), or that of a skirted warrior fighting a swastika of nude men (Legrain 1936 No. 286) may point to powers inimical to Ur. The same impression may be conveyed by swastika patterns composed jointly of humans and bulls (Legrain 1936 Nos. 394, 398 and 399). On the other hand, swastika patterns do figure on "city-league seals", where a social configuration friendly to Ur is likely to be alluded to (Legrain 1936 Nos. 412, 454, 461, 464 and 465).

The *oecumene* images

The most numerous category of images illustrating life in the humanized world is that of the dairy scenes (6.70%). Showing a particular kind of human occupation, they offer interesting hints, alluding possibly to the activities of the divine shepherd Dumuzi, to acquire great significance in the future, as we shall presently see. For the time being, let us notice the labelling of some of such activities with the spread-eagle emblem (Legrain 1936 Nos. 349, 350, 360 and 361).

One of the more frequently occurring image categories is represented by the combination of the spread-eagle icon, animals and humans, outlining certain ideas which percolated through the society of archaic Ur (4.53%). The spread eagle denotes both scenes in which humans defend animals (Legrain 1936 Nos. 242, 243, 244, 246) and those in which animals are hunted as game (Legrain 1936 Nos. 288, 296?, 305, 306, 312 and 322). Our combination links with the world of fertility symbolism by means of association with bulls and scorpions (Legrain 1936 No. 324). The same message may be intended in scenes where the spread eagle turns up in dairy scenes, sometimes as an emblem on shepherds' huts (Legrain 1936 Nos. 349, 350, 360, 361). Some banquet scenes do nonetheless include humans with the spread-eagle emblem but without animals (Legrain 1936 No. 373). Sometimes the likeness of the mighty bird takes on a form of a religious symbol to which offerings are brought (Legrain 1936 Nos. 323 and 387), but in one case a dancing performance may rather be implied (Legrain 1936 No. 327, on fertility implications of dancing cf. Kilmer 1995, 2610–2611). Rather significantly, the spread-eagle icon denotes "city-league seals" (Legrain 1936 Nos. 415, 416, 417, 420 and 421). The relevant scene combinations, showing the spread-

-eagle image as a fitting emblem of sovereignty over both the humanized and the natural world, lend thus an eloquent bacground information for the archaic-Ur personal name Lugal-anzu (cf. supra).

At archaic Ur , a considerable number of depictions of humans belonged to shepherds (Legrain 1936 Nos. 308, 309, 310, 312, 313, 314, 315, 316, 317, 318, 319, 320, 321 and possibly 380). Some of them might have nonetheless been occupied at other pursuits: orchardry work (Legrain 1936 No. 264), bringing of fish (Legrain 1936 Nos. 302 and 303) and handling jars (Legrain 1936 No. 330). They exercise their tasks under the emblems of a rosette (Legrain 1936 Nos. 315, 380) and a spread eagle (Legrain 1936 No. 312).

The category of humans defending animals features such nature lovers under the ensigns of spread eagle (Legrain 1936 Nos. 242, 243, 244 and 246) and rosette (Legrain 1936 Nos. 241, 253, 254, 256 and 257).

The human figures may sometimes be arranged in a way suggesting files of dancing figures (Legrain 1936, Nos. 328?, 329, 374, 375 and 376). The fact that one of these depictions shows a scorpion on butt (ibid. No. 376) may imply that a file of young dancers, evoking fertility capacities of the earth, may be meant (Kilmer 1995, 2610–2611).

The scorpion image probably conferred procreation force on both humans and animals.Thus their depictions accompanied animal icons (such as an ibex: Legrain 1936 No. 263), but especially various settings within human society. Some of these display coherent scenes: a dairy group (Legrain 1936 No. 348) is followed by a banquet- (Legrain 1936 No. 382) and dance compositions (Legrain 1936 No. 376). The sense of the general idea conveyed by the scorpion images is borne out by their presence in erotic scenes (Legrain 1936 Nos. 366 and 368).

Among others, groups of jars, symbolizing probably storage of some product of human toil, are present. Some of such jars may consitute cargoes of boats (Legrain 1936 No. 301), the depictions of which now seem to have acquired a profane character. A jar is also present in a scene combining a human and animals (Legrain 1936 No. 325, one animal only), a category represented by no more than 0.72% of the archaic Ur icons, i e. much less than in Late Uruk – Jemdet Nasr.

The *anoecumene* images

Wild animals, once so popular in the Late Uruk – Jemdet Nasr seals, do still constitute a numerous category of archaic Ur icons (4.53%). These come in either complete or represented by their heads only (Legrain 1936 Nos. 275, 276 and 277). In addition to quadruped depictions, frogs (Legrain 1936 Nos. 282 and 283, the latter with snakes and a rosette), snakes (Legrain 1936 Nos. 283 and 284) and what may be an insect (Legrain 1936 No. 290, two bears and a bee?) complete the picture.

Attacks by beasts of prey on other animals feature rather frequently at archaic Ur (3.44%); the relevant scenes include a monstrous giant snake devouring perhaps a kid or lamb (Legrain 1936 No. 285). In two cases such scenes may stand for warlike events in human society. The vultures pecking at animals heads may symbolize a fateful end of a social body denoted by the accompanying swastika (Legrain 1936 No. 274). The latter, composed of human bodies, may be depicted in conflict with skirted warriors. The author of a seal, displaying a parallel between a warrior defeating an enemy and a lion attacking an ibex (and, strangely enough, including a rosette design), rounded up the message by carving an image of a wild boar on the butt of the relevant seal (Legrain 1936 No. 297). Was the bearer of the seal notorious for his assertive character and warrior qualities?

Some of such designs bear out our suspicion, voiced as early as the Late Uruk – Jemdet Nasr times, that they do but stand as symbols for other entities, some of which may be situated beyond the sphere of sensory perception. This is the case of the animals files denoted by the icon of the spread eagle, making up a fairly numerous category of *anoecumene* motifs (4.53%). Accompanied by pictures of jars (Legrain 1936, Nos. 211, 331), lizard (ibid. No. 212), scorpions (ibid. Nos. 214, 272, 273 and 280), lions attacking bulls or antelopes (ibid. Nos. 215, 216 and 217) and rosettes (ibid. Nos. 272 and 273), it tallies very well both with the idea of a symbol of a supernatural donor of fertility and procreation force, suggesting also a clue for the linking of such faculties with the LUGAL (the above cited name Lugal-anzu). In Late Uruk and Jemdet Nasr times, the association of the scorpion image with animals and people and especially with females implies fertility symbolism (Rova 1994, p. 84). The same may go for the rosette which had once embodied a divine aspect of the plant world (Rova 1994, p. 95, Nos. 172, 175).

The hunting scenes do represent a rather numerous category of images of archaic Ur. The ecological niches in which the "hunters of the east" got their game show a remarkable degree of variation. Hunting expeditions roamed through highland areas from which ibex and (wild?) goats were brought (Legrain 1936 Nos. 287, 291, 294, 295 and 296). Trophies of the Ur chiefs did also come from woodland areas supplying various other quadrupeds

(Legrain 1936 Nos. 304, 305 and 306), including bear (Legrain 1936 No. 289). Open woodland-steppe areas offered to the daredevils a chance to hunt lions (Legrain 1936 No. 293) and grassy plains gave access to antelopes and gazelles (Legrain 1936 Nos. 288 and 322). The mythical implications of such scenes may be read off images like that of a fight with big lizards (Legrain 1936 No. 281), as well as off complementary emblems such as a rosette (Legrain 1936 No. 281), the spread eagle (Legrain 1936 Nos. 288, 296, 306) or the chequerboard-cum-"hourglass" (Legrain 1936 No. 291).

The combination of animals with pots, likely to hark back to Late Uruk – Jemdet Nasr times, may activate the fertility inherent in animals as human resources. In many instances such animals of the steppe as antelopes (Legrain 1936 Nos. 190, 192 and 198), which may be attacked by lions (Legrain 1936 No. 238), pose in icons of this kind. Fertility symbolism in likely to be alluded to by depictions of the spread eagle (Legrain 1936 Nos. 211, 223, 280 and 331), scorpions (Legrain 1936 No. 280) and rosettes (Legrain 1936 No. 317). Among the human actors of such compositions we find an armed warrior (Legrain 1936 No. 251) and a shepherd (Legrain 1936 No. 317).

The scorpion icon, referring presumably to the sphere of fertility, associates both with beasts of prey attacking (Legrain 1936 No. 261) and with a depiction of a nude human figure (Legrain 1936 No. 263). More frequently, however, it links up with the spread-eagle image (Legrain 1936 Nos. 272, 273 and 280) and with rosettes (Legrain 1936 Nos. 272, 273). A different meaning may be hinted at by the occurrence of a scorpion in an animal-banquet scene together with a wild-boar image and with depiction of a dagger on the seal butt (Legrain 1936 No. 384). Is a personal inclination towards aggresivity implied in the bearer of the seal here?

Icons involving fish (Legrain 1936 Nos. 44, 169, 237, 300 and 301 = 0.91%) do all point to them in settings where they seem to play their natural role of denizens of the watery kingdoms. In one single instance (Legrain 1936 No. 169) they associate with a worship scene and the "hourglass" symbol. It may thus legitimately be asked whether they also do not allude to the sphere of fertility symbolism.

Images of war

In actual fact, war conflicts may be hinted at by the numerous human- and animal-contest scenes. This is implied by the imagery of a seal in which the image of a defeat of a human enemy finds a parallel in the depiction of the victory of a lion over an ibex (Legrain 1936 No. 297). A likeness of a skirted hero fighting a swastika of nude, and thus socially inferior humans (Legrain 1936 No. 286) joins a design of a war chariot accompanied by mythical animals (Legrain 1936 No. 298) in suggesting mythological implications of war images in the archaic Ur society. This again brings out the truly spiritual character of the office of the LUGAL, in whom the personal names of the epoch praise their military-leader qualities.

The ritual scenes

Already on the decline in Late Uruk – Jemdet Nasr times, such designs constitute a category not overabundant (6.88%), but do display some interesting features. With the 29th–28th century material, we may be getting a closer hold on the "hourglass" image (2.17%). It accompanies icons such as a gardener and a shepherd (Legrain 1936 No. 167), animal file (ibid. No. 168), a banquet entertainment with music (No. 169), and hunting scenes (ibid. No. 291). Let us focus a particular attention on a depiction combining a square panel of nine fields filled in by "hourglass" motifs, lumped together with images of a bull, a lion, rampant goats, a hilly landscape, a "star-flower", a scimitar and a pentagram (ibid. No. 239). The significance of such symbols is explained, in a highly illuminating fashion, by an erotic scene ornated with symbols of a rosette, a scorpion and a disc divided, in a chequerboard manner, into seven fields. In these, we may eventually surmise the "hourglass" fillings, but they can as well stand independently for the chequerboard motif (ibid. No. 368). The disc of seven squares, representing unquestionably a simplified form of chequerboard and "illuminating" a scene in which a man and a woman embrace to produce offspring, refers in an unveiled manner to fertility- and procreative-force symbolism. This, however, contributes a most welcome hint at the interpretation of chequerboard patterns, perhaps as early as the Halaf-culture times (cf. supra).

In the archaic Ur imagery, erotic scenes constitute a subject of prime importance, as they allude directly to activities triggering off fertility- and procreation forces. Let us notice that these icons show a measure of cultural vulgarization as against Late Uruk – Jemdet Nasr times. For the ancestors of the seal-bearers of archaic Ur, hints and implications such as the image of the impenetrably robed lady, plaiting the tassels of a "temple" gonfanon in the company of nude men walking in a garden and bearing cups, sufficed entirely (Rova 1994, pp. 72 and 327, No. 768 Tav. 46). In the 29th–28th centuries, however, erotic scenes do point to the significance of a host of emblems, sometimes of respectable antiquity, the meanings of which thus receive a clearcut illumination. Such ensigns do include images of the scorpion (Legrain 1936 Nos. 366 and 368), rosette (Legrain 1936 Nos. 368 and 385) and the highly significant seven-compartment disc, representing a variant of the chequerboard motif (Legrain 1936 No. 368). One of the two other reference points is represented by the depiction of musicians (Legrain 1936 No. 369), alluding perhaps to the old cultic obligations of the NIN arch-priestess as (erotic) partner of the EN arch-priest (Charvát 1997, 85). The other features a man holding two hares (Legrain 1936 No. 370). The mythical connotation of such scenes is borne out by a depiction of an embracing couple, accompanied by what apparently represents a worship scene involving an URI_3 symbol with a rosette (Legrain 1936 No. 385).

We have already seen that banquet scenes may constitute a case of the fertility-sphere symbolism. An eloquent proof thereoff is offered by the presence of musicians, frequently called on to enliven banquet settings (Legrain 1936 Nos. 371, 372 and 373), accompanying once an erotic scene (Legrain 1936 No. 369). The same target area seems to be implied by the presence of such emblems as the spread eagle (Legrain 1936 No. 373) and scorpion-cum-rosette (Legrain 1936 No. 382). Even an animal-banquet scene has received a supplement in the form of a scorpion (Legrain 1936 No. 384).

Scenes of bringing offerings, once so popular, have strongly declined in popularity on archaic Ur seals. Their cultic settings are in some instances denoted by symbols like a rosette (Legrain 1936 No. 378) or a spread eagle (Legrain 1936 No. 387). A curious scene which may fall under this heading includes a nude human figure tearing at his or her hair (Legrain 1936 No. 388). It may thus usher in a mourning ceremony and depict a rare case of a funerary scene.

Four instances (Legrain 1936, Nos. 389, 390, 391 and 392) may display facades of shrines or other buildings of this kind.

Surprisingly, the Ur icons also feature our old friend, the spread-legged female, this time cultivating the company of scorpions (Legrain 1936 Nos. 42, 258?, 268, 269 and 270 = 0.91%). Having fallen out of the ensign role which she might have assumed in Late Uruk – Jemdet Nasr times, she may still stand for a fitting symbol of fertility and procreation force.

In a summary fashion, let us now review the results in tabellary form.

The *anoecumene* – SIS 8–4

Wild animals	25	4.53%
Spread eagle with animals	24	4.35%
Beasts of prey attacking	19	3.44%
Hunting scenes	14	2.54%
Animals and pots	11	1.99%
Animals with scorpions	10	1.81%
Fish	5	0.91%
Anoecumene total	**108**	**19.57%**

The *oecumene* – SIS 8–4

Dairy scenes	37	6.70%
Spread eagle, animals and humans	25	4.53%
Humans at work	18	3.26%
Humans defending animals	16	2.90%
Human figures	12	2.17%
Humans and scorpions	9	1.63%
Groups of jars	6	1.09%
Humans and animals	4	0.72%
Shrines	4	0.72%
Humans and (or in) boats	4	0.72%
Oecumene total	**135**	**24.46%**

War among humans – SIS 8–4

	3	**0.54%**

Ritual scenes – SIS 8–4

"Hourglass"	12	2.17%
Erotic scenes	8	1.45%
Banquet scenes	8	1.45%
Bringing offerings	5	0.91%
Spread-legged female with scorpions	5	0.91%
Ritual total	**38**	**6.88%**

"City league" seals including		
the EDINU sign	77	13.95%
Rosette in various combinations	58	10.51%
Geometrical compositions	53	9.62%
Swastika patterns	13	2.35%
Other motifs total	**201**	**36.41%**

The archaic Ur seal imagery 2:
Icons from strata contemporary with, or overlying, the "Royal cemetery" (SIS 3–1)

The unusually productive find contexts of the Early Danstic city of Ur enable, together with the meticulous methods of the sites's excavation, an assessment of developments in seal iconography which took place during the later segment of the Early Dynastic epoch (ED II–III). The finds from the SIS 3–1 strata come from layers superimposed over the then defunct "Royal cemetery" (Leonard Woolley's Introductory note in Legrain 1936, vii-viii). A rare chance to analyze these later sealings as source material for our case, and to see whether, and in what extent and measure, transformations which took place within the archaic Ur society may be reflected in them, lies thus ahead of us.

Though the overall number of finds is much lower than that of the earlier SIS 8–4 contexts, the categories in which these images fall do show up evidence for a change. In this time, most of the seal impressions fall into the *oecumene* range (33 items = 5.98%). These are followed by the *anoecumene* icons (15 cases = 2.72%), ritual scenes (8 instances = 1.45%) and other motifs (6 examples = 1.09%).

Of the most frequent category among the later Ur seals, the *oecumene* images, the human-cum-animal contest scenes do show a degree of difference from the earlier state of affairs. Cases like a fight between a hero and a swastika composed of human beings do, of course, boast a respectable ancestry in the earlier Ur evidence, evoking possibly the military supremacy of the Ur post-"Royal-cemetery" commanders (Legrain 1936 No. 518). A conclusion if this kind seems to be buttressed by the fact that the seal in questions belonged to Mesanepada, king of Kish and husband of the Lofty One (lugal kiši dam nu-gig$_6$), and another one of this kind to the lady Ninbanda, a NIN (Legrain 1936 No. 516). On the other hand, such scenes frequently display supplementary emblems which had earlier presumably referred to the sphere of fertility and procreation force. Here belong such items as the scorpion (Legrain 1936 Nos. 513, 514, 515 and 517), monkey(?) musicians (Legrain 1936 Nos. 503 and 504), a lizard (Legrain 1936 Nos. 510 and 513) much as a snake (Legrain 1936 Nos. 513 and 514), as well as the spread eagle icon (Legrain 1936 No. 517). It may thus be legitimately asked whether the meaning of such icons has not changed since the SIS 8–4 times and whether they now do not stand for mere emblems of the "civilized" Ur world. In fact, there is a fair chance that contest seals, associating with containers, tools and weapons, and with copper items, denote male (or classificatory-male) burials (Rathje 1977, esp. pp. 28–29, and Charvát 2002, 172 and 207).

The one single occurrence of a dairy scene, a theme rather popular even in the archaic Ur (Legrain 1936 No. 484), is surprising, as it represents a sharp fall from its earlier popularity. This fact enhances our suspicion that the archaic dairy scenes had carried a symbolic meaning which, in SIS 3–1 times, was taken over by other iconic compositions. Now, the human-cum-animal contest scenes may be strongly suspected to take over the charge of a sovereignty emblem, with which, in earlier times, the dairy scenes, alluding perhaps to the Dumuzi-related activity sphere, might have been endowed.

An interesting development may be perceived in the sphere of boat scenes, which, with 6 items (1.09%), displays a certain rise in popularity as against the archaic Ur period. A strong connection links such scenes with those of the banquet, as they frequently feature persons seated aboard and drinking either from jars by means of long tubes (Legrain 1936 Nos. 522?, 523, 534) or from cups (Legrain 1936 No. 521). In two instances, however, boats associate with personages wearing horned caps of divinity. Once such a personage takes a boat ride himself or herself (Legrain 1936 No. 492). In the other instance, a seated bald-headed human, putting hand before mouth and seated in a boat, approaches a gigantic figure wearing a horned cap and lifting a hand (Legrain 1936 No. 531). In these instances it may well be asked whether a particular cultic setting, such as, for instance, a *ki-a-nag* ancestor-worship shrine, or some other kind of an open-air cultic installation, is not alluded to (Reiter 1991).

The following observations on the anoecumene icons may be put forward:

The animal-contest scenes fall in with the general characteristics of the human-cum-animal icons of this type (7 instances = 1.27%).

Landscapes overgrown with woods, sheltering sometimes wild animals, constitute another category of such images (4 items = 0.72%). They may again simply stand for what they are – depictions of natural settings free of human interference.

We would indeed be hard put to judge how far the spread-eagle symbol, present in three instances (0.54%), actually belongs to the *anoecumene* sphere. Nevertheless, its repeated association with a pair of horned quadrupeds strongly alludes to a symbolism related to the copper bas-relief ornating the entrance to the Ninhursag temple built by Aanepada at al-Ubaid. An association of the spread-eagle icon with a scorpion image points in the same general direction, though it denotes a human-cum-animal contest scene (Legrain 1936 No. 517).

The scorpion icon invariably accompanies human-cum-animal or animal-contest scenes (7 instances = 1.27%). In one instance, a human-cum-animal contest carries, in addition to the scorpion- and spread-eagle icons, an inscription identifying the bearer as LÚ.BA or LÚ.IGI (Legrain 1936 No. 517).

Ritual settings:

Traditional banquet scenes on seals, which may now denote persons employed in internal court service, frequently wearing a splendid attire and handling a variety of precious materials, possibly ladies of rank (Rathje 1977, 28–30), are present in four instances (0.72%).

Images of worship now include icons clearly heralding the "presentation scenes" of the later periods (4 items = 0.72%). The seated divinities are offered libations, either from spouted jars (Legrain 1936 No. 533) or from cups (Legrain 1936 Nos. 534, 535). One of such sealings was found in a much later, Larsa-period context, and its chronological relevance thus stands open to doubt (Legrain 1936 No. 536).

The "other" category includes, as its most numerous sample, geometrical compositions, on which silence is the only conclusion that we may hazard (5 items = 0.91%).

One single instance of a swastika motif again represents a considerable departure from the earlier state of things (= 0.18%; Legrain 1936 No. 518).However, figuring on the seal of Mesanepada, thus motif clearly carries a high measure of prestige.

Trying to conclude from these scanty data, we cannot escape the conclusion that a significant narrowing of the thematic sphere of the later Ur icons takes place. The *répertoire* of seal imagery contemporary with the Mesanepada dynasty seems to be limited to patterns carrying the highest-prestige connotations. This goes either for the sacred themes (boats, banquet, worship, spread eagle) of for the profane activity spheres (human-cum-animal contest, animal contest).

Seal impressions from strata contemporary with, or overlying, the "Royal Cemetery" (SIS 3–1)

The *anoecumene* – SIS 3–1

Animal contest	7	1.27%
Landscapes	4	0.72%
Spread eagle	3	0.54%
Scorpion, spread eagle and inscription	1	0.18%
Anoecumene total	**15**	**2.72%**

The *oecumene* – SIS 3–1

Human and animal contest	26	4.71%
Dairy scenes	1	0.18%
Boat scenes	6	1.09%
Oecumene total	**33**	**5.98%**

Ritual – SIS 3–1

Banquet scenes	4	0.72%
Worship scenes	4	0.72%
Ritual total	**8**	**1.45%**

Other motifs – SIS 3–1

Geometrical compositions	5	0.91%
Human and animal contest with human swastika	1	0.18%
Other motifs total	**6**	**1.09%**

The archaic Ur seal imagery 3: Surviving cylinder seals of Early Dynastic Ur

The iconography of actual cylinder seals, preserved throughout the various find contexts datable into the pre-Akkadian time period, strongly warns against chronological conclusions based solely on analyses of existing cylinder seals.

The most numerous category – that of geometrical compositions – looms large in SIS 8–4 but falls to the average values in SIS 3–1. As to wild animals, parading so frequently on actual cylinders, in seal impressions they make up a major component of the entire range of *anoecumene* icons in SIS 8–4; however, in SIS 3–1 they vanish altogether. Depictions of animals of the steppe, as well as two "Royal-cemetery" instances in which such motifs combine with banquet scenes (Legrain 1951 Nos. 120 and 122), may point to symbolism pertaining to female deities of open landscapes (Ninhursag?). The same may go for the spread-eagle icons, also linking montane landscapes, animals of the steppe and banquet seals, though one single animal-contest instance (Legrain 1951 No. 154) may provide a link to the male world. Similar ideas may also be alluded to by fish- and scorpion images.

Hunting scenes again involve animals of the steppe and also, surprisingly, boat- (Legrain 1951 No. 88) and banquet themes (Legrain 1951 No. 123). Is the competence sphere of Ninhursag again referred to? Possibly, as the perhaps gender-related banquet scenes imply (Rathje 1977). These last ones combine steppe-animal depictions with the spread-eagle emblem.

One of the boat-scene images turned up in a Late Jemdet Nast grave 113 (Legrain 1936 No. 88). This is a very peculiar treatment of the theme, showing animal occupants of a boat in the act of hunting other animals. Such a rendering, bearing out a fairly high level of abstraction, brings the iconography current in the city of Ur of the 30th century B. C. rather close to its illustrious predecessors, the foremost centres of the Late Uruk – Jemdet Nasr world such as Susa, in the art of which some animals may take over human roles (Lebrun 1985, Fig. 1 on p. 33).

Human- and animal-contest scenes may again be gender-related (Rathje 1977). The picture is rounded up by one single offering scene (Legrain 1951 No. 222).

All this indicates that (at least a part of the) surviving seals do tend to stem from epochs that are distinctly earlier than their deposition contexts, that is, from a time compatible with the earlier SIS strata at Ur. This observation attests to the longevity of such examples of the glyptic art, quite logical in the light of the compact nature of the seal cylinders, their decorative nature, especially in terms of seals made of more coloured stones, as well as their small size and lightness.

On the other hand, it must be pointed out that there exist iconographical patterns that are attested to predominantly, and chiefly, by surviving cylinder seals. A group of nine cylinders does display a rather remarkable composition, combining a large-scale zigzag line, arranged on the whole surface of the seal in question and going from one edge of the cylinder to the other, with images of spread eagles inserted in the triangular spaces delineated by the folds of the zigzag line (Legrain 1951 Nos. 53, 54, 58, 59, 60, 61, 62, 97 and 98). This composition does find but two counterparts in seal impressions, one in the SIS 8–4 strata (Legrain 1936 No. 222) and another one in SIS 3–1 (Legrain 1936 No. 555). In overall layout, however, this pattern may noticeably be paralleled by a motif borne by the painted pottery of Susa (de Mecquenem 1943, p. 6, Fig. 2 : 1). The diversity of materials used for manufacturing the seals decorated with this composition (lapis lazuli, shell, various kinds of steatite) does imply that it was carved into a variety of imported materials at Ur itself, and that ideational, rather than regional of professional (or better "status"), factors might have resulted in its application to seal-cutting.

Imagery of actual cylinder seals found at Ur

Geometrical compositions	21	3.00%
Wild animals	17	2.43%
Spread eagle	15	2.14%
Fish and similar	9	1.29%
Scorpions	5	0.71%
Hunting scenes	5	0.71%
Banquet scenes	4	0.57%
Boat scenes	3	0.43%
Human and animal contest	3	0.43%
Animal contest	3	0.43%
Tame animals	1	0.14%
Offering scenes	1	0.14%

The archaic Ur seal imagery: conclusions

There is a considerable difference between the images on Late Uruk – Jemdet Nasr age and those of the archaic Ur period in terms of their iconography. After c. 3000 B.C., the earlier preponderance of animal- and human files gave way to patterns carrying highly symbolical, reference-loaded messages. In the SIS 8–4 layers, these are represented, first and foremost, by the "city-league seals" with geometrical compositions, and by motifs like the rosette and swastika, with probably overtly mythical undertones. At the onset of the Early Dynastic age, emphasis clearly shifted to depictions of *oecumene* settings, may these have featured human-activity themes such as dairy scenes, humans at work or humans defending animals, or the clearly emblematic spread-eagle images. There are fairly good chances that such icons might have referred to even higher entities, as we shall presently see.

The symbolism inherent in seal images might have been carried even farther during the later time to which the SIS 3–1 images belong. This age was characterized by the predominance of a few symbolic devices (e. g. contest scenes), featured very frequently as emblems of high social standing of the seal-bearers rather than as conveyors of symbolic messages and myth-coded meanings. It may well be asked whether the absence of the "city-league seals" is to be understood as a sign of extinction of this now lifeless institution, or whether, by any chance, this phenomenon reflects the now unquestionable political supremacy of the Ur kingdom.

Actually preserved seals complicate the ensuing picture even farther. In addition to geometrical devices, they frequently display wild animals and the spread-eagle emblem, which does not quite fall in with any of the seal-impression classification schemes. Yet, they do tend to be closer to the earlier, SIS 8–4 images than to the later ones, attesting thus to the long circulation periods of cylinder seals, and thus also perhaps giving indirect historical evidence for the stability of the personages and (or) collectives they were attached to, and employed by, in society. Nevertheless, the Ur evidence points to the conclusion that though the surviving cylinder seals and seal impressions from one single site do not match, both these categories supply unique and irreplaceable kinds of information. The questions with which future students of the matter are confronted, are, then,

– how to interpret this evidence,
– what weight must be assigned to each of the find categories (seals vs. seal-impressions),
– and what kind of informations both find categories supply.

The Ur LUGAL and NIN cemetery:
Dumuzi and his entourage

In this section of the text I take the liberty of coming back to the "royal tombs" or Ur, a phenomenon quite beyond any ordinary kind of evidence and a major challenge to human imagination of the twentieth post-Christian century. I have dedicated a considerable part of my lately published text to an attempt at interpretation of their evidence (Charvát 2002, 224–229), and here I entreat my readers to be indulgent to me for taking up the matter again. This time, I hope, I shall succeed in presenting my views in a much more succinct, but more considerate and less blurred manner.

To make a long story short, here are the main points. We have already seen that the EN of Ur, being a female as the chief deity, Nannar, was male, had to provide the local NIN a partner with whom the NIN could perform the NA_2 ceremony. This launched into a trajectory of public visibility the LUGAL, and undoubtedly also triggered off the debate on the character of his office. How far a direct borrowing of the situation at Uruk, the EN of which, being a consort of Inanna, was identified with Dumuzi, could have taken place, must be investigated by future research (Weadock 1975, 102).

Judging from the archaic Ur seal imagery, the local LUGAL office, though integrated into a network of cooperating communities of more or less the same standing ("city-league seals"), hovered between the adoption of two devices as emblems of its status. One of these was the spread eagle, commending itself for the icon of Anzu, the well-known lion-headed bird of the later ages, and likely to be interpreted as a symbol of one of the atmospheric deities presiding over weather, wind, rain and storm and thus like unto their chief representative, Enlil. The other much frequented symbol, that of the dairy scene, coupled with images linking humans with animals or showing humans defending animals, is likely to refer to the activity sphere of the shpeherd Dumuzi, the dying and reviving god.

The Kish kings, as we already know, ultimately assumed the status of human beings. The Ur theoreticians of government saw the matter in a different light. Theirs was a question: Enlil or Dumuzi?

At one point within the incipient third Early Dynastic period, probably sometime in the 27th–26th pre-Christian centuries (Julian Reade will pardon me), a group of the foremost thinkers of Ur opted for the latter solution and elevated the local kings to the status of Dumuzi, the youthful deity and eternal lover of Inanna, the embodiment of femininity. Such a solution was neither permanent nor, in our eyes, very convincing. Nevertheless, it produced a deep impression both on Early Dynastic perception of statehood and on contemporary social practice.

The heart of the matter has been put forward, in a masterly simplification, by Frans Wiggermann whose words are worth quoting in full:

*The dead, however, have no choice in the matter; they must travel westwards through the desert and cross the Hubur to reach the kur, "mountainland", the other world. The same route is taken by Lamaštu and the witches…, **and once a year by Dumuzi who takes the dead with him…** . They travel by means of a chariot…, a donkey and a boat;… (relevant are also the ships found in tombs, especially those from the royal tombs of Ur…)* (Wiggermann 1996, 211–212, note 52 with ref., underlined by P. Ch.).

In the light of what has been said above, it seems quite logical to me that unlike the Kish kings, the LUGAL and NIN of Ur assumed the roles of (earthly incarnations of?) Dumuzi and Inanna. As such, they might have gone down to their graves accompanied by those who died in the same year. These last-named personages, or rather their kith and kin, might, in their turn, have demonstrated their loyalty to the then current ideology of "royal" power by having their deceased ones laid to rest together with those who were perceived as divine beings exercising their sovereign right to take their entourage wherever it pleased them, guarantors of a good and orderly voyage to the land of no return, and lawful visitors of the nether world. In short, those who passed away trusted their dead LUGAL and NIN to secure them a safe conduct to the empire of shadows.

Is anything of this order conceivable at all? How would the Sumerians have gotten hold of bodies of dead community members, once the LUGAL or NIN died? How would these have been handled, and how would it have been determined who will be solemnly dressed and lie down in glory, and who not?

Admittedly, such questions are difficult to answer but hints do exist. First and foremost, it may be helpful to return to the oft-quoted passage from the inscription of Gudea's Statue B in which the solemnities, surrounding the building of Ningirsu's temple, are described. One of the relevant passages expressedly says that "no hoe was used at the city cemetery, no bodies were buried" (col. V, lines 1–2: ki-mah-iri-ka al nu-ĝar, adda$_x$ ki nu-túm; Edzard 1997, 30–38, on p. 32 col. V : 1–2).

This highly important text conveys two capital information items: under normal conditions the dead could have been expected to be buried in excavated pits; but there could be a time when no dead body was buried.

In actual fact, the Lagash people would not have stopped dying, just because a sovereign deemed it dignified to have his pious feat graced by a denial of the laws of nature. This proves that ways and means to retain the corpses above ground, and presumably to bury them subsequently, did exist, and could have been resorted to when an occasion presented itself.

Most recently, true secondary interments, involving disposal of dead bodies from which the soft tissues had been removed and sometimes laid to rest in a state of partial decomposition, have now, for the very first time, been borne out in Sumer by archaeological excavations at the site of Larsa. The relevant evidence dates to the Jemdet Nasr age, and allows thus an assumption of the knowledge of such practices in the 27th–26th centuries B. C. (David 2003; Sellier 2003).

But this, in fact, is exactly what may be assumed in the cases of bodies accompanying our LUGAL and NIN of Ur into their graves. The simpler part of the task, identification of those who died after the respective LUGAL and (or) NIN, would entail keeping of the relevant corpses above ground for the deposition within a LUGAL- or NIN burial retinue, just as Gudea's panegyrist says. As for those who died in the same year, but prior to the demise of the illustrious personage in question, their post-mortal voyage might have involved some twists and turns. Exposure of the dead to the elements, for instance, could have been done for the purpose of removal of the soft tissues and reducing the body to the state of a skeleton which is much easier to handle. I need not remind here of the fates of many a great personage of the Middle Ages, who died abroad and was carried back home as a neat bundle of bones. The followers invariably resorted to the macabre custom of boiling the body in a cauldron and scraping off the soft parts.

Let us now see how far the proposition advanced above may be corroborated by facts established by archaeological excavations of the Ur "royal tombs". We are fortunate in being able to benefit from a thorough re-assessment of the Ur evidence, carried out prior to a major travelling exhibition of the Ur remains thanks to the initiative of the staff of the Museum of Archaeology and Anthropology, University of Pennsylvania (Zettler-Horne 1998).

Vegetal, and thus presumably fertility-related, symbolism percolates throughout all strata of the Ur "royal" jewellery, being especially prominent among the trappings of the most ostentatious graves such as that of PG 800 (Pu-abi). Witness, for instance, the magnificent Pu-abi's head-dress (Pittman 1998, 89–92), and even more so her "diadem", probably a collection of several exquisite jewellery items, comprising not only a series of four paired animal (long-haired sheep, cervids, bearded bulls, antelopes), but clearly displaying identifiable flower and a bunch of fruit of a date palm, alluding thus directly to the fertility- and procreation sphere (Pittman 1998, 92–94; Miller 1999).

The Ur interments have also yielded beads and pendants in the form of flies. Donald Hansen and Holly Pittman have noticed that the images of these ubiquitous insects may refer to the concepts of procreation and proliferation and thus to fertility. Fly icons associate with mother goddesses, as well as with the sphere of death, normally also falling into the competence spheres of female deities. Most importantly, however, such symbols also turn up in connection with the Inanna-Dumuzi texts, pointing thus in the very direction that I propose here (Hansen 1998, 47; Pittman 1998, 110–111).

The evidence that may shed light on practices linked with fertility symbolism may include the curious and hitherto unexplained shallow vessels of irregular rhomboid outlines with spouts protruding from one of the acute angles which their edges form. The fact that one of such vessels, made of sheet silver, was found lying across the body of Pu-abi in PG 800 may imply that such receptacles played a certain role in fertility rites, indeed, perhaps in symbolic fertilization- or fertility-triggering rituals. Such an explanation would be most interesting, as it could furnish us with a more concrete idea as to the manner in which the NA_2 ceremony could have been performed (Zettler 1998, 35; Weber-Zettler 1998, 137).

From all this it follows that the identification of the chief occupants of the "royal tombs" or Ur with personages likely to have been credited with achievements equal to those of Dumuzi and Inanna can be substantiated (cf. above, the Uruk reference: Weadock 1975, 102). Unlike the Kish court, of which the intellectuals ultimately settled on the assignment of human status to the Kish LUGAL, the Ur thinkers did not, at one moment of the city's long and eventful history, shirk from conferrring a quasi-divine status on the chief representatives of the Ur community. We do not know whether the LUGAL and NIN of Ur actually enjoyed the status of Dumuzi and Inanna, whether they could, in a time and space defined by a certain ritual procedure, perhaps have acted as receptacles of the divine substance, or whether they were perceived as mere earthlings whose act, emulating the upper-sphere divine proceedings, constituted a plea to the gods to shower down abundance and plenty.

Still, all this defines the role of the LUGAL and NIN of Ur in a rather peculiar manner. Calling them "kings" and "queens" goes apparently amiss their particular ritual, as well as social, roles. "Priests" or "clergy" are terms too specific to be used for persons whose activities are difficult to subsume under the notion of officiation of a particular divine cult. Should a definite designation be expected from me, I would opt for something like "providers", "purveyors", those thanks to whom abundance and plenty spring forth. Indeed, the semantics of the Ur titles of LUGAL and NIN do approach the Old English pair of social-role names out of which the denominations for "lord" and "lady" evolved, namely hláford and hláfdiga, meaning "bread-giver", "bread-provider".

Incidentally, the setting of this complex ideational scheme into motion required a substantial effort on behalf of the entire Ur society. The plentiful and well-excavated evidence for historical development of Early Dynastic Ur does show convincingly that the third Early Dynastic period, into which the Ur "royal tombs" belong, brought about not only an intensification of the Ur economy, but also a considerable re-alignment of the energy flows within her socio-economic structures.

I propose to adopt as a vector of explanation the relation between "contest seals", made predominantly of shell and designating persons which we may imagine as men-at-arms, and "banquet seals", most of which are made of lapis lazuli and which are highly likely to have constituted social markers of court ladies of rank (Rathje 1977, esp. pp. 26–27 and 29–31). The introduction of practical measures visualizing such a dichotomy, which may well reflect the male and female poles of social structuration, must have required the emergence of a provisioning system geared to the needs of such social classification.

In fact, the time of the Ur "royal tombs" must have seen a deep-reaching transformation, and expansion, of the entire long-distance trade network supplying the city with imported materials. This involved, first and foremost, the cessation of imports of some materials designating the earlier high-rank personages of Ur of the preceding ED I–II times, such as volcanic stones for the production of stone vessels (Moorey 1999, 44).

Within the "royal-tomb" period, some of the earlier economic links of Ur, reaching up the Euphrates and Tigris rivers, remained in function. This is especially visible in the case of supplies of woodland materials which might have still been coming in from the northwest down the Euphrates river, particularly from the Anatolian (and Levantine?) hills. Both images of northern animals borne by art creations of the south (a stag on a lyre from Ur: de Schauensee 1998, 22) and actual finds from the tombs of Ur point in this direction (ibid., 25 – the stag figure carved from box- and pistachio wood). A similar case may be argued for obsidian, likely to come from Eastern Anatolia but sometimes elaborately carved at Ur herself (an obsidian bowl copying a local metal shape: Moorey 1999, 45, 70). Also, the Ur centre may have been furnished by supplies delivered in Syrian jars (Reade 2001, 25–26).

On the other hand, the needs for luxurious and showy materials moved the entrepreneurs of Ur to breach new roads into faraway, foreign, wild and potentially dangerous landscapes (cf., in general, also Horne 1998). I have already noted the renewed presence of lapis lazuli, likely to have come from distant Baluchistan where the blue stone could have been mined only with great difficulty (Moorey 1999, 88–89). The same general direction is indicated by finds of fine limestone artifacts, likely to have been supplied by manufacturers of present-day eastern Iranian or Afghanistan (Moorey 1999, 45).

Not content with inroads into the rugged mountain ranges along the eastern frontier of Sumer, the Ur prospectors even braved the maritime expanses of the Persian Gulf and the seas beyond it. The fact that this is the first time when some utterly banal artifacts, such as harvesting sickles, start to be made of copper shows that this metal was in plentiful supply (Moorey 1999, 63). Whatever future investigations may find out, it still seems probable that specialists used Persian-Gulf ores to manufacture most of the Early Dynastic copper artifacts of Sumer (Moorey 1999, 248–249). In addition to this, cornelian beads with etched patterns, highly likely to have been delivered by Indian suppliers, show another innovation resulting from the burgeoning of the Ur enterprise machine, fuelled by the needs of a symbolic system proposed by the Lords temporal, but especially by the Lords spiritual, of Early Dynastic Ur (Moorey 1999, 171, cf. also Reade 2001, 26).

Of course, it might be legitimately asked what was the source of all this wealth which the "maiores" of Ur invested into ostentatious consumption of both material and immaterial goods. The answer is likely to be found in the political predominance of Ur, which at that time might have rendered herself master of a considerable part of Sumer. Taking into account the martial and military aspect visible in the male-oriented grave goods of the "royal tombs", as well as the fact that the Ur model of government was apparently the only one that was not only proposed but successfully put through by the sovereigns of Ur, we may safely assume that they commanded a vast territory, the economic surplus of which could have been converted into the paraphernalia needed for the paerformance of what might have been one of the first "theatre state" of history. The same conclusion is borne out by the titles boasted by the followers of the "lords of fabulous treasures" such as Mesanepada, who was "lugal kiši dam nu-gig$_6$," (cf. infra).

Let us also notice that the newly opened territories, the resources of which were by now tapped by the Ur entrepreneurs, do, in fact, perfectly fit into the description of "kur", the Other World, to which Dumuzi takes his host of the dead. The "kur" frontier was constituted by such rivers as Hubur in Syria, but also Ulaya in Elam (Wiggermann 1996, 212). The materials which ended up in the Ur "royal tombs" thus really came from the "kur", realms of Dumuzi. In fact, the LUGAL and NIN of Ur frequented "kur" even in their lifetimes, acting as Dumuzi and Inanna, and (their emissaries) returned from there laden with precious gains. The LUGAL and NIN could thus be trusted to know the way which they ultimately took with their ghastly retinues.

Let us notice the fact that this whole ideational setup could have been revived under the kings of the Third Dynasty of Ur, perhaps with an eye on enhancing the legitimity of their rule which, in fact, they had usurped. There does exist a text in which king Urnama is rewarded for his piety by birth of a son, of whom an *entu* priestess of Nannar is delivered at Nippur (Weadock 1975, 102). Šusin, Urnama's grandson, demonstrated an even stronger predilection for history by moving his residence from the Ehursag directly into the Gipar-ku, residence of the EN of Ur (Frayne 1997, 329–330, text Šusin E3/2.1.4.19). We may appreciate his particular but, in this place, most welcome modesty in dealing with matters divine: he dedicates one of his inscriptions to the goddess Annunitum, his consort (sic! dam-a-ni-ir), whose name is written without the divine determinative, unlike that of Šusin which is duly provided with it (Frayne 1997, 330–331, text Šusin E3/2.1.4. 20). This transfer of the Ur royal residence into the Gipar could have had permanent consequences, as the substantial rebuilding of the Ur sacred area by the Kassite king Kurigalzu I, seems to have bypassed its walls (Clayden 1996, esp. pp. 118–119).

It can thus be put forward that in seeking the answer to the question of the status and function of the LUGAL, whom the EN of Ur provided to her NIN for the performance of the NA$_2$ ceremony, the Ur "chosen ones" entrusted to their LUGAL and NIN the discharge of functions of the Sumerian deities Dumuzi and Inanna. The LUGAL and NIN thus rose to positions of unquestionable authority, assuming posts endowed with considerable spiritual, but also temporal power. The whole ideational scheme proved to be so persuasive that it infused into the armies of Ur enough martial spirit to subject to their command a considerable part of Sumer (and perhaps even Akkad?). All the territories subjected to the Ur supremacy then delivered their surplus products to the city of Nannar, where most of them paid the costs of public performances of social and cultic significance, and of articles of ostentatious consumption. In the quest for legitimation of their supreme power by means of public employment of exotic materials, obtained from lands that were so faraway that for most of the average public they were to all purposes identical with the "kur", outer edge of the world inhabited by gods, demons, dead people and wild beasts, the LUGAL and NIN of Ur now initiated a whole series of exploratory and prospecting voyages, which brought to their city products of distant lands as visible proofs of the quasi-divine status and powers of the initiators of such undertakings.

Postscript

The two categories of Early Dynastic lordship – the human one of Kish and the divine one of Ur – may be first seen in coalescence on the seal of Mesannepada of Ur who styles himself both "king of Kish" and "husband of the nu-gig$_6$", the nu-gig$_6$ standing for Inanna and the king assuming thus the role of Dumuzi (Legrain 1936 No. 518; cf. on this Zgoll 1997). Both traditions persisted in the South and in the North separately, merging only in the times of the Old Akkadian dynasty.

Sargon, Rimush and Manishtusu, faithful to the heritage of their ancestors, take up the "king of Kish" title. It is only under Naramsin that both traditions ultimately fuse together, having been expressed by the elevation of the sovereign to the divine status clearly demarked as such by a divine determinative preceding his name in the official inscriptions.

It thus also becomes clear why there are only three cities which continuously exercise kingship in the Early Dynastic times. Of all the Sumerian capitals, the sovereigns of which had wielded varying amounts of power, only the primeval Uruk and her subsequent followers, Ur and Kish, have proposed original solutions to the problem of exercise of profane power. The three models were evidently considered as binding and regulating state life in Early Dynastic Sumer. At that time, ancient administrators saw secular government as unequivocally defined by one of the models proposed by these three pristine capitals of the Land between two rivers, and bound to them. Take, for instance, the sovereign Lugalkinišedudu who exercised nam-en at Uruk and nam-lugal at Ur (Sollberger-Kupper 1971, 85, IE1c, IE1d). The administrative centre at Fara is likely to have been affiliated to the Kish kingdom, and, as it conferred the *énsi* title on a number of local and regional rulers, these were perceived as derivatives of the Kish model. Such an interpretation undoubtedly applied also to Lagash, whose early rulers, as we know, were in actual fact subordinated to the Kish sovereigns. There is thus no reason, for instance, why the Lagaš sovereigns wiould have been included in the Sumerian King List; their power was deemed to derive from Kish and had nothing original in it.

CONCLUSIONS

Let us now pass in review the long trajectory which the Mesopotamian world had to pass before all the essential elements created, by their interaction, a world that was to become a home for generations and that contributed so much to the successive human civilizations which followed it in due course.

Our journey begins in an epoch very distant in time, in the dim light of the prehistoric phase of the Near East. At that time, the domestic fires on which food was cooked in chiefly households constituted civilization agents fulfilling one of the tasks of prime importance of contemporary human society. Perceiving in the food their chiefs were offering them the external manifestation of the supreme qualities of the chief's body, their followers desired to embody and to digest such qualities in the form of the successive meals they ate at the chiefly banquets.

Some of the ornaments borne by the Halaf-culture tableware reveal at least a glimpse into what kinds of values these early villagers longed for. The rosette- and cross patterns are likely to stand for the "properly structured universe", stabilization of the social equilibrium viewed as just an proper. The chequerboard patterns, likely to refer to the sphere of fertility and proliferation, perhaps conferred the same qualities on those who ate or drank from vessels so decorated. In combination with he rosette- or cross patterns, however, they could have expressed the idea of "may the properly structured world be fruitful and multiply", or, "let civilization grow". The bull's heads, or *bucrania*, could then refer to the virtue of fortitude and courage, needed to combat the forces of chaos, evil and perdition. Findings at the site of Khirbet Derak with its Halaf-style pottery but Ubaid-style seal impressions may show that sometimes, the highly ranked groups of Halaf culture could have performed various services in reward for material goods supplied by Ubaid-culture "commoners".

In this manner, all the three "estates" of any human society – the specialists in matters spiritual, the managers and commanders, and the providers – enter our field of vision in the Eneolithic Near East, more than seven thousand years ago.

The picture acquired more depth and perspective with the advent of Late Ubaid times, at the end of the 5th pre-Christian millennium. At that time, the first settlers of the site that was to become known as Susa established either a cemetery of graves bordering on one another, or a huge funerary tumulus, within the precint of their habitation site. This cemetery seved as a place in which personages laid to rest with the exquisite painted pottery items, as well as personal ornaments, weapons and other belongings found eternal repose. Analysis of the motifs borne by the painted pottery have shown that these elements constituted components of a system of sometimes intelligible signs, arranged on the pot- and cup walls into patterns and recurrent schemes which may be surmised to convey not only particular semantic units, but possibly certain messages of a degree of complexity. These sign complexes referred again to the "three estates" of prehistoric society.

The primeval "Lords Spiritual" displayed symbols like the sun image (An?), the arc (the verb RU, "to dedicate", "to consecrate") or the "hourglass" (Ninhursag or similar?). Even the name of the god Enlil appears on the painted pottery of Susa, while the chequerboard patterns refer to the sphere of fertility and the triangular compositions perhaps to ideas concerning "the whole world".

The business of the first "Lords Temporal" took the visual form of the squares and square compositions, likely to refer to the establishments of new "civilized communities" (image of the "city" reflecting the structure of the four quarters of the world). Their charges and tasks were also evoked by images of the hunting expeditions, likely to reflect the effort to "humanize" the wild and thus dangerous and chaotic world, as well as the rare designs showing military triumph scenes. Design deriving their origin from what may be images of reed mats, possibly as nuptial beds which sometimes occur in pairs, may refer to marriages between high-rank groups.

Finally, the "Commons" adopted as their ensigns the images of water, watercourses as well as what appears to be images of water-management schemes (irrigation channels?) and icons related to grain and harvesting.

In all the three social spheres, however, the attention of the Susa pot painters focused on individual personages rather than on humans conceived of as representatives of social groups. This is visualized by the numerous depictions of combs, likely to refer to the particular individuals to whom the feats described on the painted pots were ascribed, and for which they were venerated.

Pottery decorated in this manner turns up all over the settled area of Susiana. It must thus have played a special social and symbolic role but the most important site of its deposition was obviously the funerary precinct of Susa. Both the stabilized character of the sign *répertoire* occurring on the pots and the apparently established role of prominent administrators in society make me think of a chiefly ritual, in which the Susa cemetery in general, and the sign- and message-bearing pots in particular, did play their role.

Instead of the domestic scenes of food consumption from the exquisite painted pottery of the preceding Halaf-culture period, I imagine the focal point and the "constitutive act" of the Susa chiefdom as an open-air ritual of inthronization of a paramount. This chiefly figure became, at the moment of assumption of the directing function, mystically united with all his ancestors resting in the funerary precinct who, at this moment, re-enacted all the memorable feats for which they were remembered. However, in order to accomplish this there must have been a record of such feats, and this record had to be preserved and intelligible. This is a reasoning that makes me think of the patterns on the Susa painted pottery as of a first system of conventional signs arranged into commonly understood and legible patterns. In other words, we witness here a decisive step towards the creation of sscript.

The next step, at which the first iconic seals left their impressions at Susa (Ubaid-Uruk transition to Early Uruk, early 4th pre-Christian millennium). This age witnessed two important transformations. First and foremost, the extinction of the painted-pottery tradition left in their place only figurative seal impressions as carriers of socially relevant icons. Secondly, the continuity between both individual emblems and whole patterns observable on the painted pottery of Susa and subsequent signs of writing or their sequences do imply that the first true script of mankind saw the light of day in this very period of time.

The seal imagery continues the old tradition of depiction of the "three estates". The "Lords Spiritual" are represented by priestly(?) figures performing the libation ritual, as well as the "dompteur" or "Maître d'animaux" figure, who, as I believe, is to be understood as a chif magician charging with the procreative force, the triggering-off of which is entrusted to him by the gods, the entire nature.

The "Lords Temporal" re-assume now the role of city founders (square designs, likely to repeat the symbolic image of a city as incarnation of the "civilized" four-quarter concept) and military victors. In addition to this, however, there are the "hand in armpit" scenes in which a chiefly figure, raising his hands, is approached by a human of smaller stature who puts his hand into the chief's armpit. I do believe that this is a legitimation scene, as human hair is considered the embodiment of a true nature of each individual in question. As it grows out of the interior of every human, it carries with itself the innermost nature of that particular human and his or her most intimate perosonal characteristics. Touching of human hair – and especially the armpit hair, comprehended as standing for the very nature of the individual in question – may thus be interpreted as taking over the characteristic features of the donor's personality. In this case, I believe that chiefly authority is being transmitted.

The relevant scene thus visualizes a most important step forward in human reasoning – the sovereign authority now becomes dissociated from individual personhood and assumes a form of an invisible force, filling the body of its carrier and transferable to other persons apt to take over the charge. "Statehood" has now become visible.

The question of the pristine development of script is most delicate, chiefly because no carrriers of writing datable to this early time have survived. nevertheless, isolated occurrences of signs on objects of this age (Susa) do bear out the existence of writing.

The use to which the script is now put compares well to the now defunct usage of the Susa painted pottery: a) script does not address dead ancestors but living communities – which, in fact, is much the same thing, given the status of ancestors as the embodiment of a living community; b) script is not used for the benefit of one single paramount, but in the interest of the whole community in question; and c) the use of script is not confined to one single moment within a lifetime of a generation when a new paramount assumes his power, but is repeated regularly, in a yearly or seasonal cycle.

It follows from what has been said the I envisage as the chief function of this pristine script the participation of the community, whose name is recorded in writing, in a rite carried out, on behalf of the participating communties, by one of the contemporary "Lords Spiritual", perhaps the arch-priest performing the libation rite. This rite is likely to have loosened the forces of fertility and procreation force both in the nature and in human beings by means of an act involving pouring out of fresh water as a metaphor for this. I imagine the ritual procedure involved, in one way or another, a written document recording the names of those communities for the benefit of which the officiant celebrates the rite. This, of course, involved subordination of the communities denoted by the written names to the spiritual and possibly (later?) secular power of the abovementioned participant. This may be the reasoning hidden behind the "Enmerkar and the Lord of Aratta" story.

This idea of human beings as carriers of "higher forces", chiefly authority or ability to release fertility, is then carried over into the fully protohistoric world of the Late Uruk and Jemdet Nasr communities of the late and final 4th pre-Christian millennium. The ability of magical creation of whatever spatiotemporal contexts may be conceivable is now incorporated in the new invention of (possibly) lowland Mesopotamia, the cylinder seal. It embodies the combination of cyclical and linear time peculiar to Mesopotamian civilization, as well as its capacity to perceive space as a function of time (rolling of the seal creates an artifical space), and vice versa. The world of this time seems to have comprised the ancient and traditional Susa centre, which might have represented a cult centre sanctioned by age and venenrated for some of the rites performed there on behalf of the entire literate community. The chief social forces, however, might have been represented by the fertility-releasing ceremony of NA_2 performed by the "pontifical couple", the arch-priest EN and the arch-priestess NIN. Only after they had carried out this ceremony properly, might natural and human fertility have acquired a full swing and have resulted in abundance and bounty conferred by the gods on the fields, meadows, wild and tame animals, and, ultimately, on the humans themselves. This procedure also constituted the chief theme of contemporary socially relevant icons. Images of the wild animals and of human files both producing and offering a share of the goods produced to deities as donors of fertility lead the field in iconography of cylinder seals of the Late Uruk and Jemdet Nasr ages. Thus the good mother earth responded kindly to those efforts of her children aimed at rendering her fertile and fruit-bearing.

Nonetheless, the age of full maturity came forth with the synthesis of all preceding elements in the earlier part of the 3rd pre-Christian millennium. Those cities in which there were no twin deities as at Uruk, where EN and NIN acted for An and Inanna, faced a problem. The EN, regardless of whether these were males (where the chief deities were female) or females (with the chief deities male) could not perform the NA_2 ceremony with their NIN. Wedded to their divine consorts, they could not well maintain any legitimate relations to any earthly partners. This made the respective NIN usher in, as their partners, the LUGAL, who thus represent a new element on the ritual scene, involving a necessary definition of their status and nature of their function.

Starting from the roles of EN and NIN as defined by the Uruk pattern, Mesopotamian sages gave two types of answer to the question of the nature of the LUGAL roles. The northern, Kish answer, embodied in the Sumerian cycle of the Gilgamesh tales, opted for the human nature of the LUGAL. Gilgamesh, performing the "sacred marriage" act with Inanna in the "Gilgamesh and the Bull of Heaven", tries to rememedy his ill-becoming conduct by obeying the irate goddess in "Gilgamesh and the Huluppu-Tree". Yet, even in this story the ominous underworld already makes its appearance with the ghastly journey of Enkidu, who cannot fail to remind us of the Biblical parallel of his story with that of Lazarus. Gilgamesh receives the fateful answer — thou art the MAN (not god) – in "Gilgamesh and the Land of the Living". The last act remaining of the drama is, of course, the "Death of Gilgamesh". The Kish answer is thus: the LUGAL are no gods – they are humans, however noble and well-born they may be.

A different trajectory was taken by the thinkers of archaic Ur. Hesitating between the assignation of the role of one of the weather deities (Anzu) and of the shepherd gods (Dumuzi) to their LUGAL, they opted at one time for the "king" as Dumuzi and his "queen" (NIN) as Inanna. Those who died in the same year as the "king" or "queen" had apparently the right to be buried with them, in allusion to the journey to the nether world undertaken by Dumuzi once in a year. That the LUGAL of Ur played the role of Dumuzi is also borne out by their prospecting expeditions to foreign lands, frequently montane and far from Ur. Such landscapes were likely to be equated in popular imagination with the "kur", foreing land but also land of no return. By organizing expeditions into the "kur" and returning with abundant earnings including precious materials like gold or gems, the LUGAL of Ur confirmed before the community their status of incarnations of Dumuzi.

Ultimately, the LUGAL of Ur took over both roles in the person of Mesannepada, who styled himself "lugal Kiš dam nu-gig$_6$ (king of Kish and husband of the Lofty One = Inanna)". This is likely to have brought their power to a climax where no more powerful sovereign title could be conceived, and thus the comprehension of the LUGAL title as designation of supreme authority could ahve been born. Nevertheless, this tradition fell into oblivion after the demise of the first Ur dynasty and the rest of the Early Dynastic age was spent in competition between the two traditions, the Kish one of human kings (Gilgamesh) and the Ur one of divine kings (Dumuzi). Both traditions were re-united by Naramsin of the Akkad dynasty. His predecessors styled themselves modestly after the Kish manner; only with Naramsin does the divine aspect of the royal blood prevail, and constitutes from that time on one of the constant features of Mesopotamian kinghood.

Such a comprehension of the political ideas behind the Early Dynastic royalty also explains why there are only three "royal" cities, properly speaking – Uruk, Ur and Kish – in the "Sumerian King List". In fact, only these three communities proposed original solutions in the course of emergence of statehood in Mesopotamia. The city of Uruk, leaning on its twin sacerdotal office endowed with quasi-divine power and respected also as secular rulers, gave way to its successor states of Kish and Ur. The Kish tradition saw in the LUGAL human sovereigns while the Ur idea was to equate them with earthly incarnations of the dying god Dumuzi.

Apparently, the other powers, paramounts and sovereigns of Early Dynastic Sumer were perceived as mere imitators of these three models. The Fara kingdom, which conferred on the power figures of later Early Dynastic Sumer the title of ensi$_2$ (PA.TE.SI), obviously represented an agency of the Kish kingdom (but why not the Ur kingdom, after all?). The Lagash sovereigns, styling themselves in this manner, obviously based their power on one of the models proposed above, and were thus not worth mentioning in the "List". They had put forward no original solution to the problem of secular rule in Sumer.

And this is the true end of the story. Secular rule is what all these goings-on contributed to the world history. Adopting this course of events, the Mesopotamian statesmen and stateswomen took a path radically different from that of Egypt, the kings of which never divested themselves of their divine status. Ancient Susians and Sumerians thus created an organism of long-term duration, a form of government dominating the daily life of the later centuries and millennia of human history.

The tale should end in the serene and customary "and they lived happily ever after". But did they, in fact?

BIBLIOGRAPHY

ALBERTI, A. 1990:
125) en < emen, "N. A. B. U." 1990 No. 4 (décembre), 102–103.

ALGAZE, G. 1993:
The Uruk World System, Chicago-London: The University of Chicago Press.

ALSTER, B. 1991:
6) An enigmatic line in a mystical/mythological explanatory work as agriculture myth, "N. A. B. U." 1991 No. 1 (mars), 5–6.

AMIET, P. 1972:
Glyptique susienne, des origines à l' époque des perses achéménides. Paris: Geuthner.

AMIET, PIERRE 1986:
L'âge des échanges inter-iraniennes, 3500–1700 avant J. C., Paris: Ministère de la Culture et de la Communication, Editions de la Réunion des Musées Nationaux.

ATU:
A. Falkenstein: Archaische texte aus Uruk. Berlin and Leipzig: Deutsche Forschungsgemeinschaft and Kommissionsverlag Otto Harrassowitz.

AURELL, M. 1998:
Aux origines de la Catalogne: Le mythe fondateur de la maison de Barcelone dans l'historiographie du XIIe siècle, in: Comptes-rendus de l'Académie des Inscriptions et de Belles-Lettres, séances de l' année 1998, janvier–mars, fasc. I, Paris: de Boccard, 7–18.

AUSTIN, ALEXANDER 1988:
The Human Body and Ideology – Concepts of the Ancient Nahuas I, Salt Lake City: University of Utah Press.

BACHE, CH. 1936:
The Joint Assyrian Expedition, "Bulletin of the Amercian Schools of Oriental Research" No. 62, 6–9.

BASDEN, G. T. 1966:
Niger Ibos; a description of the primitive life, customs and animistic beliefs, and c. of the Ibo people of Nigeria by one who, for thirty-five years, enjoyed the privilege of their intimate conference and friendship, London: Frank Cass & Co. Ltd.

BERMAN, J. 1994:
The Ceramic Evidence for Sociopolitical Organization in 'Ubaid Southwestern Iran, in Stein – Rothman 1994, 23–33.

BERNBECK, R. 1994:
Die Auflösung der häuslichen Produktionsweise – Das Beispiel Mesopotamiens, B. B. V. O. vol. 14, Berlin: Dietrich Reimer Verlag.

BIELENSTEIN, H. 1997:
The Six Dynasties II, "Bulletin of the Museum of Far Eastern Antiquities" No. 69, Stockholm, 5–246.

BOESE, J. 1995:
Ausgrabungen in Tell Sheikh Hassan I: Vorläufige Berichte über die Grabungskampagnen 1984–1990 und 1992–1994, Saarbrücken: Saarbrücker Druckerei und Verlag.

BOILEAU, G. 2002:
Wu and shaman, "Bulletin of the School of Oriental and African Studies of the University of London" 65/2, 350–376.

BOLLWEG, JOHANNES 1999:
Vorderasiatische Wagentypen (O. B. O. 167), Freiburg: Universitätsverlag. Reviewed by Peter Miglus in "Bibliotheca Orientalis" 58/3–4, 2001, 456–458.

BOTTÉRO J., KRAMER, S. N. 1993:
Lorsque les dieux faisaient l'homme – Mythologie mésopotamienne. Paris: Editions Gallimard.

BRENIQUET, CATHERINE 1996:
La disparition de la culture de Halaf – Les origines de la culture d'Obeid dans le Nord de la Mésopotamie. Paris: Editions Recherche sur les Civilisations.

BRENIQUET C., MINTSI E., 2000:
Le Peintre d'Amasis et la glyptique mésopotamienne pré- et protodynastique,"Revue des Études Anciennes" 102/3–4, 333–360.

LE BRETON, LOUIS 1947:
Note sur la céramique peinte aux environs de Suse et à Suse, "Mémoires de la Mission Archéologique en Iran (Mission de Susiane)" XXX, 120–219.

BRUCE, S. 2001:
The Origins of Cistercian Sign Language, "Cîteaux – Commentarii cistercienses" 52/3–4, 193–208 (reference courtesy Prof. K. Charvátová, Faculty of Education, Charles University Prague).

CAD:
Chicago Assyrian Dictionary:
Vol. G edited by A. L. Oppenheim as Editor-in-Charge, Chicago-Glückstadt: Oriental Institute and J. J. Augustin Verlagsbuchhandlung 1956.
Vol. I/J edited by A. L. Oppenheim as Editor-in-Charge, Chicago-Glückstadt: Oriental Institute and J. J. Augustin Verlagsbuchhandlung 1960.

Vol. K edited by A. L. Oppenheim as Editor-in-Charge, Chicago-Glückstadt: Oriental Institute and J. J. Augustin Verlagsbuchhandlung 1971.

Vol. N 1 edited by E. Reiner as Editor-in-Charge, Chicago-Glückstadt: Oriental Institute and J. J. Augustin Verlagsbuchhandlung 1980.

Vol. Š II edited by E. Reiner as Editor-in-Charge, Chicago-Glückstadt: Oriental Institute and J. J. Augustin Verlagsbuchhandlung 1992.

CAMILLE, M. 2000:
Adam's House at Angers: Sculpture, Signs and Contrasts in the Medieval Street, in Kontraste im Alltag des Mittelalters, Internationaler Kongress Krems an der Donau, 29. September bis 2. Oktober 1998, Wien: Verlag der Österreichischen Akademie des Wissenschaften, 173–178.

CARTER E., STOLPER M.W., 1984:
Elam – Surveys of Political History nad Archaeology. Berkeley – Los Angeles – London: The University of California Press.

CHARPIN, D. 1990:
A Contribution to the Geography and History of the Kingdom of Kahat, in: S. Eichler, M. Wäfler, D. Warburton (edd.), Tall al-Hamīdīya 2 – Symposion Recent Excavations in the Upper Khabur Region, Berne, December 9–11, 1986, Freiburg and Göttingen: Universitätsverlag and Vandenhoeck und Ruprecht, 67–85.

CHARVÁT, P. 1992:
Out of Sight, out of Mind: the Limits of Archaeological Vision, in: J. Prosecký (ed.), Ex pede pontis – Papers presented on the occasion of the 70th anniversary of the foundation of the Oriental Institute, Prague, Prague, 86–92.

CHARVÁT, P. 1993:
Uruk IV society: Evidence of the script. In: J. Zablocka, St. Zawadzki (edd.): ŠULMU IV – Everyday life in ancient Near East. Papers presented at the International Conference Poznań, 19–22 September 1989. Poznań: Wydawnictwo naukowe UAM, 53–61.

CHARVÁT, P. 1994:
Pig, or, on Ethnicity in Archaeology, „Archív Orientální" 62, 1994, 1–6.

CHARVÁT, P. 1995:
Early Texts and Sealings: "Divine Journeys" in the Uruk IV period? "Altorientalische Forschungen" 22/1, 30–33.

CHARVÁT, P. 1996:
On sealings and officials. Sumerian DUB and SANGA, c. 3500–2500 B.C., in P. Zemánek (ed.), Studies in Near Eastern Languages and Literatures – Memorial Volume of Karel Petráček, Prague: Academy of Sciences of the Czech Republic, Oriental Institute, 181–192

CHARVÁT, P. 1997:
On People, Signs and States – Spotlights on Sumerian Society, c. 3500–2500 B.C. Prague: The Oriental Institute, Academy of Sciences of the Czech Republic.

CHARVÁT, P. 2002:
Mesopotamia Before History, London and New York: Routledge.

CHATTERJEE, I., GUHA, S. 1999:
Slave-queen, waif-prince: Slavery and social capital in eighteenth-century India, "The Indian Economic and Social History Review" XXXVI/2, 165–186.

CLARKE D., HEALD A. 2002:
Beyond Typology: Combs, Economics, Symbolism and Regional Identity in Late Norse Scotland, "Norwegian Archaeological Review" 35/2, 81–93.

CLAYDEN, T. 1996:
Kurigalzu I and the restoration of Babylonia, "Iraq" 58, 109–121.

DAMEROW P., ENGLUND R. K., LAMBERG–KARLOVSKY C. C. 1989:
The Proto-Elamite Texts from Tepe Yahya (The American School of Prehistoric Research Bulletin 39). Harvard University, Cambridge, Massachusetts: Peabody Museum of Archaeology and Ethnology.

DAVID, H. 2003:
Une tombe collective de l'époque de Djemdet Nasr à Larsa, in Huot 2003, 15–20.

DIETERLEN, G. 1970:
La serrure et sa clef (Dogon, Mah), in J. Pouillon, P. Maranda (edd.), Echanges et Communications, Mélanges offerts à Claude Lévi-Strauss à l'occasion de son soixantième anniversaire I–II, The Hague-Paris: Mouton, 7–28.

DOLLFUS, G. 1971:
Les fouilles à Djaffarabad de 1969 á 1971, in "Cahiers de la Délégation Archéologique Française en Iran" 1, 17–161.

DOLLFUS, G. 1973:
"Cachets" en terre cuite de Djaffarabad et "cachets" apparentés, "Revue d'Assyriologie" 67/1, 1–19.

DONALDSON, B. A. 1938:
The Wild Rue – A Study of Muhammadan Magic and Folklore in Iran. London: Cuzac & Co.

DOUAIRE-MARSAUDON, FRANCOIS 2001:
D'un sexe, l'autre. Le rituel du kava et la reproduction de l'identité masculine en Polynésie, "L'homme" 157, 7–34.

DURAND, J.- M. 1989:
112) Tombes familiales et culte des Ancêtres à Emâr, "N. A. B. U." 4/1989, Décembre, 85–88.

EDZARD, D. O. 1976–1980:
Kamm A. Philologisch, in D. O. Edzard (ed.), Reallexikon der Assyriologie Band V (Ia… – Kizzuwatna), Berlin – New York: Walter de Gruyter Verlag, 332.

EDZARD, D. O. 1987–1990:
ME-barage-si, in D. O. Edzard et al. (edd.), Reallexikon der Assyriologie VII (Libanukšabaš-Medizin), Berlin – New York: Walter de Gruyter, 614.

EDZARD, D. O. 1990:
Gilgameš und Huwawa A. I. Teil, "Zeitschrift für Assyriologie" 80/2, 165–203.
EDZARD, D. O. 1991:
Gilgameš und Huwawa A. II. Teil, "Zeitschrift für Assyriologie" 81/2, 165–233.
EDZARD, D. O. 1993:
"Gilgameš und Huwawa" – Zwei Versionen des sumerischen Zedernwaldepisode nebst einer edition von Version "B". Bayerische Akademie der Wissenschaften, Philosophisch--historische Klasse, Sitzungsberichte, Jahgang 1993, Heft 4. München: Verlag der Bayerischen Akademie der Wissenschaften.
EDZARD, D. O. (ed.) 1997:
Royal Inscriptions of Mesopotamia – Early Periods vol. 3/1 – Gudea and His Dynasty, Toronto-Buffalo-London: University of Toronto Press.
EMBERLING G., MCDONALD H. 2001:
Excavations at Tell Brak 2000: Preliminary Report, "Iraq" LXIII, 21–54.
EMERSON, JOHN 1996:
Yang Chu's Discovery of the Body, "Philosophy East and West" 46/4, 533–566.
ENGLUND R. K., BOEHMER R. M. 1994:
Archaic Administrative texts from Uruk – The Early Campaigns, Berlin: Gebr. Mann Verlag.
ENGLUND R. K., GRÉGOIRE J. – P., MATTHEWS R. J. 1991:
The Proto-Cuneiform Texts from Jemdet Nasr. Materialien zu den frühen Schrifterzeugnissen des Vorderen Orients (MSVO) Bd. 1. Berlin: Gebr. Mann Verlag.
ENGLUND R. K., MATTHEWS R. J. 1996:
Proto-Cuneiform Texts from Diverse Collections. Materialien zu den frühen Schrifterzeugnissen des Vorderen Orients (MSVO) Bd. 4. Berlin: Gebr. Mann Verlag.
EVES, RICHARD 1998:
The Magical Body – Power, Fame and Meaning in a Melanesian Society, s. l. (no place): harwood academic publishers.
FERIOLI P., FIANDRA E., FISSORE G. G., FRANGIPANE M. (edd.) 1994:
Archives before Writing – Proceedings of the International Colloquium Oriolo Romano, October 23–25, 1991, Torino: Scriptorium and Ministero per i Beni Culturali e Ambientali, Ufficio Centrale per i Beni Archivistici.
FIRTH, R. 1970:
Rank and Religion in Tikopia, Boston: Beacon Press.
FOREST, J.-D. 1983:
Les pratiques funéraires en Mésopotamie du cinquième millénaire au début du troisième, étude de cas, Paris: Editions Recherche sur les Civilisations.
FOREST, J.-D. 1993:
Çatal Höyük et son décor: Pour le dechiffrement d'un code symbolique, in J. de Courtils, A. Tibet (edd.), Anatolia Antiqua – Eski Anadolu II, Travaux et recherches de l'Institut Français d'Etudes Anatoliennes, Paris: Librairie d'Amérique et d'Orient Adrien Maisonneuve – Jean Maisonneuve Successeur, 1–42.

FORMOSO, B. 2001:

Des sacs chargés de mémoire. Du jeu des tambours à la résistance silencieuse des Wa de Xuelin (Yunnan), "L'Homme" 160, 41–66.

FRANGIPANE, M. 2002:

The 2001 Campaign at Arslantepe. A lecture held at the 24th International Symposium of Excavations, Surveys and Archaeology, organized by the General Directorate of Monuments and Museums, Ministry of Culture of the Republic of Turkey, at the National Library, Ankara, on 27–31 May 2002, on the day of 29 May 2002.

FRAYNE, D. 1997:

Royal Inscriptions of Mesopotamia – Early Periods vol. 3/2 – Ur III period (2113–2004 B.C.), Toronto-Buffalo-London: University of Toronto Press.

GARFINKEL, Y. 2000:

The Khazineh painted style of western Iran, "Iran" XXXVIII, 57–70.

GAYDUKEVITCI I, V. Г. (ГАЙДУКЕВИЧ, В. Ф.) 1952:

К вопросу о ткацком ремесле в боспорских поселениях, (On the question of the weaver's craft in Bospor settlement sites, in Russian), in: В. Ф. Гайдукевич, М. И. Макарова (edd.), Боспорские "орода I, МИА No. 25, Москва-Ленинрад 1952 (V. F. Gaydukevitch, M. I. Makarova, Bosporskiye goroda I, "Materialy i issledovaniya po arkheologii SSSR" vol. 25, Moscow-Leningrad: Izdatel'stvo Akademii Nauk SSSR), 395–414.

GELL, ALEXANDER 1992:

The Anthropology of Time – Cultural Constructions of Temporal Maps and Images, Oxford and Providence: Berg.

GEORGE, A. 1997:

Assyria and the Western World, in S. Parpola and R. M. Whiting (edd.), Assyria 1995, Helsinki: Academia Scientiarum Fennica, 69–75.

GIFFORD, E. W. 1929:

Tongan Society. Honolulu, Hawaii: Bernice P. Bishop Museum.

GLASSNER, J. - J. 1993:

Chroniques mésopotamiennes, Paris: Les Belles Lettres.

GLASSNER, J.- J. 1999:

Savoirs secrets et écritures secrétes des scribes mésopotamiens, "Politica Hermetica" No. 13: Les langues secrètes, 15–30.

GLASSNER, J.- J. 2000:

Écrire à Sumer – L'invention du cunéiforme, s.l. (no place): Editions du Seuil.

GLASSNER, J.- J. 2000a:

Historical Times in Mesopotamia, in: A. de Pury, Th. Römer, J.- D. Macchi (edd.), Israel Constructs its History – Deuteronomistic Historiography in Recent Research. Journal for the Study of the Old Testament: Supplement Series 306, 2000, 189–211.

GODELIER, MAURICE 1992:

Corps, parenté, pouvoir(s) chez les Baruya de Nouvelle-Guinée, "Journal de la Société d'Océanistes" 94/1, 3–24.

GRANERO, F. S. 1986:
Power, ideology and the ritual of production in lowland South America, "Man" N. S. 21/4, 657–679.

GREAVES A., HELWING B. 2003:
Archaeology in Turkey: The Stone, Bronze, and Iron Ages, 2000, "American Journal of Archaeology" 107/1, 71–104.

GREEN, M. M. 1964:
Igbo village affairs, chiefly with reference to the village of Umueke Agbaja. Second edition.London: Frank Cass & Co. Ltd.

GRONENBORN, D. 2001:
Zum möglichen Nachweis von Sklaven/Unfreien in prähistorischen Gesellschaften Mitteleuropas,"Ethnographisch-Archäologische Zeitschrift" 42/1, 1–42.

GUSTAVSON-GAUBE, CARRIE 1981:
Shams ed-Din Tannira 4: The Halafian pottery of Area A, "Berytus" XXIX, 9–182.

HANNA, J. L. 1976:
The Anthropology of Dance Ritual: Nigeria's Ubakala Nkwa Di Iche Iche, Ann Arbor, Michigan: Xerox University Microfilms [1980 copy].

HANSEN, D. 1998:
Art of the Royal Tombs of Ur: A Brief Interpretation, in Zettler-Horne 1998, 43–72.

HARPER PRUDENCE, ARUZ JOAN, TALLON FRANÇOISE 1992:
The Royal City of Susa – Ancient Near Eastern Treasures in the Louvre, New York: The Metropolitan Museum of Art.

HEIMPEL, W. 2000:
Nin-hursaĝa A, in D. O. Edzard (ed.), Reallexikon der Assyriologie, Band IX, Lieferung 5–6 (Nimrud -Ninlil), Berlin – New York: Walter de Gruyter Verlag, 378–381.

HENDERSON, H. K. 1970:
Ritual roles of women in Onitsha Ibo society, Ann Arbor, Michigan: University Microfilms [1980 copy].

HENDERSON, R. N. 1972:
The king in every man; evolutionary trends in Onitsha Ibo society and culture, New Haven and London: Yale University Press.

HICKS, D. (ed.) 1999:
Ritual and Belief – Readings in the Anthropology of Religion. Boston etc. (up to Toronto): McGraw-Hill College.

HOLDER, G. 1998:
Esclaves et captifs au pays dogon, "L'homme" 145, 71–108.

HOLE, F. 1992:
The Cemetery of Susa: An Interpretation, in: Harper-Aruz-Tallon 1992,26–31.

HOLE F., JOHNSON G. A. 1986–1987:
Umm Qseir on the Khabur: Preliminary Report on the 1986 Excavation, "Annales Archéologiques Arabes Syriennes" 36–37, 172–220.

HORNE, L. 1998:
Ur and Its Treasures: The Royal Tombs, "Expedition" 40/2, 4–11.

HOROWITZ, WAYNE 1998:
Mesopotamian Cosmic Geography, Winona Lake, Indiana: Eisenbrauns.

HUOT, J.-L. (ed.) 2003:
Larsa – Travaux de 1987 et 1989, Beyrouth: Institut Français d'Archéologie du Proche-
-Orient. I owe this reference to my learned friend and colleague, Jean-Louis Huot.

HUROWITZ, V. (A.) 1992:
I Have Built You an Exalted House. Temple Building in the Bible in Light of
Mesopotamian and Northwest Semitic Writings, Sheffield: Sheffield Academic Press.

JACKSON, M., KARP, I. (edd.) 1990:
Personhood and Agency – The Experience of Self and Other in African Cultures, "Acta
Universitatis Upsaliensis" 14, Uppsala.

JACOBSON-WIDDING, A. 1990:
The Shadow as an Expression of Individuality in Congolese Conceptions of Personhood,
in Jackson-Karp 1990, 31–58.

JAMES, K. E. 1991:
The female presence in heavenly places: Myth and sovereignty in Tonga, "Oceania" 61/4,
287–308.

JAMISON, S. W. 1999:
Penelope and the Pigs: Indic Perspectives on the Odyssey, "Classical Antiquity" 18/2,
227–272.

JÉQUIER, GUSTAVE 1905:
Cachets et cylindres archaiques, "Mémoires de la Délégation en Perse (Ministère de
l'instruction publique et des beaux-arts)" VII,, 1–27.

JOANNÈS, F. 1989:
šêpê ina ṭiṭṭi šakânu, "N. A. B. U." 1989 No. 4, décembre, 81–82.

KANK, RACHEL 2000 [1992]:
Land-God-man: concepts of land ownership in traditional cultures in Eretz-Israel, in: A.
R. H. Baker, G. Biger (edd.), Ideology and Landscape in Historical Perspectives – Essays
on the Meaning of Some Places in the Past, Cambridge – New York – Victoria:
Cambridge University Press, 63–82.

KARVOUEN-KANNAS, K. 1995:
The Seleucid and Parthian terracotta figurines from Babylon in the Iraq Museum, the
British Museum and the Louvre. Firenze: Casa editrice Le Lettere.

KEEL, O. 1990:
V. Berichtigungen und Nachträge zu den Beiträgen II–IV: A) Nachträge zu "Der Bogen
als Herrschaftssymbol", in O. Keel, M. Shuval, Ch. Uehlinger, Studien zu den
Stempelsiegeln aus Palästina/Israel Bd. III: Die Frühe Eisenzeit – Ein Workshop,
Freiburg (Schweiz) – Göttingen: Universitätsverlag and Vandenhoeck und Ruprecht,
263–279.

KILMER, A. D. 1995:

Music and Dance in Ancient Western Asia, in Sasson et al. 1995, pp. 2601–2613.

KIRK, GEORGE 1970:

Myth, its meaning and functions in ancient and other cultures, Cambridge – Berkeley – Los Angeles: Cambridge University Press and University of California Press.

KOCHER, G. 1992:

Zeichen und Symbole des Rechts. Eine historische Ikonographie. München: Verlag C. H. Beck.

KONDRAT'YEVA, (КОНДРАТЬЕВА) O. A. 1999:

„Язик" гребня. К вопросу о семиотическом статусе вещи (The "language" of combs. On the question of semiotical status of an object, in Russian), в Е. Н. Носов, Раннесредневековые древности северной Руси и её соседей, Санкт-Петербург" (E. N. Nosov (ed.), Rannesrednevekovye drevnosti severnoy Rusi i yeyo sosedej, Sankt-Peterburg: Institut istorii material'noy kultury Rossiyskoy Akademii Nauk), 80–88.

KOUCHOUKOS, N. 2001:

Satellite Images and Near Eastern Landscapes, "Near Eastern Archaeology" 64/1–2, 80–91.

KREBERNIK, M. 2000:

Ninlil, in D. O. Edzard (ed.), Reallexikon der Assyriologie, Band IX, Lieferung 5–6 (Nimrud -Ninlil), Berlin – New York: Walter de Gruyter Verlag, 452–461. The caption reaches over into

D. O. Edzard (ed.), Reallexikon der Assyriologie, Band IX, Lieferung 7–8 (Ninlil-Nuzi), Berlin – New York: Walter de Gruyter Verlag 2001.

KRYUKOV, VALENTIN 1995:

Symbols of power and communication in pre-Confucian China (On the anthropology of de). Preliminary assumptions, "Bulletin of the School of Oriental and African Studies of the University of London" 88/2, 314–333.

LAFONT, S. 1989:

45) AEM I/1, 251: "poser le pan de son vêtement". "N. A. B. U." 1989 No. 2, p. 29.

LAMBTON, A. K. S. 1953:

Landlord and Peasant in Persia. A Study of Land Tenure and Land Tenure Administration, London – New York – Toronto: Oxford University Press.

LEACH, E. R. 1999 [1958]:

Magical Hair, in: Hicks (ed.) 1999, 221–239. Originally published in "Journal of the Royal Anthropological Institute" 88/2, 1958, 147–164.

LEACH, E. R. 1999 [1968]:

Ritual, in: Hicks (ed.) 1999, 176–183. Originally published in International Encyclopaedia of Social Sciences, London 1968.

LEACH, E. R. 1968:

Political systems of highland Burma. Boston: Beacon Press (second edition).

LEBRUN, A. 1978:
L'origine de l'écriture à Suse, "Cahiers de la Délégation Archéologique Française en Iran" 8, 11–59.

LEBRUN, A. 1985:
Le niveau 19 de l'Acropole de Suse. Mémoire d'argile, mémoire du temps, "Paléorient" 11/2, 31–36.

LECLANT, JEAN, CLERC, GENEVIEVE 1998:
Fouilles et travaux en Egypte et au Soudan, 1996–1997, "Orientalia" N. S. 67/3, 315–444.

LEGRAIN, L. 1921:
Empreintes de cachets élamites, "Mémoires de la Mission Archéologiqe de Perse (Mission de Susiane)" XVI, 1–59.

LEGRAIN, L. 1936:
Ur Excavations vol. III: Archaic Seal-Impressions, New York: British Museum London, University Museum Philadelphia, Trustees of the two Museums by the aid of a grant from the Carnegie Corporation.

LEGRAIN, L. 1951:
Ur Excavations vol. X: Seal Cylinders, New York: British Museum London, University Museum Philadelphia, Trustees of the two Museums by the aid of a grant from the Carnegie Corporation.

LEMAIRE, ANDRE 1998:
Une inscription araméenne du VIIIe siècle av. J. C. trouvée a Bukân (Azerbaidjan iranien), "Studia Iranica" 27/1, 15–30.

LEVI-STRAUSS, C. 1966:
Tristes tropiques. I quote from "Smutné tropy," the translation of the work into Czech, published at Praha by the "Odeon" publishing house.

MacGINNIS, J. 2002:
The use of writing boards in the neo-Babylonian temple administration at Sippar, "Iraq" 64, 217–236.

MALINOWSKI, B. 1922:
Argonauts of the Western Pacific, London – New York: G. Routledge & sons, Ltd., and E. P. Dutton & Co.

MALINOWSKI, B. 1929:
The Sexual Life of Savages in Northwest Melanesia, New York-London: H. Liveright & G. Routledge and Sons.

MALINOWSKI, B. 1935:
Coral Gardens and their Magic. A Study of the Methods of Tilling the Soil and of Agricultural Rites in the Trobriand Islands, vol. II, New York-Cincinnati-Chicago: American Book Company.

MALLOWAN M., ROSE J. C. 1935:
Excavations at Tall Arpachiyah, 1933, "Iraq" II, 1–178.

MANDER, P. 1999:
Janua hominum et deorum in the Sumerian Mythological Texts, "Annali de l'Istituto Universitario Orientale" 59/1–4, 93–108.

MARTIN H. P., MATTHEWS R. J. 1993:
Seals and Sealings, in Anthony Green (ed.), Abu Salabikh Excavations Volume 4, The 6G Ash-Tip and its contents: cultic and administrative discard from the temple?, London: British School of Archaeology in Iraq, 23–81.

MASSÉ, H. 1938:
Croyances et Coutûmes Persanes, suivies de Contes et Chansons Populaires I–II, Paris: Librairie Orientale et Americaine. I am quoting the English translation of this work, made for the Behavior Science Translations by Ch. A. Messner, available at the Bibliothèque of the Laboratoire d'Anthropologie Comparée, Collège de France, 52, rue Cardinal Lemoine, 75005 Paris.

MATNEY, T. 1995:
Re-excavating Cheshmeh Ali, "Expedition" 37/2, 26–51.

MATTHEWS, R. J. 1993:
Cities, seals and writing: archaic seal impressions from Jemdet Nasr and Ur. Materialien zu den frühen Schrifterzeugnissen des Vorderen Orients (MSVO) Bd. 2. Berlin: Gebr. Mann Verlag.

MAXWELL-HYSLOP, K. R. 1992:
The goddess Nanše. An attempt to identify her representation, "Iraq" 54, 79–82.

McGOVERN, P. E. et al. 1997:
P. E. McGovern, U. Hartung, V. R. Badler, D. L. Glusher, L. J. Exner: The beginnings of Winemaking and Viniculture in the Ancient Near East and Egypt, "Expedition" 39/1, 3–21.

MEAD, M. 1975 [1928]:
Coming of age in Samoa, s.l.(no place): William Morrow & Company.

DE MECQUENEM, ROLAND 1911:
Constructions élamites du tell de l'Acropole de Suse, "Mémoires de la Délégation en Perse (Ministère de l'instruction publique et des beaux-arts)" XII, 65–78.

DE MECQUENEM, R. 1912:
Catalogue de la céramique peinte susienne conservée au Musée du Louvre, "Mémoires de la Délégation en Perse (Ministère de l'instruction publique et des beaux-arts)" XIII, 105–158.

DE MECQUENEM 1920–1921:
Fouilles de Suse, Compte rendu de la campagne 1920–1921. Unpublished manuscript in the *Archives Mecquenem* file, not numbered, Département des Antiquités Orientales, Musée du Louvre, Paris.

DE MECQUENEM, R. 1922–1923:
Journal de Fouilles à Suse 1922–1923. Unpublished manuscript in the *Archives Mecquenem* file, not numbered, Département des Antiquités Orientales, Musée du Louvre, Paris.

DE MECQUENEM, R. 1924a:
Journal de fouilles archéologiques à Suse, saison 1924. Unpublished manuscript in the *Archives Mecquenem* file, not numbered, Département des Antiquités Orientales, Musée du Louvre, Paris.

DE MECQUENEM, R. 1924b:
Annexe III. Suse 1924: Inventaire des Antiquités. Unpublished manuscript in the *Archives Mecquenem* file, not numbered, Département des Antiquités Orientales, Musée du Louvre, Paris.

DE MECQUENEM, R. 1925:
Journal de fouilles, 1925. Unpublished manuscript in the *Archives Mecquenem* file, not numbered, Département des Antiquités Orientales, Musée du Louvre, Paris.

DE MECQUENEM, R. 1926:
Fouilles archéologiques de Perse 1926, Annexe II: Inventaire des Antiquités, Série H. Unpublished manuscript in the *Archives Mecquenem* file, not numbered, Département des Antiquités Orientales, Musée du Louvre, Paris.

DE MECQUENEM, R. 1927:
Fouilles archéologiques en Perse 1927. Rapport de mission – Annexe II: Inventaire des antiquités expédiées au Musée du Louvre. Unpublished manuscript in the *Archives Mecquenem* file, not numbered, Département des Antiquités Orientales, Musée du Louvre, Paris.

DE MECQUENEM, R. 1928a:
Rapport de mission 1928. Unpublished manuscript in the *Archives Mecquenem* file, not numbered, Département des Antiquités Orientales, Musée du Louvre, Paris.

DE MECQUENEM, R. 1928b:
Rapport de mission, 1928. Annexe II, série K. Unpublished manuscript in the *Archives Mecquenem* file, not numbered, Département des Antiquités Orientales, Musée du Louvre, Paris.

DE MECQUENEM, R. 1929:
Rapport de mission 1929, Annexe II: Liste générale des antiquités inventoriées en 1929, série L. Unpublished manuscript in the *Archives Mecquenem* file, not numbered, Département des Antiquités Orientales, Musée du Louvre, Paris.

DE MECQUENEM, R. 1932a:
Inventaire des objets rapportés au Louvre, et provenant des campagnes 1919, 1930, 1931, 1932, Séries L, M, N. Unpublished manuscript in the *Archives Mecquenem* file, not numbered, Département des Antiquités Orientales, Musée du Louvre, Paris.

DE MECQUENEM, R. 1932b:
Fouilles archéologiques de Perse, Mission en Susiane, Campagne 1932, Inventaire des antiquités, Série N, 12ème inventaire. Unpublished manuscript in the *Archives Mecquenem* file, not numbered, Département des Antiquités Orientales, Musée du Louvre, Paris.

DE MECQUENEM, R. 1933:
Fouilles archéologiques de Perse, Mission de Susiane, Emballages des antiquités,

campagne 1933, 13ème inventaire. Unpublished manuscript in the *Archives Mecquenem* file, not numbered, Département des Antiquités Orientales, Musée du Louvre, Paris.

DE MECQUENEM, R. 1934:
Fouilles de Suse, Campagne 1934, Inventaire des objets. Unpublished manuscript in the *Archives Mecquenem* file, not numbered, Département des Antiquités Orientales, Musée du Louvre, Paris.

DE MECQUENEM, R. 1934–1935:
Mission Archéologique de Suse, Inventaire des Antiquités recueillies, campagne 1934–1935. Unpublished manuscript in the *Archives Mecquenem* file, not numbered, Département des Antiquités Orientales, Musée du Louvre, Paris.

DE MECQUENEM, R. 1936:
Journal de Fouilles, campagne 1936. Unpublished manuscript in the *Archives Mecquenem* file, not numbered, Département des Antiquités Orientales, Musée du Louvre, Paris.

DE MECQUENEM, R. 1936–1937:
Mission archéologique de Susiane, Saison 1936–1937, Journal des fouilles et Emploi du temps. Unpublished manuscript in the *Archives Mecquenem* file, not numbered, Département des Antiquités Orientales, Musée du Louvre, Paris.

DE MECQUENEM R. 1938:
Journal de Fouilles – Campagne 1938. Unpublished manuscript in the *Archives Mecquenem* file, not numbered, Département des Antiquités Orientales, Musée du Louvre, Paris.

DE MECQUENEM, ROLAND 1943:
Fouilles de Suse, 1933–1939, "Mémoires de la Mission Archéologique en Iran (Mission de Susiane)" XXIX, 3–119.

DE MECQUENEM, R. hist.:
Historique de Suse: Les fouilleurs de Suse. Unpublished manuscript in the *Archives Mecquenem* file, not numbered, Département des Antiquités Orientales, Musée du Louvre, Paris.

DE MECQUENEM, R. s.d. (not dated):
Section drawing entitled "Coupe du premier Sondage de l'Acropole", in: Correspondence, Divers, *Archives Mecquenem* file, not numbered, Département des Antiquités Orientales, Musée du Louvre, Paris

MEEK, CH. K. 1970:
Law and authority in a Nigerian tribe: a study in indirect rule, New York: Barnes and Noble.

MICHALOWSKI, P. 1997:
Sumerians, in Myers 1997, 95–101.

MICHALOWSKI, P. 1998:
The Unbearable Lightness of Enlil, in J. Prosecký (ed.), Intellectual Life of the Ancient Near East, Papers Presented at the 43rd Rencontre Assyriologique Internationale, Prague, July 1–5, 1996, Prague: Oriental Institute, 237–248.

MILLER, N. F. 1999:

Date Sex in Mesopotamia!, "Expedition 41/1, 29–30."

MILLER, R., BERGMAN, CH., AZOURY, I. 1982:

Additional Note on Reconstructing Aspects of Archery Equipment at Shams ed-Din Tannira, "Berytus" XXX, 53–54.

MOOREY, P. R. S. 1999:

Ancient Mesopotamian Materials and Industries – The Archaeological Evidence, Winona Lake, Indiana: Eisenbrauns.

DE MORGAN, JACQUES 1900a:

Ruines de Suse, "Mémoires de la Délégation en Perse (Ministère de l'instruction publique et des beaux-arts)" I, 50–54.

DE MORGAN, JACQUES 1900b:

Travaux du tell de la Citadelle. Travaux souterrains, "Mémoires de la Délégation en Perse (Ministère de l'instruction publique et des beaux-arts)" I, 81–87.

DE MORGAN, J. 1900c:

Description des objets d'art, "Mémoires de la Délégation en Perse (Ministère de l'instruction publique et des beaux-arts)" I, 139–198.

DE MORGAN, JACQUES 1912:

Observations sur les couches profondes de l'Acropole à Suse, "Mémoires de la Délégation en Perse (Ministère de l'instruction publique et des beaux-arts)" XIII, 1–25.

DE MORGAN JACQUES, LAMPRE GUSTAVE, JÉQUIER GUSTAVE 1900:

Travaux de l'hiver, 1897–1898, "Mémoires de la Délégation en Perse (Ministère de l'instruction publique et des beaux-arts)" II, 55–99.

MOSKO, MICHAEL 1992:

Other messages, other missions, or, Sahlins among the Melanesians, "Oceania" 63/2, 97–113.

MYERS, E. (ed.) 1997:

The Oxford Encyclopaedia of Archaeology in the Near East, vols. I–V. New York – Oxford: Oxford University Press.

NEUMANN, H. 1996:

Review of Englund-Grégoire-Matthews, "Bibliotheca Orientalis" 91/1, 22–27.

NZIMIRO, F. I. 1972:

Studies in Ibo political systems; chieftaincy and politics in four Niger states, Berkeley-Los Angeles: University of California Press.

Ó CORRÁIN, D. 1995:

Ireland, Scotland and Wales to the early eleventh century, in R. McKitterick (ed.), The new Cambridge Medieval History vol. II, c. 700 – c. 900, Cambridge – new York – Melbourne: Cambridge University Press, 43–63.

OATES D., OATES J. 1993:

Excavations at Tell Brak, 1992–1993, "Iraq" 55, 155–200.

OBEYESEKERE, G. 1981:

Medusa's Hair. An Essay on Personal Symbols and Religious Experiences, Chicago and London: The University of Chicago Press.

OTTENBERG, S. 1975:

Moshed rituals of Afikpo; the context of an African art, Seattle and London: for the Henry Art Gallery by the University of Washington Press.

OVERMYER, DAVID et al. 1995:

D. L. Overmyer, D. N. Keightley, E. L. Shaughnessy, C. A. Cook, D. Harper: Chinese Religions – The State of the Field I. Early Religious Traditions: The Neolithic Period through the Han Dynasty (ca. 4,000 B. C. E. to 220 C. E.), "The Journal of Asian Studies" 54/1, 124–160.

OVESEN, J. 1990:

Initiation: A Folk Model among the Lobi, in Jackson-Karp 1990, 149–167.

PÉZARD, M. 1911:

Etude sur les intailles susiennes, "Mémoires de la Délégation en Perse (Ministère de l'instruction publique et des beaux-arts)" XII, 79–141.

PITTMAN, H. 1994a:

Towards an understanding of the role of glyptic imagery in the administrative systems of Proto-Literate Greater Mesopotamia, in: Ferioli – Fiandra – Fissore – Frangipane (edd.) 1994, 177–203.

PITTMAN, H. 1994b:

The Glazed Steatite Glyptic Style. The Structure and Function of an Image System in the Administration of protoliterate Mesopotamia (Berliner Beiträge zum Vorderen Orient Bd. 11), Berlin: Dietrich Reimer Verlag.

PITTMAN, H. 1997:

Susa, in E. Myers (ed.), The Oxford Encyclopaedia of Archaeology in the Near East vol. 5, New York – Oxford: Oxford University Press, 106–110.

PITTMAN, H. 1998:

Jewelry, in Zettler-Horne 1998, 87–124.

PLOTNIKOVA, A. A. (ПЛОТНИКОВА) 1999:

Caption „Давать взаймн" ("davat' vzaymi" – Mutual exchange, in Russian), in Н. И. Толстой (ed.), Славянские древности – Этнолингвистический словарь т. 2 (Д–К), Москва (N. I. Tolstoy (ed.), Slavyanskiye drevnosti – Etnolingvisticheskiy slovar', vol. 2, D-K, Moskva: "Mezhdunarodniye otnosheniya"), 14–16.

POMPONIO F., BIGA M. G. 1989:

114) Pa$_4$-ba$_4$, épouse d'Iblul-il, roi de Mari, "N. A. B. U." 1989 No. 4 (décembre), 89–90.

POTTIER, E. 1912:

Etude historique et chronologique sur les vases peints de l'Acropole de Suse, "Mémoires de la Délégation en Perse (Ministère de l'instruction publique et des beaux-arts)" XIII, 27–104.

POTTS, D. T. 1999:
The archaeology of Elam: formation and transformation of an ancient Iranian state. Cambridge: Cambridge University Press. Reviewed by M. Roaf in "Bulletin of the School of Oriental and African Studies of the University of London" 63/2, 2000, 286–287.

PRADELLES DE LATOUR, CH.-H. 1996:
Les morts et leurs rites en Afrique, "L'homme" 138, 137–142.

PUETT, MARVIN 1998:
Sages, Ministers and Rebels: Narratives from Early China Concerning the Initial Creation of the State, "Harvard Journal of Asiatic Studies" 58/2, 425–479.

PULLEN, D. J. 1994:
A Lead Seal from Tsoungiza, Ancient Nemea, and Early Bronze Age Aegen Sealing Systems, "American Journal of Archaeology" 98/1, 35–52.

QUAY, S. 2001:
Signs of Silence: Two Examples of Trappist Sign Language in the Far East, "Cîteaux – Commentarii cistercienses" 52/3–4, 211–229 (reference courtesy Prof. K. Charvátová, Faculty of Education, Charles University Prague).

RATHJE, W. L. 1977:
New Tricks for Old Seals: A Progress Report, in McG. Gibson and R. Biggs (edd.), Seals and Sealing in the Ancient Near East, Bibliotheca Mesopotamica volume Six, Malibu: Undena Publications, 25–32.

READE, J. 2001:
Assyrian King-Lists, the Royal Tombs of Ur, and Indus Origins, "Journal of Near Eastern Studies" 60/1, 1–29.

REITER, K. 1989:
107) kikkilu/kilkillu, "Raum zu Aufbewahrung des Eidleistungssymbols" (šu. nir = šurinnum) des Šamaš, "N.A.B.U." 1989/4, décembre, 79–80.

REITER, K. 1991:
84) Kilkillu, archäologisch. "N. A. B. U." 1991 No. 3 (septembre), 55–57.

ROTHMAN, M. 1994:
Seal and sealing findspot, design, audience and function: Monitoring changes in administrative oversight and structure at Tepe Gawra during the fourth millennium B. C., in Ferioli-Fiandra-Frangipane-Fissore 1994, 97–119.

ROVA, ELENA 1994:
Ricerche sui sigilli a cilindro vicino-orientali del periodo di Uruk/Jemdet Nasr, Roma: Istituto per l'Oriente C. A. Nallino.

RUHE, D. 1993:
Gelehrtes Wissen, "Aberglaube" und pastorale Praxis im französischen Spätmittelalter. Der *Second Lucidaire* und seine Rezeption (14. – 17. Jahrhundert), Wiesbaden: Dr. Ludwig Reichert Verlag.

SAFAR F., MUSTAFA M. A., LLOYD S. 1981:
Eridu. Baghdad: Republic of Iraq, Ministry of Culture and Information, State Organization of Antiquities and Heritage.

SANDAY, P. R. 1997:
Eggi's Village – Reconsidering the Meaning of Matriarchy, "Expedition" 39/3, 27–36.

SASSON, J. M. et al. (edd.) 1995:
J. Sasson, J. Baines, G. Beckman, K. S. Rubinson (edd.): Civilizations of the Ancient Near East, volumes I–III, New York: Charles Scribner's Sons and Macmillan Library Reference USA, Simon and Schuster Macmillan 1995.

DE SCHAUENSEE, M. 1998:
The "Boat-Shaped" Lyre – Restudy of a Unique Musical Instrument from Ur, "Expedition" 40/2, 20–28.

SELLIER, P. 2003:
La tombe collective de Larsa (époque Djemdet Nasr): paléoanthropologie et pratiques funéraires (résumé), in Huot 2003, 21–22.

SELZ, G. 1998:
Über Mesopotamische Herrschaftskonzepte. Zu den Ursprüngen mesopotamischer Herrscherideologie im 3. Jahrtausend, in M. Dietrich, O. Loretz (edd.), dubsar anta-men, Studien zur Altorientalistik, Festschrift für Willem H. Ph. Römer zur Vollendung seines 70. Lebensjahres, Münster: Ugarit-Verlag, 281–344.

SELZ, G. 1999:
Von "Vergangenen Geschehen" zu "Zukunftsbewältigung", Überlegungen zur Rolle der Schrift in Ökonomie und Geschichte, in: B. Böck, E. Cancik-Kirschbaum, Th. Richter (edd.), Munuscula Mesopotamica – Festschrift für Johannes Renger, Münster: Ugarit--Verlag, 465–512.

SELZ, G. 2000:
Five Divine Ladies: Thoughts on Inanna(k), Ištar, In(n)in(a), Anunnītum, and Anat, and the origin of the Title "Queen of Heaven" in NiN, thematic issue "Journal of Gender Studies in Antiquity" vol. 1, Styx Publications, 29–62.

SOLLBERGER E., KUPPER J.-R. 1971:
Inscriptions royales sumériennes et akkadiennes, Paris: Les Editions du Cerf.

STEIN, G. 1998:
Heterogeneity, Power, and Political Economy: Some Current Research Issues in the Archaeology of Old World Complex Societies, "Journal of Archaeological Research" 6/1, 1–44.

STEIN, G. 2001:
"Who Was King? Who Was Not King?" Social Group Composition and Competition in Early Mesopotamian State Societies, in J. Haas (ed.), From Leaders to Rulers, New York: Kluwer Academic/Plenum Publishers, 205–231.

STEIN G., ROTHMAN M. (edd.) 1994:
Chiefdoms and Early States in the Near East: The Organizational Dynamics of Complexity, Madison (Wisconsin): Prehistory Press.

STEINER, G. 1996:
Huwawa und sein "Bergland" in der sumerischen Tradition, "Acta Sumerologica" (Japan) 18, 187–215.

STEINKELLER, P. 1995:
Review of ZATU, in "Bibliotheca Orientalis" 52/5–6, 689–713.

STRECK, M. P. 2001:
Ninurta/Ningirsu A. I. In Mesopotamien, in D. O. Edzard (ed.), Reallexikon der Assyriologie Band IX, Lieferung 7–8 (Ninlil-Nuzi), Berlin – New York: Walter de Gruyter Verlag, 512–522.

SUPPLÉMENT 2002:
Sumer, in Supplément au Dictionnaire de la Bible, fascicules 72–73, tome XIII, Paris: Letouzey & Ané, 77–359.

TASSIE, G. J. 1996:
Hair-Offerings – An Enigmatic Egyptian Custom, "Papers from the Institute of Archaeology" 7, 59–67.

THOMAS, N. W. 1913:
Anthropological report on the Ibo-speaking peoples of Nigeria I. Law and custom of the Ibo of the Awka neighbourhood, southern Nigeria, London: Harrison & Sons.

THOMAS, N. W. 1914:
Anthropological report on the Ibo-speaking peoples of Nigeria IV: Law and custom of the Ibo of the Asaba district, southern Nigeria, London: Harrison & Sons.

TOBLER, A. J. 1950:
Excavations at Tepe Gawra, vol. II. Philadelphia – London: University of Pennsylvania Press and G. Cumberlege, Oxford University Press.

TOLSTOY, N. I., USACHEVA, V. V. (ТОЛСТОЙ, Н. И., УСАЧЕВА, В. В.) 1995:
Волосы (Volosy = Hair), in: В. Я. Петрухин, Т. А. Авалкина, Л. Н. Виноградова, С. М. Толстая, Энциклопедический Словарь – Славянская Мифология, Москва (V. Ya. Petrukhin, T. A. Avalkina, L. N. V. Vinogradova, S. M. Tolstaya, Entsiklopedicheskiy slovar' – Slavyanskaya mifologiya, Moskva: Ellis Lak), 105–107.

VAN DER TOORN, K. 1995:
The Significance of the Veil in the Ancient Near East, in D. P. Wright, D. N. Freedman, A. Hurvitz (edd.), Pomegranates and golden bells. Studies in Biblical, Jewish and Near Eastern Ritual, Law and Literature in Honour of Jacob Milgrom, Winona Lake: Eisenbrauns, 327–339.

TOSCANNE, P. 1911:
Etudes sur le serpent – Figure et symbole dans l'antiquité élamite, "Mémoires de la Délégation en Perse (Ministère de l'instruction publique et des beaux-arts)" XII, 153–229.

TRAMONTANA, SILVIO 1999:
Il Regno di Sicilia – Uomo e natura dall'XI al XIII secolo, Torino: Giulio Einaudi editore.

UERPMANN, HANS-PETER 1982:
Faunal remains from Shams ed-Din Tannira, a Halafian site in nothern Syria, "Berytus" XXX, 3–52.

UET II:

E. Burrows: Ur Excavation Texts vol. II: Archaic texts. London and Philadelphia: Trustees of the two Museums 1935.

VALLAT, F. 1990:

Les cornes élamites, "N. A. B. U." 1990 No. 4 (décembre), 111–112.

VANSTIPHOUT, H. L. J. 1989:

98) The Akkadian word for grain and Lahar and Ashnan, "N.A.B.U." 1989 No. 4 (décembre), 72–73.

VANSTIPHOUT, H. L. J. 1990:

57) A *double entendre* Concerning Uttu, "N. A. B. U." 1990 No. 2 (juillet), 40–44.

VANSTIPHOUT, H. L. J. 1994:

Another attempt at the "spell of Nudimmud", "Revue d'Assyriologie" 88, 135–154.

VANSTIPHOUT, H. J. L. 1997:

Why did Enki organize the world?, in I. L. Finkel, M. J. Geller (edd.), Sumerian Gods and their Representations, Cuneiform Monographs No. 7, Groningen: Styx Publications,117–134.

VANSTIPHOUT, H. L. J. 2002:

Sanctus Lugalbanda, in Tz. Abusch (ed.), Riches Hidden in Secret Places – Ancient Near Eastern Studies in Memory of Thorkild Jacobsen, Winona Lake, Indiana: Eisenbrauns, 259–289.

VINOGRADOVA, L. N. (ВИНОГРАДОВА, Л. Н.) 1999:

Материальные и бестелесные формы существования души (Material and immaterial forms of existence of the soul, in Russian), in Славянские етносы – Сборник к юбилею С. М. Толстой, Москва: Издательство Индрик (Slavyanskiye etnosy – Sbornik k yubileyu S. M. Tolstoy, Moscow: Izdatel'stvo "Indrik"), 141–160.

WARDEN, P. G. 1992:

Gift, Offering, and Reciprocity – Personalized Remembrance and the "Small Finds", "Expedition" 34/1–2, 50–58.

WATANABE CH. E. 1998:

Symbolism of the Royal Hunt in Assyria, in J. Prosecký (ed.), Intellectual Life of the Ancient Near East – Papers Presented at the 43rd Rencontre Assyriologique Internationale, Prague, July 1–5, 1996, Prague: Oriental Institute, 439–450.

WEADOCK, P. N. 1975:

The Giparu at Ur, "Iraq" 37, 101–128.

WEBER J., ZETTLER R. 1998:

Metal Vessels, in Zettler-Horne 1998, 123–140.

WEIPPERT, M. 2002:

"König, fürchte dich nicht!": Assyrische Prophetie im 7. Jahrhundert v. Chr., "Orientalia" N. S. 71/1, 1–54.

WHYTE, S. R. 1990:

The Widow's Dream: Sex and Death in Western Kenya, in Jackson-Karp 1990, 95–114.

VON WICKEDE, A. 1990:
Prähistorische Stempelglyptik in VorderAsien, München: Profil Verlag.

WIGGERMANN, F. 1992:
Mesopotamian Protective Spirits – The ritual texts, Groningen: Styx and PP Publications.

WIGGERMANN, F. 1996:
Scenes from the shadow side, in M. E. Vogelzang, H. L. J. Vanstiphout (edd.), Mesopotamian poetic language: Sumerian and Akkadian, Groningen: Styx Publications, 207–230.

WILLIAMSON, M. H. 1979:
Powhatan Hair, "Man" N. S. 14, 392–413.

WINTER, I. 2000:
Le palais imaginaire: scale and meaning in the iconography of neo-Assyrian royal seals, in Ch. Uehlinger (ed.), Images as media – Sources for the cultural history of the Near East and the Eastern Mediterranean (1st millennium BCE), Orbis Biblicus et Orientalis 175, Fribourg – Göttineg: University Press and Vandenhoeck & Ruprecht, 51–87.

WRIGHT, G. A. 1978:
Social Differentiation in the early Natufian, in Ch. L. Redman et al. (edd.), Social Archaeology – Beyond Subsistence and Dating, New York – San Francisco – London: Academic Press, 201–223.

YELIZARENKOVA, T. Ya. (ЕЛИЗАРЕНКОВА, Т. Я.) 1993:
Язик и стиль ведийских риши (Language and style of the Vedic rishis, in Russian), Москва: "Наука", Издательская фирма "Восточная литература" (Moscow: "Nauka" and Publishing agency "Vostochnaya literatura").

YOFFEE, N. 1998:
The economics of ritual at late Old Babylonian Kish, "Journal of the Economic and Social History of the Orient" 41/3, 312–343.

ZATU:
M. Green, H.- J. Nissen, Zeichenliste der Archaischen Texte aus Uruk (Archaische Texte aus Uruk Band 2), Berlin: Gebrüder Mann Verlag 1987.

ZETTLER, R. 1992:
The Ur III temple of Inanna at Nippur (Berliner Beiträge zum Vorderen Orient Bd. 11), Berlin: Dietrich Reimer Verlag.

ZETTLER, R. 1998:
The Burials of a King and Queen, in Zettler-Horne 1998, 33–38.

ZETTLER R., HORNE L. (edd.) 1998:
Treasures from the Royal Tombs of Ur, Philadelphia: University of Pennsylvania Museum of Archaeology and Anthropology.

ZGOLL, A. 1997:
Inanna als nugig, „Zeitschrift für Assyriologie" 87/II, 181–195.

INDEX

SB 2010 (my No. 117) – p. 18–19, 115
SB 2011 (my No. 114) – p. 18, 115
SB 2012 (my No. 118) – p. 19, 115
SB 2013 (my No. 111) – p. 17, 115–116
SB 2048 (my No. 116) – p. 18, 117
SB 2061 (my No. 115) – p. 18, 115
SB 2107 (my No. 110) – p. 17, 119
SB 2136 (my No. 109) – p. 17, 119
SB 2139 (my No. 112) – p. 17–18, 119
SB 2227 (my No. 108) – p. 16–17, 119
SB 2228 (my No. 130) – p. 21, 115
SB 2229 (my No. 129) – p. 21, 115
SB 2245 (my No. 132) – p. 22, 119
SB 2246 (my No. 113) – p. 18, 117–118
SB 2247 (my No. 131) – p. 22, 117
SB 2248 (my No. 128) – p. 21, 117
SB 2265 (my No. 133) – p. 22, 122
SB 2265 (my No. 134) – p. 22, 122
SB 2266 (my No. 127) – p. 21, 116
SB 2267 (my No. 126) – p. 20, 116
SB 2862 (11 385, A5) (my No. 85) – p. 15
SB 3123 (my No. 86) – p. 15
SB 3124 (12.550) (my No. 99) – p. 16
SB 3125 (12 686) (my No. 87) – p. 16
SB 3127 (22) (my No. 92) – p. 16
SB 3128 (my No. 100) – p. 16
SB 3129 (10 054) (my No. 102) – p. 16
SB 3130 (my No. 24) – p. 13, 84
SB 3131 (my No. 138) – p. 23
SB 3132 (my No. 103) – p. 16

SB 3134 (12 160) (my No. 31) – p. 13
SB 3135 (12.679) (my No. 105) – p. 16
SB 3136 (13.876) (my No. 16) – p. 13, 82
SB 3137 (12 934, A 7934) (my No. 30) – p. 13, 84
SB 3138 (A 6864) (my No. 96) – p. 16, 89
SB 3140 (A 6.618) (my No. 34) – p. 13, 87, 90
SB 3141 (13.906) (my No. 59) – p. 14, 90–91
SB 3142 (12.403) (my No. 60) – p. 14, 91, 93
SB 3143 (A 6.618) (my No. 18) – p. 13, 79, 88
SB 3144 (12.115) (my No. 15) – p. 12, 84
SB 3145 (12.316) (my No. 52) – p. 14, 90
SB 3146 (12.689) (my No. 57) – p. 14, 95
SB 3148 (10.026) (my No. 10) – p. 12, 87
SB 3149 (A. 7918) (my No. 12) – p. 12, 87–88,
SB 3152 (12.675) (my No. 14) – p. 12
SB 3153 (11.617) (my No. 6) – p. 12
SB 3154 (my No. 141) – p. 23
SB 3155 (12.130) (my No. 91) – p. 16, 88
SB 3156 (15.316, A 7908) (my No. 104) – p. 16
SB 3157 (my No. 136) – p. 23
SB 3158 (12.410) (my No. 81) – p. 15
SB 3159 (12 348) (my No. 83) – p. 15
SB 3160 (13.912) (my No. 94) – p. 16, 84
SB 3161 (12.491) (my No. 17) – p. 13, 88
SB 3162 (12.693) (my No. 22) – p. 13
SB 3163 (11 620) (my No. 33) – p. 13, 87, 90
SB 3164 (12.677) (my No. 84) – p. 15
SB 3165 (my No. 142) – p. 23
SB 3166 (10 038) (my No. 98) – p. 16
SB 3167 (my No. 144) – p. 23
SB 3168 (my No. 137) – p. 23
SB 3169 (12 138) (my No. 42) – p. 14
SB 3170 (12.313) (my No. 58) – p. 14, 93
SB 3171 (A. 7957) (my No. 71) – p. 15
SB 3172 (13.922) (my No. 97) – p. 16, 81, 98
SB 3174 (my No. 135) – p. 23
SB 3175 (11.613) (my No. 27) – p. 13, 79
SB 3176 (A 7.011) (my No. 7) – p. 12
SB 3178 (my No. 139) – p. 23
SB 3179 (my No. 143) – p. 23
SB 3180 (Strasbourg) (my No. 36) – p. 13

SB 3181 (13.926) (my No. 53) – p. 14, 80, 88, 92
SB 3182 (my No. 146) – p. 23
SB 3183 (12.613) (my No. 8) – p. 12
SB 3184 (A 7.938) (my No. 43) – p. 14, 80, 91
SB 3186 (9.794) (my No. 5) – p. 12, 79, 81
SB 3187 (A 7.908) (my No. 80) – p. 15
SB 3188 (12 470) (my No. 69) – p. 15
SB 3189 (12.647) (my No. 55) – p. 14
SB 3190 (12.581) (my No. 51) – p. 14, 88
SB 3191 (12.143) (my No. 21) – p. 13
SB 3193 (12.244) (my No. 20) – p. 13
SB 3194 (12.101) (my No. 3) – p. 12, 108
SB 3195 (13 892) (my No. 32) – p. 13, 84
SB 3196 (12 218) (my No. 35) – p. 13
SB 3197 (my No. 48) – p. 14, 79, 91
SB 3198 (A. 7956) (my No. 62) – p. 14, 80, 88
SB 3199 (12 395) (my No. 46) – p. 14, 87, 91
SB 3200 (A. 7041) (my No. 28) – p. 13, 79
SB 3202 (12 698) (my No. 40) – p. 14, 80, 87
SB 3204 (181, 26, 13 896) (my No. 41) – p. 14
SB 3206 (A 7.930) (my No. 64) – p. 15, 80, 88, 90
SB 3208 (my No. 140) – p. 23
SB 3211 (12.569) (my No. 82) – p. 15
SB 3212 (12.121) (my No. 72) – p. 15, 91
SB 3213 (12.618) (my No. 79) – p. 15
SB 3218 (A 7.936) (my No. 4) – p. 12, 108
SB 3223 (11.623) (my No. 1) – p. 12, 81, 92, 109
SB 4819 (12.609) (my No. 2) – p. 12
SB 4820 (12 694) (my No. 26) – p. 13, 89
SB 5300 (my No. 123) – p. 20, 115
SB 5301 (my No. 124) – p. 20, 115
SB 6936 (my No. 121) – p. 19, 115
SB 6938 (my No. 122) – p. 19–20, 119
SB 6940 (my No. 125) – p. 20, 117–118
SB 6941 (my No. 119) – p. 19, 117–119
SB 6943 (my No. 120) – p. 19, 117–118
SB 9503 (270, 16 046, 10 046?) (my No. 37) – p. 13
SB 14 265 (A 7045, 184) (my No. 38) – p. 13, 87, 90
SB 14 266 (12 330, 64) (my No. 63) – p. 15, 80, 88
SB 14 267 (12 174 = Louvre 106) (my No. 11) – p. 12, 87
SB 14 268 (12 494) (my No. 70) – p. 15

SB 14 269 (11 600, B1) (my No. 56) – p. 14, 82
SB 14 270 (12 961, 4?3, 50) (my No. 65) – p. 15, 88, 91
SB 14 271 (my No. 145) – p. 23
SB 14 272 (12 305, 58) (my No. 54) – p. 14, 88
SB 14 273 (12 599, 38) (my No. 50) – p. 14, 89
SB 14 274 (12 120) (my No. 49) – p. 14, 91
SB 14 275 (12 138, 25?) (my No. 44) – p. 14, 80, 87, 91
SB 14 276 (12 138, 25?) (my No. 39) – p. 13, 80, 84, 87
SB 14 277 (12 553, 97) (my No. 101) – p. 16
SB 14 278 (12 442, 77) (my No. 67) – p. 15, 91
SB 14 279 (A 6879) (my No. 106) – p. 16, 80
SB 14 280 (12 640, 242) (my No. 89) – p. 16
SB 14 281 (12 339, 2279) (my No. 93) – p. 16, 80
SB 14 282 (12 678, 254) (my No. 95) – p. 16
SB 14 283 (A 6453, 260) (my No. 88) – p. 16
SB 14 284 (14 065, 212) (my No. 77) – p. 15
SB 14 285 (A 6455) (my No. 78) – p. 15, 88, 92
SB 14 286 (228) (my No. 75) – p. 15
SB 14 287 (A 6859, 229) (my No. 76) – p. 15
SB 14 288 (12 453, 24) (my No. 9) – p. 12
SB 14 289 (10 058bis, 94bis) (my No. 73) – p. 15
SB 14 290 (A 7932, 56) (my No. 66) – p. 15, 89, 91, 109
SB 14 291 (12 591) (my No. 47) – p. 14, 79, 88, 91
SB 14 292 (5?) (my No. 74) – p. 15, 89
SB 14 293 (11 596) (my No. 45) – p. 14
SB 14 294 (M 237) (my No. 61) – p. 14, 82
SB 14 381 (A 6568) (my No. 23) – p. 13
SB 14 382 (12 487) (my No. 19) – p. 13, 79
SB 14 383 (12 695) (my No. 13) – p. 12
SB 14 384 (11 619) (my No. 29) – p. 13, 87
SB 14 385 (7009) (my No. 68) – p. 15, 91
SB 14 386 (AS 15 460, 2) (my No. 90) – p. 16
SB 19 354 (B 223 et R 773) (my No. 107) – p. 16, 84, 90
SB 19 519 (As 12 522) (my No. 25) – p. 13, 79

Numbers of painted-pottery items used in this book:

135. SB 3174 – p. 23, 80, 90
136. SB 3157 – p. 23, 82, 84, 108
137. SB 3168 – p. 23, 82, 108
138. SB 3131 – p. 23, 80

139. SB 3178 – p. 23
140. SB 3208 – p. 23
141. SB 3154 – p. 23, 84
142. SB 3165 – p. 23, 88, 91
143. SB 3179 – p. 23, 80
144. SB 3167 – p. 23
145. SB 14 271 – p. 23, 84
146. SB 3182 – p. 23, 87
147. de Morgan 1912, Pl. XIX: 8; Amiet 1986, 235 fig. 2 (*in situ* sketch by de Morgan). – p. 24
148. de Morgan 1912, Pl. IV: 1 – p. 24, 80, 91
149. de Morgan 1912, Pl. IV: 3 – p. 24, 80, 84, 88
150. de Morgan 1912, Pl. IVa: 4 – p. 24, 90, 91
151. de Morgan 1912, Pl. V: 2 – p. 24
152. de Morgan 1912, Pl. V: 4 – p. 24
153. de Morgan 1912, Pl. V: 5 – p. 24, 80, 88
154. de Morgan 1912, Pl. V: 7 – p. 24
155. de Morgan 1912, Pl. Va: 2 – p. 24
156. de Morgan 1912, Pl. Va: 4 – p. 24, 87
157. de Morgan 1912, Pl. Va: 6 – p. 24, 87
158. de Morgan 1912, Pl. Va: 7 – p. 24
159. de Morgan 1912, Pl. Va: 9 – p. 24
160. de Morgan 1912, Pl. VI: 1 – p. 24, 91
161. de Morgan 1912, Pl. VI: 2 – p. 24, 90
162. de Morgan 1912, Pl. VI: 4 – p. 24, 91–92
163. de Morgan 1912, Pl. VI: 5 – p. 24, 88, 91
164. de Morgan 1912, Pl. VI: 6 – p. 24
165. de Morgan 1912, Pl. VIa: 1 – p. 24, 92
166. de Morgan 1912, Pl. VIa: 3 – p. 24
167. de Morgan 1912, Pl. VII: 1 – p. 24
168. de Morgan 1912, Pl. VII: 2 – p. 24, 91
169. de Morgan 1912, Pl. VII: 4 – p. 24, 91
170. de Morgan 1912, Pl. VII: 6 – p. 24, 80, 88
171. de Morgan 1912, Pl. VIII: 2 – p. 24, 91
172. de Morgan 1912, Pl. VIII: 4 – p. 24
173. de Morgan 1912, Pl. VIII: 6 – p. 24, 88, 91
174. de Morgan 1912, Pl. VIII: 7 – p. 24, 88
175. de Morgan 1912, Pl. IX: 2 – p. 24, 88, 91
176. de Morgan 1912, Pl. IX: 5 – p. 24
177. de Morgan 1912, Pl. IX: 6 – p. 24
178. de Morgan 1912, Pl. X: 5 – p. 24

179. de Morgan 1912, Pl. X: 6 – p. 24
180. de Morgan 1912, Pl. X: 7 – p. 24, 82, 88
181. de Morgan 1912, Pl. X: 8 – p. 24
182. de Morgan 1912, Pl. XI: 2 – p. 24, 87
183. de Morgan 1912, Pl. XI: 3 – p. 24, 87
184. de Morgan 1912, Pl. XI: 5 – p. 25
185. de Morgan 1912, Pl. XII: 2 – p. 25
186. de Morgan 1912, Pl. XII: 3 – p. 25
187. de Morgan 1912, Pl. XII: 4 – p. 25, 90
188. de Morgan 1912, Pl. XII: 5 – p. 25
189. de Morgan 1912, Pl. XII: 6 – p. 25, 87
190. de Morgan 1912, Pl. XIII: 1 – p. 25
191. de Morgan 1912, Pl. XIII: 3 – p. 25, 87
192. de Morgan 1912, Pl. XIII: 7 – p. 25
193. de Morgan 1912, Pl. XIV: 1 – p. 25, 95
194. de Morgan 1912, Pl. XIV: 2 – p. 25
195. de Morgan 1912, Pl. XIV: 4 – p. 25
196. de Morgan 1912, Pl. XIV: 6 – p. 25
197. de Morgan 1912, Pl. XIV: 8 – p. 25
198. de Morgan 1912, Pl. XV: 1 – p. 25
199. de Morgan 1912, Pl. XV: 2 – p. 25
200. de Morgan 1912, Pl. XV: 3 – p. 25
201. de Morgan 1912, Pl. XV: 5 – p. 25
202. de Morgan 1912, Pl. XV: 7 – p. 25
203. de Morgan 1912, Pl. XVI: 6 – p. 25
204. de Morgan 1912, Pl. XVI: 7 – p. 25
205. de Morgan 1912, Pl. XVII: 4 – p. 25, 84
206. de Morgan 1912, Pl. XVIII: 4 – p. 25
207. de Morgan 1912, Pl. XVIII: 5 – p. 25
208. de Morgan 1912, Pl. XIX: 4 – p. 25
209. de Morgan 1912, Pl. XIX: 6 – p. 25
210. de Morgan 1912, Pl. XIX: 7 – p. 25
211. de Morgan 1912, Pl. XIX: 9 – p. 25
212. de Morgan 1912, Pl. XX: 1 – p. 25
213. de Morgan 1912, Pl. XX: 2 – p. 25
214. de Morgan 1912, Pl. XX: 3 – p. 25
215. de Morgan 1912, Pl. XX: 4 – p. 25
216. de Morgan 1912, Pl. XX: 6 – p. 25
217. de Morgan 1912, Pl. XX: 7 – p. 25
218. de Morgan 1912, Pl. XXI: 1 – p. 25
219. de Morgan 1912, Pl. XXI: 3 – p. 25

220. de Morgan 1912, Pl. XXI: 6 – p. 25
221. de Morgan 1912, Pl. XXI: 8 – p. 25
222. de Morgan 1912, Pl. XXII: 1 – p. 26
223. de Morgan 1912, Pl. XXII: 2 – p. 26
224. de Morgan 1912, Pl. XXII: 6 – p. 26, 90
225. de Morgan 1912, Pl. XXII: 7 – p. 26
226. de Morgan 1912, Pl. XXII: 8 – p. 26
227. de Morgan 1912, Pl. XLI: 3 – p. 26
228. de Morgan 1912, Pl. XLI: 5 – p. 26
229. de Morgan 1912, Pl. XLII: 4 – p. 26
230. de Morgan 1912, Pl. XLII: 6 – p. 26, 87

GENERAL INDEX

Aanepada – p. 197
AB (EŠ$_3$) – p. 167, 175, 179
Abu Salabikh – p. 180
Abydos – Umm el Ga'ab (Egypt) – p. 45
Abzu (= *apsû*) – p. 143–144
Afikpo people (E Ibo tribes, Nigeria) – p. 64
Africa – p. 63–66, 116
Akkadian period – p. 121, 184, 199, 209
ALAN – p. 145, 169–170, 174
ALIM or PIRIG – p. 82
Amazonia – p. 51, 70
America – p. 56, 62, 68–71
An (Anu) – p. 40, 43, 46, 48–49, 73–74, 95, 112, 122, 143–144, 151, 158, 173, 212, 215–217
Anaku (land) – 144
Anatolia – p. 121, 126, 138, 143–144, 149, 166, 206
Ancestors – p. 52, 55, 71, 83
ANŠE – p. 82
Anunnitum – p. 208
Anzu – p. 185, 202, 216–217
Apsě cf. Abzu
Aratta – p. 93, 135
Architecture – p. 142–146
Arpachiyah – p. 42, 44–49, 51, 92, 143–144
Arslantepe – p. 121, 138
Assurbanipal – p. 185

Austria – p. 106
Babylon – p. 92
BAD$_3$ – p. 76
Baluchistan – p. 207
Barcelona (Catalonia, Spain) – p. 68
Beowulf – p. 184
Bevelled–rim bowls – p. 29, 33, 34
Bororo people, Amazonia – p. 70–71,
BU = GID$_2$ = SU$_{13}$ – p. 83, 120
Bucranium motif – p. 44–45, 47, 97, 211
BUR – p. 144
Burma cf. Myanmar
Cedar Forest – p. 181–184
Cemetery – p. 26, 27, 28, 212
Chequerboard motif – p. 44–48, 72–73, 76, 78, 79–81, 89, 92, 98, 101–102, 106–109, 123–124, 162, 191, 193, 211–212
China – p. 49–52, 55, 68, 115, 128–129
Choga Mish (Iran) – p. 127, 152, 171
Chou dynasty (China) – p. 50
Cistercian (Trappist) monks – pp. 135–137
Cities – p. 76–77, 79, 87, 105–106, 115, 212
„City league" – p. 93, 165, 186–210
Commensality – p. 56, 94, 121
Cones, coloured – p. 142–144
Cord impressions – p. 17–20, 22
Cyprus – p. 144
Cyrene (Libya) – p. 68

Dalma ware (Iran) – p. 48
Dam nu-gig – p. 195, 208
DARA$_3$ – p. 82, 91
Değirmentepe – p. 126
Deshret crown (Egypt) – p. 122
Dingirmah temple (Babylon) – p. 92
Dogon (W Africa) – p. 44, 64
DUB – p. 179
Dumuzi – p. 188, 196, 202–209, 216–217
E$_2$ – p. 160, 166–169
Eagle (as an emblem) – p. 185–210
Eanedu, daughter of Kudurmabuk – p. 178
Ebla – p. 77, 181
Egypt – p. 45, 46, 63–64, 85, 110, 121–122
Ehursag temple of Ur – p. 208
Elam – p. 208
EN (sacerdotal title) – p. 146, 154, 167–170, 173–174, 177–178, 180–184, 193, 202–209, 215–217
EN.SAL – p. 178–180
ENGAR – p. 179
Enki (= Ea) – p. 80, 83, 89, 92, 95, 98, 103, 107–108, 112, 135, 139, 143–144, 170, 174
„Enki and Ninhursag" – p. 57, 168
„Enki and the World Order" – p. 139, 144, 170
Enkidu – p. 181–184, 216–217
Enlil – p. 40, 45, 79–81, 85, 95, 106–108, 112, 144, 169, 183–184, 202, 212
Enmebaragesi – p. 182, 185
„Enmerkar and the lord of Aratta" – p. 135, 215
Ensi$_2$ – p. 210, 217
Enuma eliš – p. 144
Eridu – p. 141–142, 145, 169
ERIM or ERIN – p. 85, 180
EŠ$_3$ cf. AB
Etana – p. 110
Europe (Christian) – p. 58, 62, 68–71,

128, 135–137, 158–159, 163, 184–185, 204
Eye idols – p. 143–144, 152, 154–155, 158, 161
EZEN – p. 76–77, 164, 172
EZINU – p. 88, 91
Fakaata spirit (Oceania) – p. 81
Fakatino (permanent residence of a spirit, Oceania) – p. 80
GA – p. 152, 154–155
GA + ZATU 753 – p. 150
GA$_2$ – p. 94
GA$_2$ + SUKUD – p. 180
GANA$_2$ – p. 179
GAR or NINDA – p. 93–94, 120
Gilgamesh – p. 180–184, 216–217
„Gilgamesh and the Bull of Heaven" – p. 216
„Gilgamesh and the Huluppu Tree" – p. 216
„Gilgamesh and the Land of the Living" – p. 180–184, 216–217
„Gilgamesh, The Death of" – p. 216–217
Gipar (-ku) – pp. 86–88, 98, 100–101, 106, 118, 123, 208
GIR$_3$ – p. 91
Grai Resh – p. 145
Greece – p. 56, 68, 144, 164
GU$_4$ – p. 82, 178
Gudea – p. 203–209
GUM$_2$ – p. 91
GUN$_3$ – p. 82
GURUŠ – p. 180
GUZ – p. 91
Habuba Kabira (Syria) – p. 149, 166
Halaf culture – p. 42–49, 53, 55, 59–62, 72–74, 94–95, 97, 99, 101, 104, 117, 121, 125, 143–144, 171, 173, 181, 187, 192, 211, 213
Haštu (= bur$_3$) – p. 144
Haute terrasse (Susa) – p. 113–114

Hercules – p. 56
HI – p. 179
Hikule'o – p. 60, 110
„Hourglass" – p. 91–92, 96–104, 109,
    191–193, 212
Hubur – p. 208
Humbaba – p. 181–184
„Hunch-eaters" – p. 52, 124
Huniyan – p. 70
Hunting – p. 43
I_3 – p. 134
Ibo people (Nigeria) – p. 65, 127
Ida ceremony (dance, Oceania) – p. 67
IDIGNA – p. 83
Im-ru-a – p. 94
Inanna – p. 154, 156, 161–162, 168–170,
    180, 202–209, 215–217
India – p. 51, 54, 58, 62, 68–71, 74, 85,
    112, 207
Iran – p. 56, 62–63, 89, 97, 123, 127, 143,
    148, 166, 171, 207
Jebel Aruda (Syria) – p. 124, 149, 166
Jebel Hamrin – p. 104
Jemdet Nasr – p. 178–180, 184, 189–210,
    215–217
Kachin – p. 52–53, 57
Kava drinking – p. 59–61, 110, 121, 129
Kezertu – p. 89
Khirbet Derak – p. 48–49, 73, 91, 211
KI – p. 179
Ki-a-nag – p. 196
Ki-šu-tag – p. 169
KID – p. 80
Kilns – p. 35
KIŠ – p. 82, 89, 180–184, 195, 202–210,
    216–217
KITI – p. 83
Kudurmabuk, father of Eanedu – p. 178
KUR – p. 41, 78–79, 151, 160, 208–209,
    216–217
Kurigalzu I – p. 208

LAGAB – p. 91, 179
Lagaš – p. 83, 210, 217
Lalgar – p. 143
Lamaštu – p. 203
Larsa – p. 204
Larsa age – p. 197
Leather(?) impressions – pp. 18–21,
Lelet Plateau (central new Ireland, Papua,
    New Guinea) – p. 53–54, 67
Lobi people (Nigeria) – p. 64
LU_2 – p. 166–167, 175
LU_2.BA (or LU_2.IGI) – p. 197
LU_2.IGI (or LU_2.BA) – p. 197
LUGAL – p. 167, 175, 178, 180, 184–210,
    216–217
Lugal-anzu – p. 185, 189
Lugale – p. 41
Lugalkinišedudu – p. 209
luludanitu stone – p. 43
LUM – p. 91
Madai – p. 52
MAH – p. 156
MČliktum – p. 181
Mana – p. 60–61, 120, 126–131
Manishtusu – p. 209
Marachi people (W Kenya) – p. 65,
Mari – p. 130
„Masks" (Africa) – p. 116
Mats – pp. 86–87
Me (Sumerian „ideas") – p. 129
ME_3 = *tāhāzu* – p. 85
Mesanepada – p. 195, 197, 208, 216–217
Minangkabau (Sumatra) – p. 58
Music – p. 51
$MURUB_2$ – p. 167, 175
$MUŠ_3$ (= INANNA) – p. 151
MUŠEN – p. 82–83
Myanmar – p. 52, 115, 124
NA_2 (ceremony) – p. 146, 168–170, 173,
    177–178, 180–184, 202–209, 215–217
Nabonidus – p. 92

NAM or SIM – p. 83
NAM$_2$ – p. 89
Nannar – p. 208–209
Nanše – p. 83, 144
Naqû – p. 130
Naramsin – p. 209, 217
Neo-Assyrian age – p. 125–126, 185
Neo-Babylonian age – p. 133
NERGAL$_X$ – p. 82
NI – p. 120, 134
NI + RU – p. 93–94, 150, 179
Nibelungenlied – p. 184
NIMGIR – p. 179
NIN (sacerdotal title) – p. 146, 167–170,
    173–174, 177–178, 180–184, 185–210,
    215–217
Nin$_9$ – 182
Ninbanda – p. 196
NINDA or GAR – p. 93, 120
Ninhursag (= Ninki) – p. 80, 83, 92, 95,
    101, 103, 107–109, 112, 197, 199, 212
Ninlil – p. 169
Ninurta – p. 41
Nippur – p. 183, 208
Nu-gig – p. 195, 208
Obi (ruler of the Ibo, Nigeria) – p. 65
Oceania – p. 55, 62, 66–68, 81, 127
Oikos – p. 166
Old English – p. 206
Old Testament – p. 116, 128
PA.NAM$_2$.RAD – p. 89
Peg impressions – p. 19
PIRIG or ALIM – p. 82
Pot sealings – pp. 17–21,
Proto-Elamite script – p. 77–78, 86, 91,
    95, 103, 109, 123, 134
RAD – p. 89, 109
Rimush – p. 209
Rosette – p. 45–47, 151, 153, 158, 160,
    163, 187–211
RU – p. 93–95, 107, 212

Russia – p. 69–70
SAG + MA – p. 179
SANGA – p. 93
Sargon – p. 209
Seal impression strata (Ur) – p. 186–210
Sedentarization – p. 38
Seleucid-Parthian age – p. 129
Shadip – p. 52
Shamash – p. 41, 121
Shamsuddin Tannira – p. 43–44, 47, 49
Shan – p. 52–53, 57
SIM or NAM – p. 83
Sin-leqqe-uninni – p. 184
Sippar – p. 41
Spain – p. 144
Sri Lanka – p. 70
Sumerian King List – p. 209–210, 217
Syria – p. 124, 143, 145, 148–149, 166,
    208
ŠAH$_3$ – p. 82
ŠAGAN – p. 179
Šarāku, širku – p. 94
Šassūru – p. 86
Šaššāru – p. 121
ŠE – p. 90–91, 103
ŠEG$_9$ – p. 82
ŠENNUR – p. 76
ŠUBUR – p. 82
Šuruppak (Fara) – p. 93, 148, 180, 210, 217
Šusin – p. 208
TAK$_4$.A – p. 179–180
TAK$_4$.ALAN – p. 161, 169–170
TAK$_4$.AN.KI – p. 169
TAK$_4$.SAL.AMA.NIN – p. 170, 174
Tall-i Malyan – p. 77–78,
TE – p. 179
Tell Asmar – p. 179
Tell Brak – p. 134
Tell Sheikh Hassan (Syria) – p. 143, 145
Tepe Gawra – p. 48, 95, 104, 139, 143–145,
    174

Tepe Sabz – p. 123
Tepe Yahya – p. 77–78, 86, 95
Textile impressions – pp. 17–18, 21–22, TIDNUM – p. 82
Tikopia people (Oceania) – p. 128
Tonga island (Polynesia) – p. 55, 59–60, 66–67, 85, 121, 127
Trobriand islands – p. 57
U_4 – p. 168
Ubaid culture – p. 48, 84, 91, 95–97, 105, 126, 132, 134, 141–143, 145, 171, 173, 197, 211–215
Udo spirit (Ibo people, Nigeria) – p. 65
UKKIN – p. 155, 157, 161, 167–168, 175
Ulaya – p. 208
Umeda people (Papua, New Guinea) – p. 67
Umm Qseir (Syria) – p. 143, 153

Ur – p. 46, 79, 92, 148, 151, 155, 163, 184–210, 216–217
UR_2 – p. 52
URI_3 – p. 155, 157, 160–162, 193
Urnama – p. 208
URU – p. 167
Uruk age – p. 79, 82–84, 88, 90, 93–95, 119, 121, 1
UŠUMGAL – p. 82, 108
UZ – p. 83, 91
Weaving looms – p. 156–157
Wine – p. 94, 138–139
Wood impressions – p. 16
Writing – pp. 133–139
Zababa – p. 180
ZAR = LAGAB + ŠE(+ŠE) – p. 91
ZUM = *mašādu*

APPENDIX

No. 1 (sb 3223)

No. 2 (sb 4819)

255

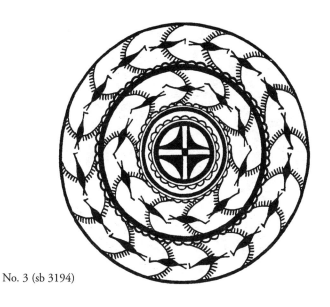

No. 3 (sb 3194)

No. 4 (sb 3218)

No. 5 (sb 3186)

No. 6 (sb 3153)

No. 7 (sb 3176)

No. 8 (sb 3183)

258

No. 9 (sb 14 288)

No. 10 (sb 3148)

259

No. 11 (sb 14 267)

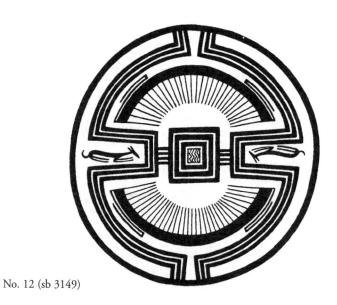

No. 12 (sb 3149)

260

No. 13 (sb 14 383)

No. 14 (sb 3152)

No. 15 (sb 3144)

No. 16 (sb 3136)

262

No. 17 (sb 3161)

No. 18 (sb 3143)

263

No. 19 (sb 14 382)

No. 20 (sb 3193)

No. 21 (sb 3191)

No. 22 (sb 3162)

No. 23 (sb 14 381)

No. 24 (sb 3130)

No. 25 (sb 19 519)

No. 26 (sb 4820)

No. 27 (sb 3175)

No. 28 (sb 3200)

No. 29 (sb 14 384)

No. 30 (sb 3137)

269

No. 31 (sb 3134)

No. 32 (sb 3195)

No. 33 (sb 3163)

No. 34 (sb 3140)

271

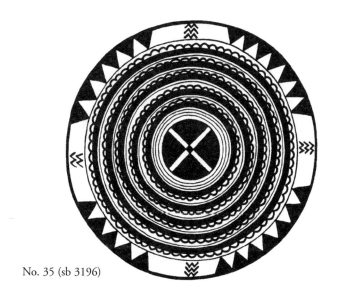

No. 35 (sb 3196)

No. 36 (sb 3180)

272

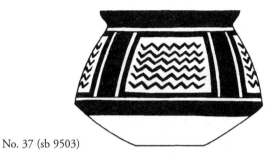

No. 37 (sb 9503)

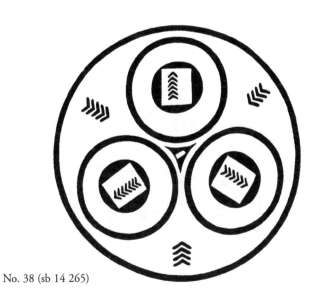

No. 38 (sb 14 265)

273

No. 39 (sb 14 276)

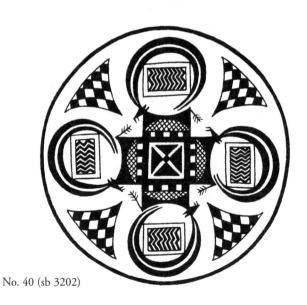

No. 40 (sb 3202)

274

No. 41 (sb 3204)

No. 42 (sb 3169)

275

No. 43 (sb 3184)

No. 44 (sb 14 275)

276

No. 45 (sb 14 293)

No. 46 (sb 3199)

277

No. 47 (sb 14 291)

No. 48 (sb 3197)

278

No. 49 (sb 14 274)

No. 50 (sb 14 273)

279

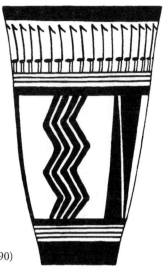

No. 51 (sb 3190)

No. 52 (sb 3145)

No. 53 (sb 3181)

No. 54 (sb 14 272)

No. 55 (sb 3189)

No. 56 (sb 14 269)

282

No. 57 (sb 3146)

No. 58 (sb 3170)

283

No. 59 (sb 3141)

No. 60 (sb 3142)

284

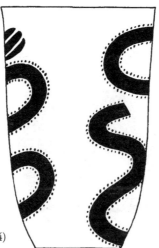

No. 61 (sb 14 294)

No. 62 (sb 3198)

285

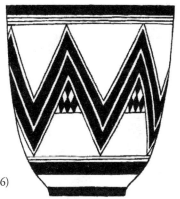

No. 63 (sb 14 266)

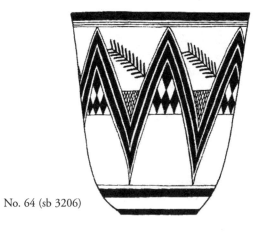

No. 64 (sb 3206)

No. 65 (sb 14 270)

No. 66 (sb 14 290)

287

No. 67 (sb 14 278)

No. 68 (sb 14 385)

288

No. 69 (sb 3188)

No. 70 (sb 14 268)

289

No. 71 (sb 3171)

No. 72 (sb 3212)

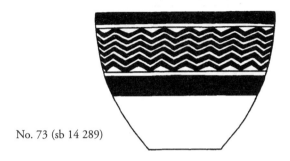

No. 73 (sb 14 289)

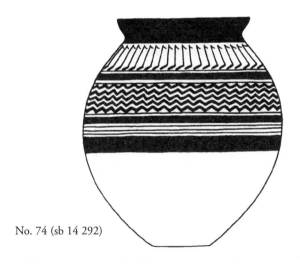

No. 74 (sb 14 292)

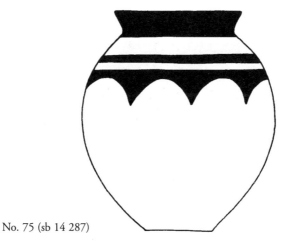

No. 75 (sb 14 287)

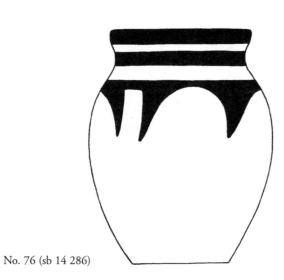

No. 76 (sb 14 286)

No. 77 (sb 14 284)

No. 78 (sb 14 285)

No. 79 (sb 3213)

No. 80 (sb 3187)

294

No. 81 (sb 3158)

No. 82 (sb 3211)

No. 83 (sb 3159)

No. 84 (sb 3164)

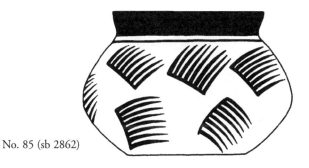

No. 85 (sb 2862)

No. 86 (sb 3123)

297

No. 87 (sb 3125)

No. 88 (sb 14 283)

298

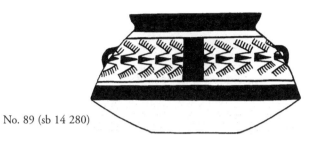

No. 89 (sb 14 280)

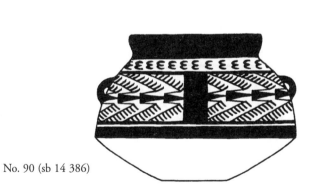

No. 90 (sb 14 386)

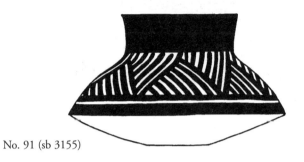

No. 91 (sb 3155)

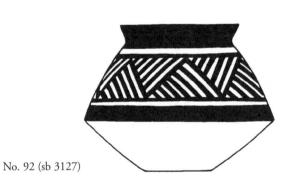

No. 92 (sb 3127)

No. 93 (sb 14 281)

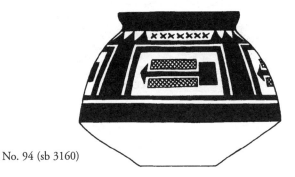

No. 94 (sb 3160)

301

No. 95 (sb 14 282)

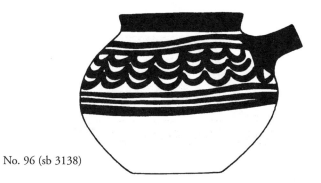

No. 96 (sb 3138)

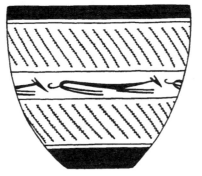

No. 97 (sb 3172)

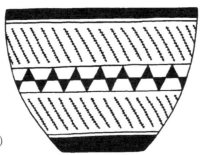

No. 98 (sb 3166)

303

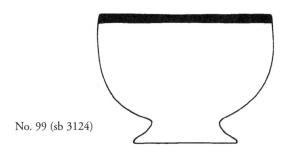

No. 99 (sb 3124)

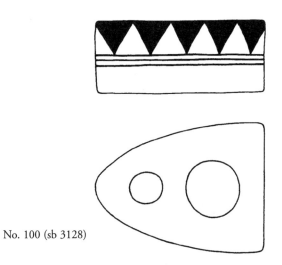

No. 100 (sb 3128)

No. 101 (sb 14 277)

No. 102 (sb 3129)

No. 103 (sb 3132)

No. 104 (sb 3156)

No. 105 (sb 3135)

No. 106 (sb 14 279)

No. 107 (sb 19 354)

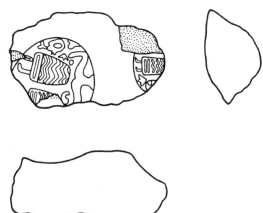

No. 108 (sb 2227)

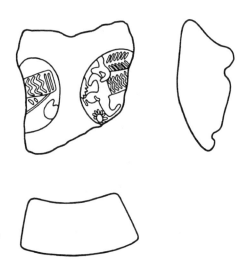

No. 109 (sb 2136)

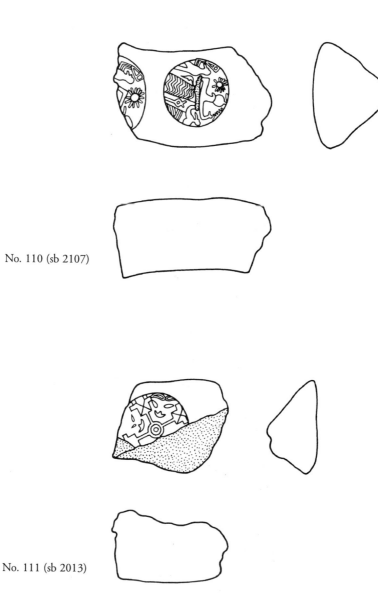

No. 110 (sb 2107)

No. 111 (sb 2013)

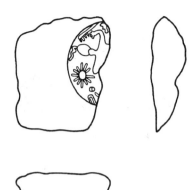

No. 112 (sb 2139)

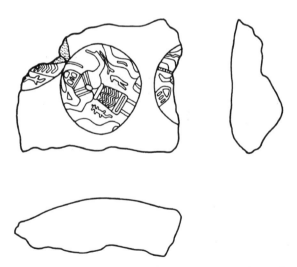

No. 113 (sb 2246)

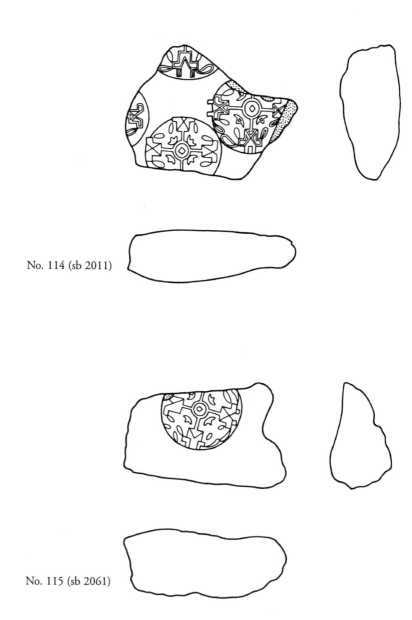

No. 114 (sb 2011)

No. 115 (sb 2061)

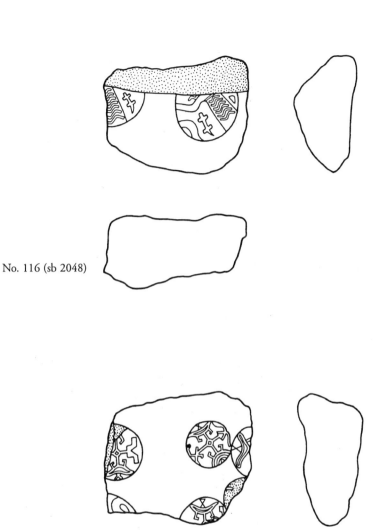

No. 116 (sb 2048)

No. 117 (sb 2010)

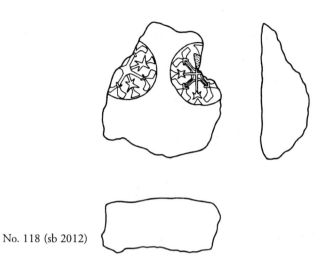

No. 118 (sb 2012)

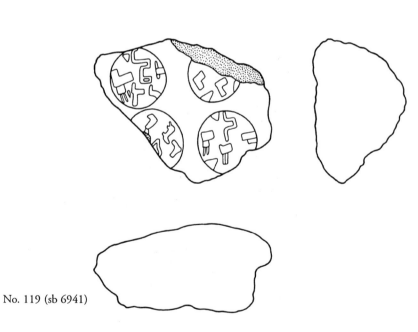

No. 119 (sb 6941)

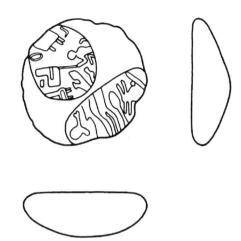

No. 120 (sb 6943)

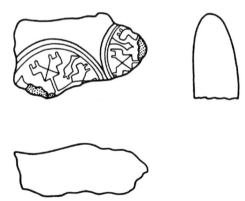

No. 121 (sb 6936)

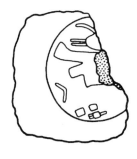

No. 122 (sb 6938)

No. 123 (sb 5300)

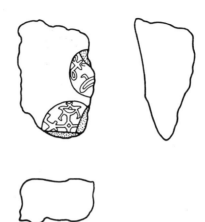

No. 124 (sb 5301)

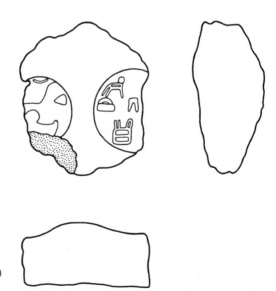

No. 125 (sb 6940)

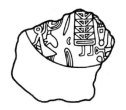

No. 126 (sb 2267)

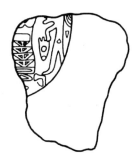

No. 127 (sb 2266)

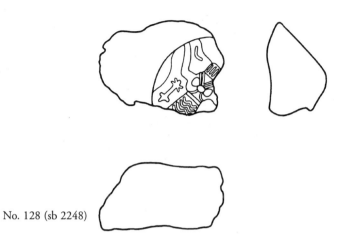

No. 128 (sb 2248)

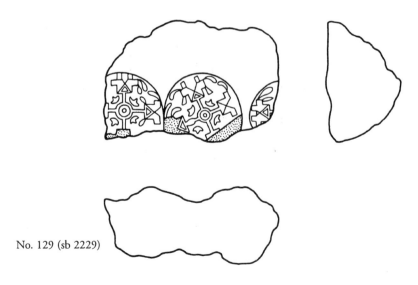

No. 129 (sb 2229)

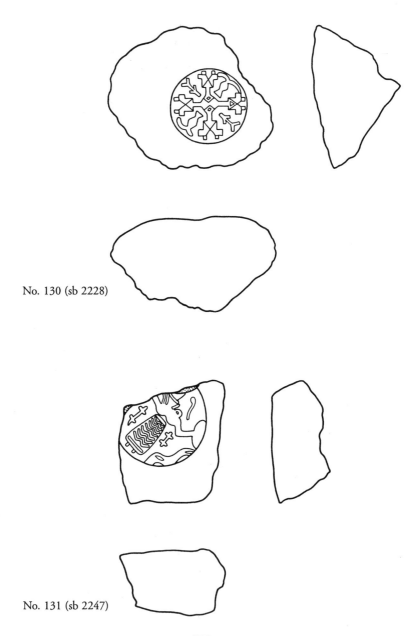

No. 130 (sb 2228)

No. 131 (sb 2247)

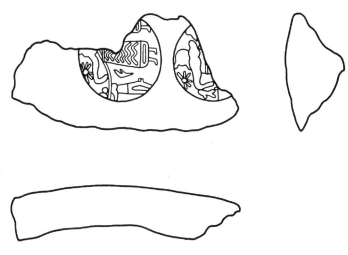

No. 132 (sb 2245)

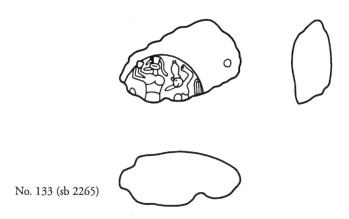

No. 133 (sb 2265)

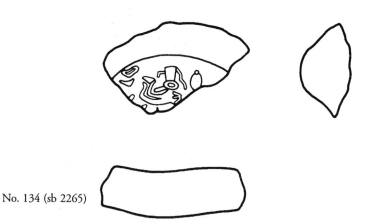

No. 134 (sb 2265)

Petr Charvát
The Iconography of Pristine Statehood
Painted pottery and seal impressions from Susa, southwestern Iran

Published by Charles University in Prague
Karolinum Press, Ovocný trh 3–5, 116 36 Prague 1
http://cupress.cuni.cz, e-mail: cupress@cuni.cz
Prague 2005

Vice-rector-editor prof. MUDr. Pavel Klener, DrSc.
Layout Kamila Schüllerová
Cover Jan Šerých
Illustration Eva Smrčinová
Typeset and printed by Karolinum Press

First edition

ISBN 80-246-0964-9